AF530800

ZONES OF CONFLICT IN AFRICA

ZONES OF CONFLICT IN AFRICA

Theories and Cases

Edited by
George Klay Kieh, Jr.
and Ida Rousseau Mukenge

PRAEGER

Westport, Connecticut
London

Library of Congress Cataloging-in-Publication Data

Zones of conflict in Africa : theories and cases / edited by George Klay Kieh, Jr. and Ida Rousseau Mukenge.
p. cm.
Includes bibliographical references and index.
ISBN 0–275–97447–2 (alk. paper)
1. Civil war—Africa, Sub-Saharan. 2. Civil war—Africa, Sub-Saharan—Case studies. 3. Africa, Sub-Saharan—Politics and government—1960– 4. Africa, Sub-Saharan—Politics and government—1960—Case studies. I. Kieh, George Klay, 1956– II. Mukenge, Ida Rousseau, 1941–
DT352.8Z66 2002
303.6'0967—dc21 2001036699

British Library Cataloguing in Publication Data is available.

Library of Congress Catalog Card Number: 2001036699
ISBN: 0–275–97447–2

First published in 2002

Praeger Publishers, 88 Post Road West, Westport, CT 06881
An imprint of Greenwood Publishing Group, Inc.
www.praeger.com

Printed in the United States of America

The paper used in this book complies with the Permanent Paper Standard issued by the National Information Standards Organization (Z39.48–1984).

10 9 8 7 6 5 4 3 2 1

Contents

Preface

The idea for this book was conceived about four years ago, following a conference on Conflict and Conflict Resolution in Africa organized by the Morehouse Center for International Studies. The conference was funded by a seed grant from the Rockefeller Foundation awarded to Emory University, Clark Atlanta University, Morehouse College, Morris Brown College, and Spelman College. The central purpose of the grant was to stimulate interest in African studies through conferences, lectures, research, seminars, and teaching. Since then, the original plan has undergone changes: Some areas have been deleted, while others have been added. The changes were dictated by the ever-fluctuating dynamics of the "Zones of Conflict in Africa." Among the additions are the chapters entiled "Theories of Conflict and Conflict Resolution," "The Context of Civil Conflicts in Africa" "Civil Conflicts in Africa: Patterns and Trends," and "Conflict and Conflict Management in the Great Lakes Region of Africa."

Clearly, conflict is an inevitable mainstay of human societies and their interactions. Nevertheless, conflicts vary in their form and impact, as well as in other characteristics. Thus, a distinction can be drawn between routine and non-routine conflicts. The former revolve around ordinary disagreements that are inherent in daily human interactions. Significantly, such conflicts are not deleterious to the body politic and its people. Conversely, non-routine conflicts are those that have a more serious, adverse, and at times catastrophic impact on the peace and stability of the polity and its citizens. This book is concerned with the latter category of civil conflict.

Various institutions and individuals have contributed to this book. First, we would like to express our gratitude to the Rockefeller Foundation for providing the seed grant that made most of the research for this book possible. In addition, we are grateful to Morehouse College for providing logistical support. Special thanks go to Ms. Livoria Hill, former Administrative Assistant at the Morehouse Center for International Studies, for providing administrative assistance. We would like to thank Dr. Edna Bay and Dr. Kristin Mann for providing encouragement and serving as liaisons with the Rockefeller Foundation. We appreciate the support, encouragement, and patience of Michael Hermann, Politics and Legal Studies Editor at Greenwood Publishing Group. Last but not least, we are grateful to the contributors to the project and the book. Without their hard work, this book would not have been possible.

PART I

BACKGROUND

1

Introduction

Ida Rousseau Mukenge

OVERVIEW

This book addresses the pervasive question of civil conflict in Africa. By civil conflict, we mean disagreement between domestic actors—government and private groups—over issues that may be economic, political, social, cultural, or any combination of these. Starting from this basic conceptual framework, the contributors analyze cases of civil conflict in Africa that have profound ramifications for peace and stability. The research represented in these case studies offers insights for prevention and management, increasing our understanding of the nature of divided societies in Africa but with implications for other parts of the world.

Conflict must be understood as potentially endemic in all political systems. There is clearly a direct connection between the escalation of civil conflict, the retardation of socioeconomic development, and the exacerbation of human misery. While the cases presented here are specific to Africa, they speak to a more generalized phenomenon; likewise, prevention or resolution of conflict in the African context may suggest conflict prevention and/or resolution in other contexts. For example, in the past, ethnicity and ethnic conflicts have been conceptualized as "tribal" and viewed as peculiarities of the African context. Recent ethnic pogroms in Eastern Europe and Central Asia as well as Africa, however, have generated a special literature that looks at the manifestations of ethnicity as a global phenomenon that is not limited to Africa and is not necessarily confined to state boundaries.

An exploration of historical circumstances is essential to explaining the context of civil conflict in Africa. Each of the contributors to this volume introduces the relevant history of the situation in question. As the contributors pursue the catalysts of civil conflict in Africa through the case studies, they also seek to balance the internal factors with the external ones that are beyond the control of national leaders. This collection represents a step toward comprehensive and integrated research on civil conflict in Africa.[1]

PART I: BACKGROUND

Part I consists of three chapters that set the background for the book: theoretical, contextual, and empirical. In chapter 2, George Klay Kieh, Jr., tackles the dual task of explaining conflict for research and for policy applications. He reviews the theoretical literature to examine three principal frameworks used to explain conflict. The *primordial theory* highlights ethnic cleavages. Previously used to explain African conflict alone, it has found recent utility in European and Asian cases. The *class theory* is rooted in classical Marxist analysis. It tends to focus on conflict between subordinate and superordinate groups defined by their control of scarce economic resources and collateral political power. The *eclectic theory* is a composite that seeks to bring out the complexity of contemporary civil conflict. This theory recognizes that civil conflict is rarely over a single issue.

Next, Kieh examines three types of theories of conflict resolution. *Peacemaking theories* involve negotiation and mediation as major processes. The success of these processes depends on both material (money, weapons, manpower) and relational (interpersonal skills, allies, goodwill) resources that may not always be readily available or equitably distributed among the concerned parties. *Peacekeeping* takes several forms: The most common is traditional peacekeeping with military force where a neutral international actor intervenes to prevent the outbreak of war, while peace observation requires a cease-fire that is monitored by neutral observers. *Humanitarian assistance theory* focuses on the provision of essentials by a third party for the innocent victims of conflict. *Peace enforcement* relies on the third party's actual coercion of compliance from all parties to the conflict. Kieh concludes chapter 2 with recommendations for refining the existing theories to make them more useful for contemporary situations.

The context within which civil conflict takes place in Africa is also the context within which peace is pursued. In chapter 3, Kieh describes the general context of civil conflict in Africa. It is beset with multiple, complex, exogenous, and endogenous forces. Some of those forces include ethnic exclusion and favoritism during the colonial period; postcolonial domination of key government sectors by select groups; one-party governments after independence; military takeovers, coups, counter-coups, and consequent unstable governments; government domination of the public sphere with little or no private sector development; and the subordination of economic development to the acquisition and maintenance of political power. When the state dominates the public sphere of civil society, competition for power and scarce resources takes place in the political arena. The private sector is also attenuated in the postcolonial era, and therefore left out of much of the competition characteristic of free society. This further magnifies the importance of the political arena. Thus, obstacles to democracy may emanate from the persistence of practices that date to colonial times, rather than from the absence of democratic institutions as such.

Each situation of civil conflict is unique; there is rarely the same configuration or even the same combination of forces, but the overall effects exhibit common patterns. Patterns and trends are the subject of Kieh's chapter 4. Civil conflict in some form is a phenomenon that can neither be ignored nor avoided in any discussion of modern Africa. Its most obvious manifestations have been seen in the recent, and unresolved as of this writing, violent clashes in Sierra Leone, Liberia, Burundi, and the Democratic Republic of the Congo (DRC), none of which is a self-contained instance of a discrete conflict situation. These situations involve crosscutting ethnic alliances compounded by political alliances. Thus, fallout from Liberia is felt in Sierra Leone; from Rwanda/Burundi in DRC; and from DRC in Uganda, Namibia, Zambia, and Angola. There is also fallout from situations in Somalia, Sudan, and Kenya that on initial examination may seem unrelated.

Ethnic, religious, and regional differences often overlap, creating multiple layers of cleavage. These multiple layers explain the apparent pervasiveness of ethnicity as discussed by Augustine Konneh in chapter 6 on Liberia. Military rule can also be a proxy for ethnic dominance. Pita Ogaba Agbese in chapter 7 and Kieh in chapter 8 discuss the complexities of this factor in Nigeria and Somalia respectively. Julius Ihonvbere's chapter 9 on Zambia addresses the challenges that ethnic issues pose to democratic consolidation and pluralistic governance. Ethnicity as a source of conflict is also exacerbated by other aspects such as those associated with social and psychological factors. As Musifiky Mwanasali explains in chapter 5 on the Great Lakes region of Africa, dehumanization, or demonization in its extreme form, is often used to justify acts against "them" that otherwise would not be possible. The case studies that constitute Part II demonstrate these patterns and trends. They also raise questions that push the reader beyond ethnicity for explanations.

PART II: CASE STUDIES

Consistent with the conceptual and methodological orientations set forth in Part I, Musifiky Mwanasali in chapter 5 begins his analysis of the African Great Lakes situations with historical background to the civil conflict that seems to have infected this region. He highlights the sociocultural, political, and economic factors leading up to the current crises in Rwanda, Burundi, Uganda, and the Democratic Republic of the Congo (DRC). This chapter examines the manifestations of both internal and external forces as they contribute to the chronic instability and violence that have overburdened humanitarian initiatives in this part of the world. Mwanasali completes his analysis with an assessment of the conflict management efforts and the prospects for the future of this region. He addresses political instability and modes of governance, focusing on issues related to systematic efforts to engender participation and definitions of citizenship. One may also generalize from the concluding remarks to other countries in Africa, at least as a warning, if not as a prediction.

Augustine Konneh's chapter on the Liberian civil war challenges us to look beyond popular political wisdom disseminated through the Western press. Such notions, however, are not limited to the media. Western scholarship typically overemphasizes the "tribal" factor in African civil wars and downplays the role of the state in creating the structural conditions that lead to such violent outbreaks. Konneh uses the war in Liberia to argue for consideration of a "multiplicity of interrelated factors" that cause civil conflict. The historical overview of Liberia sets aside long-held notions about intergroup relations, especially between Settler and non-Settler citizens, and about the role of foreign capital. The list of direct causes of the conflict includes economic stagnation, nepotism, student/labor unrest, the activities of political opposition groups, society opening up to the hinterland, absolute economic decline, and excessive spending on the Organization for African Unity (OAU) summit. Along with an account of the April 12, 1980, coup and its aftermath, Konneh reviews the role of ethnic identity in the Liberian civil conflict. His use of political economy to launch the analysis of ethnicity corrects many common misperceptions that place ethnic alliances over all others. This analysis demonstrates how economic activities, religious practices, and outside forces can exacerbate hostilities around ethnic politics. The chapter concludes with a statement of the challenges facing Liberia and an inventory of goals for democracy. These political, social, and economic challenges and goals are typical of the Liberian case but are not limited to it, as other chapters in this volume confirm.

Pita Ogaba Agbese's "Military Rule and Sociopolitical Crises in Nigeria," chapter 7, begins with a critique of Nigeria's most recent military governments. He attributes Nigeria's economic and political crises directly to the "decades of corruption and maladministration" that have characterized the military regimes. Professor Agbese notes that rather than bringing order and stability, military governments can exacerbate other problems of civil conflict in addition to harming the military institution itself. When the military is politicized, it leads to polarization within the military. As the number of roles the military appropriates for itself increases, and politics become more militarized, a culture of violence is created. This hinders the process of democratization because the use of force is too easily resorted to where dialogue and negotiation could otherwise be used. Why and how did the military in Nigeria disengage from politics? Agbese advances an analysis of the 1993 turnover by Babangida and its impact on the country. Among the explanations considered are the following: that the military takeover was temporary; and that it had accomplished its goals of bringing nonpoliticized stability, cleaning up the government, and reducing the role of the wealthy in government. He goes on to examine factors such as pro-democracy groups, ethnicity, and regionalism; ideological factors; special interest groups' concerns about unmasking corruption; and grassroots support, as they figured in the course of events surrounding the 1993 presidential elections. Agbese ends chapter 7 with a prospectus for solving Nigeria's political impasse and assuring a sound foundation for democracy. His concluding remarks suggest that a major step in this direction is the focus on a "concrete political and economic agenda," rather than just "removing the president from power."

George Kieh scrutinizes the question of primordial ethnic hostilities again in chapter 8, "The Somali Civil War." His critique of the international community's response to the crisis in Somalia accentuates the inadequacy of ethnic analyses alone for explaining the war. Kieh's central argument is that "the Somali civil war must be situated within the broader context of social formations and the attendant relations of production and distribution." From this perspective he undertakes a threefold task: (1) to delineate the political, economic, and social forces behind the civil war; (2) to assess the impact of existing efforts to resolve the conflict; and (3) to identify some essential steps toward conflict resolution in this case. In order to understand the factors that brought on the civil war, one must also understand the historical context. This Kieh accomplishes with a concise account of the precolonial and postcolonial relations on the Somali peninsula involving Somali clans, the Arabs, various European powers, and Ethiopia. The United States of America and the Soviet Union among others figure in the 1969 military coup–generated regime of Siad Barre and Somalia's consequent crises of underdevelopment. Kieh's analysis of the civil war reaffirms Agbese's observations on the serious limitations and handicapping force of military regimes. Also, Kieh demonstrates the futility of the attempts to resolve conflict and restore order that were sidetracked by actions in response to outside vested interests, rather than those of Somalia itself. Kieh's prescriptions for resolution and rebuilding, like those of the other writers, involve local, national, and international efforts.

The final case study in this volume is Julius Ihonvbere's "Democratic Consolidation and Civil Conflict in Zambia." He begins his study of Zambia by taking a closer look at both past and present pro-democracy forces in other locations on the continent. Armed with a conceptual framework for arguing the distinction between *political liberalization* and *democratization*, Ihonvbere first traces the origins of the *new* liberalization and the crisis of democratic consolidation in Africa. The challenges to consolidation and democratization that he cites echo those of Konneh, Kieh, Agbese, and Mwanasali. He gives special attention to some fractured relations, elite-mass, urban-rural, and among various religious, regional, and ethnic groups that militate against collective action by the people. Ihonvbere describes the complex ethnic element, compounded by religious considerations, various types of patronage, and the rising expectations of citizens. The case of Zambia since Frederick Chiluba presents an opportunity to take a more clinical look at rebuilding processes and how internal and external forces contribute to failed democratic consolidation. It is fitting to conclude Part II of this volume with Ihonvbere's list of conditions for conflict management in Zambia, which he calls "a typical example of the challenge, even failure, of the liberal democratic enterprise." He reminds us of the need for fundamental changes in the actions of government, citizens, and the world community.

NOTE

1. See, for example, Eghosa E. Osaghae, "Conflict Research in Africa," *International Journal of World Peace* 16 (December 1999): 53–72.

2

Theories of Conflict and Conflict Resolution

George Klay Kieh, Jr.

INTRODUCTION

The precipitous increase in the incidence of civil conflicts has occasioned two major interrelated challenges for academics, policymakers, and citizens at large. The first challenge is the daunting task of deciphering the complex milieu of conflict precipitants. In other words, a major task involves making the determination, to paraphrase Ted Robert Gurr, as to "Why [People] Rebel."[1]

The second conundrum concerns both the development and the application of modalities for resolving conflict. The issue is what model or models are appropriate for resolving civil conflicts?

Against this background, this chapter will examine some of the major theoretical frameworks that are used in the scholarly literature to explain both the root causes and the peaceful resolution of civil conflicts. These theoretical frameworks are employed in the various case studies.

THEORIES ON THE ROOTS OF CIVIL CONFLICTS

Drawing from the scholarly literature, three major theoretical frameworks on the causes of civil conflicts can be identified: the primordial, class, and eclectic theories.

The Primordial Theory

The centerpiece of the theory is primordialism and its associated loyalties and ties. Clifford Geertz provides an excellent description of these ties:

> By a primordial attachment is meant one that stems from the "givens" . . . of social existence; immediate contiguity and kin connection mainly, but beyond them the givenness that stems from being born into a particular religious community, speaking a particular language . . . and following particular social practices. These congruities of blood, speech, custom, and so on, are seen to have an ineffable, and at times overpowering coerciveness in and of themselves.[2]

Based on this premise, the theory has several characteristics. Primordial groups—clan, sub-clan, ethnic group, racial group—are the principal actors in a polity, around which cultural, economic, political, and social life is organized. Accordingly, collective action by each primordial group, including perceptions, beliefs, and expectations, is structured by ethnocultural peculiarities. Also, within the inter-primordial relational architecture there are hegemonic and subaltern groups. The former controls the levers of political and/or economic power.

The hegemonic and subordinate primordial groups have their respective agendas, which may run the gamut from a desire for political power to an interest in acquiring and retaining sizable shares of the available material resources. In the pursuance of primordially based agendas, alliances may be formed between the hegemonic group and a subordinate group or groups, and among various subordinate groups in their efforts to extract concessions from the hegemonic group.

Primordially based civil conflicts may be precipitated by various factors either singularly or collectively. For example, according to Juha Auvinan, conflict may result if the hegemonic group excludes the subordinate ones from economic and political opportunities.[3] This may assume the form of monopolization of access to cabinet posts and top positions in the military and in parastatal enterprises by the hegemonic primordial group, to the exclusion of the subordinate groups.[4] In turn, this may generate discontent among the subaltern groups directed at the sources of deprivation and entitlement failure.[5]

Another source of primordial conflict is the manipulation of differences by an external power or powers. For example, during the Cold War, many of the ethnic conflicts in the former European colonies of Asia and Africa were triggered by the superpowers pitting one ethnic group against another.

Also, ethnic conflicts may be generated by social and political change or an identity crisis propelled by the historical and political transformation of nations.[6] The cases of Yugoslavia and the Soviet Union are noteworthy.

Furthermore, ethnic diversity is a major precipitant of civil conflict, especially in developing societies. David Krymkoski and Raymond Hall argue that ethnic conflict in Africa stems in part from the legacy of European colonialism, which tended to combine, and thus enlarge, indigenous political and social territorial units, and to centralize resources, power, status, and privilege in the administrative center.[7] In many cases, these arrangements forced or strongly influenced diverse ethnic groups to enter into new social and political relationships that contravened traditional patterns.[8]

The Class Theory

The class theory has its intellectual roots in the seminal work of Karl Marx, *The Communist Manifesto*. Since then, the theory has been refined against the backdrop of the changing dynamics of industrialism and postindustrialism. The theory is based on several tenets. Every society—developed or developing—has an economic mode of production that is central to the determination of the station of the members of the society. In other words, the foundational postulates of the mode of production determine the critical issue of allocation: Who gets what? How much?

A related tenet is that each member of a society based on his or her relationship to the mode of production belongs either to the owning class or to a subaltern one. The former consists of those who own and control the major means of production on which the mode of production is anchored. Also, the propertied class determines the allocation and distribution of resources: Who gets what? The latter comprises the subaltern classes of the petite bourgeoisie, the proletariat, the peasantry, and the lumpenproletariat. The class structure leads to exploitation, which determines the sources and extent of class conflict.[9]

Another major tenet is that the exploitation of the subaltern classes by the ruling class leads to conflict. However, the major precondition for the eruption of conflict is the development of class-consciousness by the members of the subaltern classes. That is, it is not sufficient for the members of the subordinate classes to be exploited and repressed by the members of the bourgeois class; significantly, they must become cognizant of their exploitation, in order to be able to wage class struggle. According to Karl Marx,

> Along with the constantly diminishing number of the magnates of capital who usurp and monopolize all the advantages of this process of transformation, grows the mass of misery, oppression, slavery, degradation, exploitation. . . . The monopoly of capital becomes a fetter upon the mode of production.[10]

The political conflict becomes more acute as the result of both an increasing consciousness by classes of their interests and changes in their relative positions.[11] In the post–Cold War era, free market policies have broken the social safety nets and contributed to the growth of concentrated wealth and of a subproletariat.[12] Despite the end of the ideological rivalry between "East and West," and the inception of the "new globalization," the gulf between the "haves" and the "have-nots" both within and among countries is burgeoning. For example, Africa lags behind European countries and the United States in every category of development, and the gap is increasing. Within African states, there are pockets of opulence, amidst a growing landscape of poverty and mass misery.

Importantly, these class struggles are waged in the arena of the state and are often reflected in the composition of the protagonists in the civil conflict. On the one side, the regime may either defend the interests of the subaltern classes against those of the ruling class and its collaborators or defend the interests of the ruling class against those of the subaltern classes. On the other side is either an insurgency group or a constellation of insurgency groups, representing various class interests.

The Eclectic Theory

The central tenet of the eclectic theory is that civil conflicts are the products of a confluence of factors—cultural, economic, historical, political, social, and soon. That is, given the complexity of civil conflicts a single variable or factor is insufficient to explain the causes of these phenomona.

Larry Minear argues that "at the heart of the [Sudanese] conflict has been an amalgam of religious and racial, political and economic tensions defying easy description."[13] He contends further that it is the synergy of these factors that occasioned the outbreak of the Sudanese civil war in 1956.

Raymond Copson attributes civil wars in Africa to a combination of factors. Accordingly to him, poverty based on individual and regional disparities, for example, manifested in the degradation of unemployment and underemployment, works as an inducement in persuading people to engage in violence.[14] Politically, Copson cites repression, the abuse of human rights, and the concentration of power at the political center as conflict precipitants. In terms of regional and global factors, he maintains that the willingness of neighboring states to lend their support to dissident forces in countries like Angola and Mozambique and the intervention of actors from outside Africa have contributed to the continent's civil conflicts.[15]

Stephen Stedman asserts that "conflicts in Africa arise from problems basic to all populations: the tugs and pulls of different identities, the distribution of resources and access to power, and competing definitions of what is right, fair and just."[16] In other words, he posits that there is a broad universe of ethnic, economic, political, and moral factors that occasion conflicts in Africa.

Chris Garuba identifies an array of factors that contribute to civil conflicts in Africa. The paucity of resources brings even the most equitable sharing arrangements under acute stress.[17] Also, the level of ignorance among the masses makes them highly susceptible to both internal exploitation and external manipulation. Moreover, the African peoples are economically vulnerable. Furthermore, there is political instability.

Treading a similar path, T.A. Imobighe delineates a host of factors that precipitate civil conflicts in Africa. He cites inequities in access to power and resources. He laments the lack of moral and ethical standards in the management of public affairs. Another essential element is discrimination based on sex, religion, ethnic origin, and socioeconomic status.[18] There is also nondemocratic and exclusive governance.[19] Traditionally, there has been a denial of basic human rights.[20] Characteristically, governmental institutions—executive, legislative, and judicial—have performed poorly.

The precipitants of civil conflicts can be divided into two major categories: contingent and proximate. The former consists of those long-term deeply rooted conditions that date back to the very formation of society; however, they are not sufficient to precipitate a civil conflict. The latter serve as "trigger mechanisms" for the outbreak of civil conflict. As "lighting rods," they are dependent on the contingent factors.

Another postulation of the eclectic theory is that a civil conflict usually includes protagonists comprising the government and an insurgency group or groups. Each warring faction usually represents particularistic interests and their agendas.

THEORIES OF CONFLICT RESOLUTION

There are three major, interrelated types of conflict resolution theories: peacemaking, peacekeeping, and peace enforcement.

Peacemaking Theories

Peacemaking theories revolve around the traditional peaceful methods of conflict resolution—inquiry, good offices, negotiation, mediation, arbitration, and adjudication. However, theoretical frameworks have not yet been developed for inquiry, good offices, arbitration, and adjudication. Accordingly, the focus will be on negotiation and mediation, for which theories have been formulated.

Nevertheless, it is useful to sketch out the elements of inquiry, good offices, arbitration, and adjudication, because of their linkages to negotiation and mediation theories. One major linkage is that the information gathered from the aforementioned methods can be used to help negotiation and mediation. Inquiry involves the intervention of a neutral third party in a conflict for the purpose of fact-finding or information collection. The ostensible purpose is to help determine the undercurrents of the conflict.

Good offices entail an impartial third party serving as a conduit for the transmission of information between or among the parties to the conflict. Additionally, the third party may provide venues for meetings between or among the disputants. As in inquiry, the third party does not offer proposals for the settlement of the conflict.

In contradistinction to inquiry, good offices, negotiation, and mediation, arbitration and adjudication are legal methods of conflict resolution in which the decisions of the third party are legally binding. In the case of arbitration, the parties to the conflict select an arbitrator or arbitrators, determine the corpus of law to be used, choose the participants, and decide on the time and place of the hearings. Essentially, the disputants exercise full control over the fundamental rules of the process.

Although adjudication shares the legal trappings with arbitration, however, there are two major differences between the two. The third party in adjudication is usually an international tribunal, like the International Court of Justice. In addition, the international tribunal sets the parameters of the conflict resolution process, without any substantive participation by the disputants. That is, the international tribunal determines the body of law to be applied to the case, and the time and place where the case will be heard.

The Negotiation Theory. Negotiation entails the holding of face-to-face discussions between or among the representatives of the parties to the conflict. No third party is directly involved. Negotiation theory is based on several elements. At the epicenter are the actors; these are the players or the participants in the conflict; they may include the government and private groups in society—an insurgency group or groups, primordial groups, professional groups, and so on.

The issue is the focus of the negotiation process. It revolves around the raison d'être for the conflict. The raison d'être may be political, economic, social, cultural, or a mixture of these types.

Each actor has an agenda. This is the embodiment of the actor's interests, values, and goals. Interestingly, each actor wants to pursue its agenda as fully as possible. Clearly, this is what precipitates the conflict in the first place: the desire of each actor to pursue its agenda adversarially. As Hugh Midall notes, "conflict arises where actors come to have incompatible interests, values or goals."[21]

The actors have attitudes and perceptions that provide them with the compass for navigating the negotiation landscape. Their attitudes may range from unwillingness to compromise, to the use of accommodation as a "face saving exit" for peacefully resolving the conflict. Similarly, the perceptions can run the gamut from viewing the other actors as weak to perceiving them as conniving to defeat one actor.

The actors have divergent resource bases—in terms of finance, personnel, weapons, and so on. In turn, each actor's resource base affects its bargaining power during the negotiation process.

The impetus for the negotiation includes "mutual hurt," "buying time," and "public relations." In other words, the warring factions may be willing to negotiate for a variety of reasons quite apart from a genuine interest in ending the conflict.

The process is crucial to determining the outcome of the negotiation. The process involves several necessary steps. First, the various parties to the conflict must make their cases. That is, they must clearly state their agendas and their preferred solution to the conflict. Second, the structure of the conflict must be changed. This must include altering the conflict situation via, inter alia, the making of conciliatory gestures either unilaterally or mutually. Louis Kriesberg provides an excellent approach for positively transforming the structure of the conflict: "listening to discover the underlying interests of the negotiating partner; analyzing the conflict to discover possible common gains; and creating new options when negotiations become stalemated."[22]

In a similar vein, Gerald Rabow suggests that the parties should "imagine [themselves] in others' shoes; avoiding accusations; clarifying perceptions; understanding, explaining, and not escalating emotions, using appropriate symbolism; listening actively; and speaking purposefully."[23] Third, the process should focus on interests, not positions, because it is interests that the parties will need to satisfy.[24] Fourth, the parties will have to compromise and accommodate in a "give and take mode," realizing that no single party can get all it wants.

The outcome can be one of the following: successful, unsuccessful, or a mixture of the two. The major determinant of success rests on changing the situation in such a way that the conflict of interests is dissolved or transformed.[25] Conversely, an unsuccessful outcome could be propelled by a breakdown or an impasse in the negotiation, especially the unwillingness of a party or parties to compromise. Alternatively, the outcome may be a mixed bag of success and failure. That is, some issues may be resolved, while others may not. However, it is important to realize that a mixed outcome is more dynamic than an unsuccessful one in that the unresolved issues—the "failure"—could be addressed during subsequent meetings.

The Mediation Theory. Conceptually, mediation is the intervention of a neutral third party in a conflict for the purpose of proffering solutions for the peaceful resolution of the conflict. As in negotiation, the actors are the foundation of the mediation mode; these are the participants in the conflict; they may include the government and a private group or groups.

As in negotiation, the issue may cover political, cultural, economic, and social matters, such as the allocation of political power, ethnic discrimination, the inequitable distribution of resources, and poor social services. Importantly, there may be either a single issue or multiple issues at the center of a particular conflict.

In addition, central to every conflict are competing agendas. That is, each actor in the conflict has interests, values, and goals that are at variance with those of at least some of the other actors.

The various actors have attitudes and perceptions about the mediator and the other parties to the conflict. These images may either facilitate the successful resolution of the conflict or create difficulties in the way of a successful resolution.

The mediator may be invited or may volunteer. In either case, the parties to the conflict must accept the intervention of the mediator. In order to be effective, the mediator must be neutral and must be perceived as such by the parties to the conflict. The mediator must bring a perspective, skills, and information that are germane to the resolution to the conflict.

The mediation process involves the third party putting forward proposals for resolving the conflict. The mediator may use one of two approaches. At one extreme, the mediator might do no more than initiate communication between the disputing parties.[26] At the other extreme, single-text mediation, the mediator might, after a thorough exploration of the situation, offer the disputing parties a proposed solution on a take-it or leave-it basis.[27] The parties are not obligated to accept the suggestions of the mediator.[28]

In terms of the outcome, successful mediation is contingent upon a variety of factors. According to Saadia Touval, these factors can be divided into two major categories: (1) the circumstances of the mediator's intervention; and (2) the mediator's attributes and qualities.[29]

Peacekeeping Theories

The term "peacekeeping" has traditionally been used to describe various forms of legitimized collective intervention aimed at avoiding the outbreak or resurgence of violent conflict between disputants.[30] There are several modes of peacekeeping: traditional peacekeeping or military interposition, peace observation, humanitarian assistance, electoral assistance, and disarmament. So far, theoretical frameworks have been developed for traditional peacekeeping, peace observation, and humanitarian assistance. Accordingly, these theories will be examined in this section. On the other hand, electoral assistance and disarmament are still in the pre-theory stages. Schematically, electoral assistance involves a third party, usually an international organization, providing technical assistance and monitoring the holding of elections in a conflict-afflicted country. In terms of disarmament, it involves the collection of weapons from the disputants.

The Traditional Peacekeeping Theory. The traditional peacekeeping theory rests on the use of military force by a third party, usually an international organization, to intervene in a conflict that is either on the verge of breaking out into a war or is already in a state of war. The peacekeeping force should intervene in the conflict with the agreement of all or some of the parties. That is, it is important for one or more of the parties to accept the intervention of the peacekeeping force. This is because the peacekeeping force will require the assistance of one or more of the parties in order to be able to establish its foothold and subsequently traverse the local terrain.

Another major element of the theory is that the peacekeepers must be neutral and impartial. However, impartiality is difficult to find and hard to sustain for a long time under conditions of stress. But it is essential to whatever effectiveness, authority, and leverage peacekeepers have, and perhaps more than anything else it makes peacekeeping a distinctive kind of conflict resolution activity.[31]

Peacekeepers may be armed, but only for self-defense; what constitutes appropriate self-defense will vary by mission; but because the peacekeepers are almost by definition outgunned by the disputants they are sent to monitor, any recourse to force must be calibrated to localize and defuse rather than escalate violence.[32]

Importantly, if a peacekeeping force merely stifles conflict and does not facilitate its resolution, then it will only impose different forms of conflict, and violence may erupt when the peacekeeping force is withdrawn.[33] In other words, the major determinant of success is the capacity of the peacekeeping force to create an atmosphere conducive to peacemaking.

The Peace Observation Theory. The major prerequisite for peace observation is the existence of a cease-fire. That is, armed hostilities must cease, and the parties to the conflict must agree on a cease-fire arrangement. The cease-fire is enforced by a group of neutral observers usually from member states of an international organization, but acting as impartial servants of that organization rather than as representatives of their governments.[34]

The peace observers perform several interlocking functions. They may create buffer zones for keeping the combatants apart. Also, they may patrol and supervise the cease-fire agreement. The central purpose is to report both violations and compliance. Another major role that the peace observers may play is the monitoring of human rights. In this role, their major purpose is to report violations.

The Humanitarian Assistance Theory. The basis of humanitarian assistance is the provision of food, medicine, shelter, safety zones, and so on, to defenseless civilians caught up in an armed conflict. These items can be provided either within a country that is engulfed in a civil war or in other countries where there are refugees from the war-afflicted country.

Humanitarian assistance may be provided by a country, private organization, or intergovernmental organization acting singularly or in concert. Overtly, the provider's purpose is to help alleviate the suffering of innocent civilians, usually children and women.

In terms of principles, there is the need to maximize the value of the neutrality and impartiality of relief efforts.[35] Importantly, humanitarian aid must be provided only to noncombatants, solely on the basis of need, and regardless of the origins, beliefs, or ideologies of the beneficiaries.[36]

Peace Enforcement Theory

Peace enforcement theory is based on several major conditions. A third party intervener must demonstrate the will and the capacity to coerce the parties to a conflict to abide by the terms of a peace accord. In other words, the peace enforcer must have the requisite materiel and personnel to induce compliance.

The peace enforcer should be neutral. That is, the intervener must be prepared and must demonstrate its willingness to induce compliance from all of the parties to the conflict, without exception. This is critical for establishing the enforcer's credibility with both the disputants and the international community at large.

Another important element is that the enforcer must be familiar with the broader political, economic, social, and cultural dynamics of the target area.[37] Without this knowledge base, the enforcer will lack the understanding that is critical to peace enforcement.

CONCLUSION

The chapter has attempted to examine some of the major theoretical frameworks that are employed to describe and explain the roots of civil conflicts and the resolution of those conflicts. In terms of the roots of civil conflicts, the focus was on the three major theories—primordial, class, and eclectic—that are frequently used in the scholarly literature. These theories provide divergent perspectives on the causes of civil conflicts. Specifically, the primordial theory points to clan, ethnic, and racial antagonisms as the precipitants of civil conflicts. Conversely, the class theory identifies inequities among economic groups as the bases for conflicts. Between these two polar opposites is the eclectic theory. It stresses that the foundation of civil conflicts cannot be described and explained by either primordial or class antagonisms alone. Instead, conflicts are the products of a confluence of factors that may, depending on the circumstances of the conflict, include primordial and class-based factors.

In terms of conflict resolution, the chapter discusses peacemaking, peacekeeping, and peace enforcement theories. In the case of peacemaking theories, the emphasis is on negotiation and mediation. This is because negotiation and mediation have graduated to the level of theory. In contradistinction, inquiry, good offices, arbitration, and adjudication are still essentially in the pre-theory stage. Negotiation theory focuses on the centrality of direct discussions, accommodation, and compromise between and among the parties to the conflict as the bedrock of conflict resolution. On the other hand, mediation theory rests on the intervention of a neutral third party and the proffering of solutions this third party as the engine of conflict resolution. In terms of peacekeeping, the traditional peacekeeping, peace observation, and humanitarian assistance theories are discussed. The traditional peacekeeping theory is premised on the use of military force as an instrument for creating the conditions for peacemaking. The peace observation theory is based on the notion of using an impartial third party to monitor compliance with a cease-fire and on the promotion of human rights. The humanitarian assistance theory is concerned with describing and explaining the dynamics of providing aid—food, shelter, medicine, and so on—to civilians during conflicts, especially civil wars. Peace enforcement theory involves the articulation of the intricacies of a neutral third party using coercion or the threat thereof to induce compliance with a cease-fire or peace accord by the parties to a conflict.

Finally, much work needs to be done in the theory building enterprise, particularly in two areas. The existing theories on conflict and conflict resolution need to be refined from time to time, against the background of their application to various civil conflicts. This will help to improve the theories' explanatory capacities and improve their overall rigor. The other area that needs work is the formulation of new theories that embody those modes of peacemaking and peacekeeping that are in the pre-theory stage. The rationale is that this will expand the theoretical tapestry; in turn, this will give researchers more tools for describing, explaining, and predicting civil conflicts and conflict resolution.

NOTES

1. See Ted Robert Gurr, *Why Men Rebel* (Princeton, NJ: Princeton University Press, 1970). This seminal study examines the undercurrents and dynamics of civil strife.
2. Clifford Geertz, "The Integrative Revolution: Primordial Sentiments and Civil Politics in New States," in *The Interpretation of Culture: Selected Essays* (New York: Basic Books, 1973), 259.
3. See Juha Auvinen, "Political Conflict in Less Developed Countries," *Journal of Peace Research* 34, no. 2 (1997): 178.
4. Ibid.
5. Ibid.
6. George Kourvetaris, "Ethnonationalism and Subnationalism: The Cases of Former Yugoslavia," *Journal of Political and Military Sociology* 24 (Winter 1996): 165.
7. David Krymkoski and Raymond Hall, "The African Development Dilemma Revisited: Theoretical and Empirical Explorations," *Ethnic and Racial Studies* 13, no. 3 (1990): 316.
8. Ibid.
9. Terry Boswell and William Dixon, "Marx's Theory of Rebellion: A Cross-National Analysis of Class Exploitation, Economic Development and Violent Revolt," *American Sociological Review* 58 (1993): 688.
10. Karl Marx, *Capital*, vol. 1 (New York: International Publishers, 1967), 763.
11. Stephen Tansey, *Politics: The Basics* (New York: Routledge, 1995), 223.
12. James Petras and Chronis Polychroniou, "Capitalist Transformation: The Relevance of and Challenges to Marxism," in *Marxism Today*, ed. Chronis Polychroniou and Harry Targ (Westport, CT: Praeger, 1996), 107.
13. Larry Minear et al., *Humanitarianism under Siege: A Critical Review of Operation Lifeline Sudan* (Trenton, NJ: Red Sea Press, 1990), 1.
14. Raymond Copson, "Peace in Africa? The Influence of Regional and International Change," in *Conflict Resolution in Africa*, ed. Francis Deng and I. William Zartman (Washington, DC: Brookings Institution, 1991), 25.
15. Ibid.
16. Stephen Stedman, cited in O.B.C. Nwolise, "ECOMOG Peacekeeping Operations in Liberia: Effects on Political Stability in the West African Sub-Region," *African Peace Review* 1, no. 1 (1997): 39.
17. Chris Garuba, "Crisis in Africa and the Challenge of Capacity Building," in *Capacity Building for Crisis Management in Africa* (Lagos, Nigeria: Gabumo Publishing Company, 1998), 7.
18. T.A. Imobighe, "Conflict in Africa: Roles of OAU and Sub-Regional Organizations," lecture delivered at the National War College of Nigeria, Abuja, Nigeria, February 1998, 4.
19. Ibid.
20. Ibid.
21. Hugh Midall, *The Peacemakers* (New York: St. Martin's Press, 1992), 125.
22. Louis Kriesberg, *International Conflict Resolution* (New Haven, CT: Yale University Press, 1992), 125.

23. Gerald Rabow, *Peace through Agreement* (New York: Praeger, 1990), 17.
24. Ibid.
25. Midall, *The Peacemakers*, 51.
26. Rabow, *Peace through Agreement*, 23.
27. Ibid.
28. Ibid.
29. Saadia Touval, *The Peace Brokers* (Princeton, NJ: Princeton University Press, 1982), 7.
30. Mats Berdal, *Whither UN Peacekeeping?* Adelphi Papers 281 (London: Brassey, 1993), 3.
31. Larry Fabian, *Soldiers without Enemies* (Washington, DC: Brookings Institution, 1971), 21.
32. William Durch, "Introduction," in *The Evolution of UN Peacekeeping* (New York: St. Martin's Press, 1993), 4–5.
33. A.J.R. Groom, *Peacekeeping* (Bethlehem, PA: Lehigh University, 1973), 19.
34. David Wainhouse, *International Peacekeeping at the Crossroads* (Baltimore: Johns Hopkins University Press, 1973), 8.
35. United Nations High Commission for Refugees, *The State of the World's Refugees, 1995* (New York: Oxford University Press, 1995), 133.
36. Ibid.
37. George Klay Kieh, Jr., *The Economic Community of West African States and the Liberian Civil War*, Monograph (forthcoming).

3

The Context of Civil Conflict in Africa

George Klay Kieh, Jr.

INTRODUCTION

The sine qua non for understanding a civil conflict is an examination of the context in which the conflict occurs. By the conflict context, I am referring to the environment—the societal conditions—in which the conflict takes place. This is important because the conflict context provides insights into the cultural, economic, historical, political, and social conditions that germinate and nurture the seeds of civil conflict.

In the case of Africa, the various "zones of conflict" share a general conflict context. This means, because African countries have cultural, historical, economic, political, and social similarities, that a general conflict context can be constructed for the continent. However, when the conflict context is applied to a particular civil conflict, there will be some nuances, which will provide the specifics of the particular civil conflict.

Against this background, this chapter will examine two interrelated issues. What is the general context in which civil conflicts occur in Africa? How does the conflict context help to foster civil conflicts in Africa?

THE CONFLICT CONTEXT

The conflict context in Africa consists of two clusters of interrelated basic factors: colonialism and its legacy, and the postcolonial crises—the authoritarian multiplex, the crisis of economic underdevelopment, social malaise, and the ethno-cultural conundrum.

Colonialism and Its Legacy

Colonialism was one of the major stages in the dehumanization and exploitation of Africa and its peoples. Prior to the colonial era, the European imperialist powers sponsored various exploratory missions ostensibly designed to collect valuable data about the African continent. Accordingly, beginning in the sixteenth century, the European imperialists made their formal contact with African societies.

Significantly, prior to the contact with Europe, Africa had various thriving societies with their own cultural, economic, educational, political, and social systems. Vincent Khapoya provides an assessment of precolonial development in Africa:

> As early modern African states continued to develop, and trade between coastal cities and interior regions expanded throughout the continent, various African peoples established political confederations based on religious ideology, commercial linkages, and/or military authority. Such confederations were often committed to modernizing trends—for example establishing broader nationalist ideologies, promoting literacy and advancement by merit, expanding both regional and international commerce, and undertaking significant administrative and military reforms.[1]

Culturally, there were numerous ethnic groups, each with its own specific customs, norms, and values. Nevertheless, these various ethnic groups shared generic customs, norms, and values; these included an emphasis on the collectivity as opposed to the individual, respect for elders, and hospitality to neighbors and strangers.

In the economic arena, the dominant mode of production was communalism. In this mode, the major means of production were collectively owned. Also, the relations of production were based on egalitarian principles such as equity in the distribution of the goods produced. Thus, the profit motive was anathema.

The educational system and its contents were a reflection of the objective conditions of African societies.[2] That is, indigenous African education was multifaceted and relevant to both the material and the spiritual realities of African societies.[3] An excellent example was the Bemba of what was then Northern Rhodesia: Children by the age of six could name fifty to sixty species of tree plants without hesitation.[4] The explanation of this is simply that knowledge of the trees was a necessity in an environment of "cut and burn" agriculture and in a situation where numerous household needs were met by tree products.[5]

Politically, there were various clusters of state systems—confederal, federal, and unitary. Some of the famous polities included the Egyptian empires, the Malian Confederation, Songhay, and the Ashanti Kingdom. These various state systems had different organizational forms: segmented, pyramidal, and hierarchical.[6]

Socially, there were various institutions that inculcated societal values in young people and ensured compliance among the citizenry at large. At the core was the extended family, which consisted of an extensive network of relatives. Among other things, the family helped raise the children and promoted societal values and norms at the micro level. Also, the family provided the vehicle through which an individual could gain access to land; land was used to plant and produce crops primarily for consumption, not for profit.

However, such modernizing trends were interrupted by slavery, then by Europe's "Scramble for Africa" (c. 1880–1900).[7] In their stead, European colonialism imposed an alien structure complete with cultural, economic, educational, political, and social systems.

In the cultural realm, colonialism formulated and pursued a policy that was deliberately designed to create ethnic divisions and conflicts. John Mbaku explains the ethnic problems created by colonialism thus:

> To provide the appropriate environment for the exploitation of African resources for the benefit of metropolitan economies, the Europeans brought together—through force and not negotiation—many African ethnic cleavages, each with unique language, culture, traditions, and political and economic systems, to form political, economic, and administrative units that could be controlled effectively by the colonial authorities.[8]

In fact, in Burundi and Rwanda, Belgian colonialists manufactured ethnic groups—Hutu and Tutsi. The former consisted of those who made their living by farming; and the latter consisted of those who were cattle herders. For the convenience of Belgian imperialism and colonialism, what was essentially a class structure was transformed into an ethnic one. Accordingly, people were socialized to believe that they belonged to the Hutu or the Tutsi ethnic group. Significantly, given the fact that the Belgian colonialists and imperialists aligned with the Tutsis, this engendered animosity between them and the Hutus; this polarization intensified over time and was bequeathed to postcolonial Burundi and Rwanda.

Economically, colonialism formalized Africa's incorporation into the global capitalist system. There were several results. Peripheral capitalism replaced communalism as the dominant mode of production. African economies were transformed into enclaves for the production of raw materials—agricultural products, minerals—to feed the industrial-manufacturing multiplex of the metropolitan states. Similarly, the system of unequal exchange was institutionalized. Under this lopsided arrangement, which was solely controlled by the Europeans, Africans were paid little for their primary products, while they were required to pay more for often-inferior manufactured goods from the metropolitan countries. Also, the major means of production were privatized. This encouraged the penetration of African economies by metropolitan-based multinational corporations. Profit became the central raison d'être for economic activities. In turn, this laid the foundation for the exploitation of both labor and consumers by businesses. The relations of production were based on a class system, in which the individual's relationship to the major means of production determined his or her status in society. This occasioned the creation of several classes. The ruling or the propertied class owned and controlled the major means of production. The petit bourgeois class consisted of the technocrats who provided skills for the operation of the colonial bureaucracies. At the bottom of the class ladder were the subaltern classes consisting of the proletariat or the working class, the peasantry, and the lumpenproletariat. The distribution of resources favored the ruling class. The consequent inequities generated class animosities and gave rise to various class struggles that were waged by various means such as protest demonstrations and violence.

The colonial educational system was reflective of the values and needs of the colonial powers. Specifically, the contents of the curriculum reflected the dynamics of European and Western societies. Hence, Africans were forced to learn about realities to which they could not relate. Moreover, Africans were taught to believe that their indigenous cultures were inferior to European or Western ones. Accordingly, they were taught to denigrate indigenous strategies of development in favor of Western ones. In terms of needs, Africans were trained to provide labor power for various European enterprises.

The colonial political system was based on an authoritarian state and its associated institutions and undemocratic processes. At the core was the colonial bureaucracy headed by a representative of the colonial power. The colonial bureaucracy exercised unbridled power in virtually every sphere of life in the colonies. The authoritarian state had basic features. It relied on the use of brute force as the instrument for cowing the colonized African peoples into submission. As Michael Crowder asserts, "[The colonial state] engaged in burning of villages, destruction of crops, killing of women and children, and the execution of leaders of the African resistance movements."[9] Another characteristic was that the colonial state imposed laws without the approval of the colonized. Although the colonized Africans were not represented in the law-making process, they were forced to comply with these laws. Similarly, Africans were relegated to the periphery of the political process. Thus, their level of participation was seriously curtailed. Characteristically, the colonial state constantly sought to manufacture conflicts within the ranks of the various African resistance movements. The purpose was to undermine their viability, so that they would not pose major challenges to colonialism.

In the area of social services, the colonial state paid very little attention to the health, housing, and other basic human needs of the colonized Africans. State resources were used to take care of the needs of the citizens of the colonial powers that were resident in the various colonies.

The repressive and exploitative colonial multiplex provided the basis for the formation of national liberation movements in the various colonies. After years of struggle, the European colonial powers were forced to end colonialism. Thereafter, one African colony after another became politically independent.

Disappointingly, despite the attainment of independence in Africa, the vagaries of colonialism remain an albatross around the neck of independent African states. That is, African societies still retain the cultural, economic, political, and social features that were bequeathed to them by the colonial powers. Undoubtedly, since the dawn of the postcolonial era, these features have been and still are an obstruction to development and democracy in the African region and its constituent states. Julius Ihonvbere provides an excellent summation of the broad ramifications of colonialism in Africa:

> It is a truism that Africa's historical experiences of slavery deformed, distorted, disarticulated and underdeveloped the entire region. It culminated in the marginalization of Africa in the global capitalist system and its domination by profit- and hegemony-seeking transnational corporations. Post-colonial realignment of social forces has been greatly influenced by the legacies of this experience.[10]

Thus, although colonialism was formally ended beginning in the late 1950s, it was replaced by neocolonialism, an equally insidious system. As Bade Onimode aptly observes, "The nature of the colonial disengagement from most of Africa, and the rest of the Third World generally, ensured that the independent state would become a neocolonial state, in order to preserve the same basic colonial relationships of domination and exploitation."[11]

Decolonization and independence represented an opportunity for Africans to design by themselves efficient and effective laws and institutions to regulate sociopolitical interaction in the postindependence society.[12] At this time, the neocolonial state should have been reconstructed through proper constitution making to provide each country with viable laws and institutions.[13] After many years of independence, it is now evident that the opportunity made possible by independence and the departure of the Europeans was not used effectively to design the types of constitutional rules that could have maximized individual contributions to national development and allowed the various groups in each country to live together peacefully.[14] Instead, the rules adopted at independence were weak, inefficient, and not designed to reflect African realities, needs, aspirations, interests, and values.[15] The result was that the postcolonial African leadership failed to expunge the colonial legacy from African societies. In other words, independence instituted a change in leadership but failed to bring about transformative changes in institutions, processes, and public policies. To borrow from everyday African parlance, "Political independence in Africa simply changed the driver, but not the taxi."

The Postcolonial Authoritarian Multiplex

The postcolonial authoritarian multiplex in Africa is hoisted on several pillars. At the center of this arrangement are suppression and repression. By and large, since most of the governments in Africa have lost their legitimacy, they rely on the suppression and repression of the population as the primary means of maintaining control of state power. Their actions involve the violation of human and civil rights—the freedoms of association, assembly, of the press, of speech, of thought, and so on. According to Freedom House, in 1998, forty-five of the fifty-four countries in Africa were in the grip of authoritarianism: seventeen countries were making modest progress toward political democratization, while twenty-eight of them were "Not Free" at all.[16]

A related tenet is the use of force as the vehicle for addressing political dissent. For example, the pages of the annual reports of Amnesty International, Africa Human Rights Watch, domestic human rights groups in African countries, and other human rights groups are replete with cases of the arrest, torture—including beatings and other inhumane treatment by security forces—harassment, and imprisonment of scores of individuals. The centrality of the reliance on force to support authoritarianism is reflected in the allocation of public resources. In the 1980s, African countries spent a combined $20 billion on the purchase of weapons.[17] Similarly, between 1990–1991, military expenditure was 43 percent more than the combined education and health allocations in the collective budgets of African states.[18]

Another major pillar is the regimes' use of "divide and rule" as a strategy for developing needless rifts and tensions within pro-democracy groups. For example, African governments have co-opted and continue to co-opt leaders of various pro-democracy movements. In Togo, for instance, the Eyadema regime co-opted Joseph Koffigoh, a one-time highly respected pro-democracy activist: He was appointed prime minister and foreign minister. This undermined Koffigoh's credibility both within his own organization and among pro-democracy activists and the Togolese citizenry in general.

Additionally, African regimes have used primordialism as a way of building a political base amid their crises of legitimacy. In Somalia, Mohammed Siad Barre, the erstwhile dictator, pitted one clan group against another as a way of diverting the attention of the subaltern classes from the vagaries of the political economy to clan tensions and conflicts. Similarly, in Liberia during the Doe era, the regime manufactured a conflict between Doe's Krahn ethnic group and the Gio and Mano ethnic groups. This led, among other things, to needless bloodletting between the Krahns on the one hand and the Gios and the Manos on the other.

Some regimes have criminalized the state. They use their control over the levers of state power to engage in various illicit activities. For example, these African regimes provide sanctuary to drug traffickers in exchange for commissions. They allow various criminal outfits to launder money through their banking systems. They extract bribes from various organizations as the price for investing in various sectors of their economies. The criminalization of the state permeates all levels of the state's bureaucracy, from the military to the police. Military, police, and other security personnel and civil servants make the payment of bribes the precondition for providing service to an individual or group. Ultimately, the criminalization of the state leads to political instability. This is because, given the lucrative nature of the criminalization enterprise, the arena of the state becomes a major "battleground" for various groups, including warlords, seeking to control the state and the access it provides to the loot.

In related fashion, African regimes privatize the state. Accordingly, the state becomes their personal property. In such a situation, the state and its functions revolve around the personality of the president. Essentially, the institutions of the state are weakened and made subservient to the whims and caprices of the president. In other words, the state is a juridical construct, but, in reality, it is the personal fief and extension of the president. No institution of the state can make even routine decisions without seeking the approval of the president.

Since the 1990s, there has been a renewal of resistance to the authoritarian multiplex, principally by groups in civil society. Dubbed the "third wave of democratization," this development has witnessed the proliferation of civil society groups and the intensification of opposition to tyrannical regimes on the African continent. Civil society groups have employed a variety of strategies in their resistance to the authoritarian multiplex. For example, the national conference has been used as a forum for forcing authoritarian regimes to institute political reforms. The national conference was initiated in Francophone Africa in the early 1990s. It has been used in countries such as Benin, Chad, Gabon, Congo, the Democratic Republic of the Congo, Mali, Madagascar, Niger, and Togo. As John Clark states, "During the recent period of intense political reform in Africa, opposition leaders in the Francophone states focused on national conferences as perhaps the most important instrument of political change." [19] The national conference succeeded in occasioning political liberalization in Benin, Chad, Congo, Mali, and Madagascar. However, it failed to reform the authoritarian multiplex in Gabon, the Democratic Republic of the Congo, and Togo. Even in those cases where the national conference has succeeded in instituting political reforms, the neocolonial state has been left intact. The national conference has focused primarily on the control of political power and the institution of political democracy and neglected the centrality of deconstructing the neocolonial state and its peripheral capitalist mode of production. The latter strategy would have helped empower people at the grassroots level and given them a stake in the polity. In turn, this would have enabled popular forces to resist efforts to return to the authoritarian multiplex. However, since this was not done, it was therefore possible for the political democratization process to be aborted in Congo and Niger.

Another strategy has been the use of elections as vehicles for reforming the authoritarian multiplex. Toward this end, civil society groups in Africa with the assistance of Western powers (the United States, France, Britain), Western-controlled international financial institutions (the International Monetary Fund and the World Bank), and Western-based nongovernmental organizations continue to stress the importance of regular, free, and fair elections as linchpins in the political democratization enterprise. Accordingly, elections have been held in several authoritarian states in Africa. Interestingly, those elections have led to the defeat and removal from power of such legendary autocrats as Hastings Kamuzu Banda in Malawi and Kenneth Kaunda in Zambia.

Also, civil society groups have organized various public affairs programs—civic education, conferences, symposia, workshops, seminars, and lectures—for the purpose of developing a new civic culture that will revolve around a conscious populace, the rule of law, accountability, and transparency. Characteristically, there have been some successes and some limitations. In terms of successes, there is an emergent revival of interest in the affairs of the state among Africans. Also, the activities of civil society groups help to serve as checks on the activities of even the most authoritarian regimes in Africa. As for limitations, most of the civil society groups are urban-based; they lack a broad-based membership; they lack internal democracy, accountability, and transparency; some of their leaders are opportunistic and driven by the acquisitive impulse; and a number of the groups lack a real national agenda for helping to transform the society.

The Crisis of Economic Underdevelopment

The crisis of economic underdevelopment is a critical variable in the conflict context of Africa. This is because it illuminates the various problems that are inherent in the peripheral capitalist system and its relations of production and distribution. As Ufo Okeke Uzodike argues, "Despite about four decades of political independence, the sobering reality is that Africa remains a continent ravaged by various manifestations of poverty and underdevelopment."[20] The crisis of economic underdevelopment is caused by several factors. At the center is the structure of the peripheral capitalist economy. The Economic Commission for Africa poignantly stresses the ways in which the structure of the economies of African states is a precipitant of underdevelopment:

> The very structure of the African economy is the primary underlying cause of its persistent crisis. It is a structure that obliges Africa to keep producing commodities it does not need because its people consume very little of such commodities while it depends on other people for the production of its own needs. It is a structure of dependency rather than self-reliance. It is a structure that is more import-export oriented than production oriented.[21]

Another major factor involves the class system and its inequities. Under the peripheral capitalist economic system, there are two clusters of classes: the ruling and the subaltern. The former consists of two sectors. The upper sector comprises the owners of foreign-based multinational corporations and businesses who own and control the major means of production. The junior sector consists of the compradors—both state managers and local entrepreneurs. The compradors serve the interests of the foreign-based multinationals and businesses and their parent countries, and neglect those of their own countries and peoples.

Amilcar Cabral lamented the unpatriotic and dependent nature of the African compradorial classes, describing them as

> A pseudo-bourgeoisie controlled by the ruling class of the dominating country . . . thus the local bourgeoisie, however strongly nationalistic it may be, cannot effectively fulfill its historic function, it cannot freely direct the development of the productive; in belief, it cannot be a nationalistic bourgeoisie.[22]

Although the members of the various African compradorial classes constitute a minority in the population, they own and control a "lion's share" of the wealth. For example, in Liberia, one of the oldest independent African countries, the ruling class, which constitutes about 6 percent of the population, controls about 90 percent of the national wealth.

Also, African states have dependent, monocrop economies that serve as sources of raw materials for the industries of the developed capitalist states. For example, Mauritius gets 90 percent of its earnings from groundnuts and groundnut oil exports.[23] Similarly, Gabon, Libya, and Nigeria are dependent upon oil as the "life blood" of their economies. Each of the African countries is dependent upon a single product—agricultural or mineral—as the linchpin of its economy. This makes African countries vulnerable to the vicissitudes of the global capitalist market place. When the price of a particular raw material goes up, the producing African country then experiences a period of temporary prosperity. Conversely, when the price of a particular product goes down, the producing African country faces a reduction in its export earnings. In turn, this curtails the country's ability to meet the challenges of national development—education, health care, and the provision of other basic human needs. To make matters worse, there are no intersectoral linkages within the economy. Accordingly, since sectors operate as self-contained enclaves, technological innovation in one sector does not spill over to the others.

Debt bondage is one of the major causes of the crisis of economic underdevelopment in Africa. It forces African states to divert their export earnings from socioeconomic programs to debt servicing. According to the data, between 1981 and 1985, African countries spent $26.8 billion on debt servicing.[24] In 1986, some sixteen African countries transferred 350 percent more money to the International Monetary Fund than they had received from it in 1985.[25] By the 1990s, African states were collectively spending 30 percent of their export earnings or $25 billion on debt servicing.

African states have responded to their crisis of economic underdevelopment in three major ways. The external solution has been and is being provided by the International Monetary Fund (IMF) through its Structural Adjustment Programs (SAPs). Several African countries have experimented with the IMF's "SAP." SAPs assume that the problems in most African countries are a result of economic imbalances, overvalued currencies, overzealous state intervention, and deficit financing.[26] The typical IMF economic recovery program has three interrelated component parts: stabilization, structural adjustment, and growth strategy.[27] Operationally, SAP programs require African countries to devalue their currencies, reduce the workforce in the public sector, freeze employment, freeze increases in wages, remove all trade barriers, increase interest rates, and end all subsidies for social programs. Unfortunately, SAPs have exacerbated and continue to exacerbate the socioeconomic crises in Africa. First, SAPs are not tailored to the specific economic needs of an African country. Instead, they apply a "one size fits all" package to all African countries. Second, they ignore political realities. Third, overall they usually create more problems then they solve.

The other strategy for addressing Africa's crisis of economic underdevelopment was developed internally. It has two dimensions, regional or continental and sub-regional. At the regional or continental level, the principal strategy was embodied in the Organization of African Unity's Lagos Plan for the Economic Development of Africa. The plan had the following major elements:

1. the establishment of an African Economic Community by the year 2000;
2. the promotion of self-reliance through regional and sub-regional cooperation;
3. the promotion of food production;
4. the promotion of science and technology; and
5. the encouragement of national transformation.

Unfortunately, by 1986, the protocols and programs that provided the foundation of the plan had not been implemented as debt, drought, instability, and increasing maginalization in the global system pushed the African economies into desperate situations, forcing them to abandon the prescriptions of the plan for nationally based strategies and responses to economic cooperation.[28]

At the sub-regional level, the various organizations—the Economic Community of West African States (ECOWAS), the Central African Economic Community, the Maghreb Union, and the Southern African Development Community—have made efforts to find solutions to their members' shared crisis of economic underdevelopment. Each organization has experienced various levels of success and failure. However, they have one common major problem: The sub-regional organizations have failed to transform their respective economies from export-oriented enclaves for the production of raw materials to economies with industrial bases that can produce manufactured goods. This problem has hindered their ability to trade with one another. Instead, because they are all producers of raw materials, they compete for markets in the developed capitalist countries.

Social Malaise

The African continent is plagued with a plethora of social problems. In the area of health, for example, between 1985 and 1992, only 56 percent of the total population of over 650 million people had access to health services.[29] Accordingly, during the same period, life expectancy stood at fifty-two years.[30] A related issue is the food problem. African states are not producing sufficient food to feed their citizens. The effect has been a burgeoning increase in hunger. According to the Food and Agricultural Organization, about 70 percent of Africa's population did not have enough food to eat in the 1980s.[31] In terms of education, there are insufficient numbers of trained teachers, insufficient numbers of schools, inadequate infrastructure and facilities, and a lack of adequate equipment. The poor state of the educational system in the continent is reflected in the low level of literacy: By 1990, the literacy rate was only 51 percent.[32]

The Ethno-Cultural Conundrum

Africa is faced with two major types of ethno-cultural problems. One type of conflict revolves around the clamor for secession by some nationalities in post-colonial African states. For example, since the beginning of the "wave of political independence" that swept through the African continent in the 1960s, the Casamance region in Senegal has been locked in a bitter conflict with the government over the former's desire for its own independent and sovereign state. The unwillingness of the Dakar regime to grant independence to Casamance has led to a civil war. Similarly, in Niger and Mali, the Tuaregs, minorities in the two countries, have been agitating for independence. In the case of Niger, the "Tuareg problem" provided the military with the excuse to abort the process of democratization and reestablish military rule. The putschists argued that the Nigerien government had demonstrated its inability to resolve the conflict with the Tuaregs. In Mali, the new democratically elected government has been able to work out a modus vivendi with the Tuaregs. Thus, the conflict has subsided for now.

The other problem is the politicization of ethnicity by various regimes that have lost popular support and legitimacy. In other words, amidst the erosion of their legitimacy, regimes such as those of arap Moi (Kenya), Barre (Somalia), Doe (Liberia), and Eyadema (Togo) manufactured ethnic animosities between and among various groups. The goal was twofold. First, it was designed to deflect mass attention away from the crises of underdevelopment. Second, it was intended to "divide and rule" the oppressed masses, by pitting them against one another. This instrumental use of ethnicity was pivotal in the fermenting and intensification of various primordial conflicts such as the clan-based "blood bath" in Somalia and the Gio/Mano versus Krahn carnage that reigned during the Liberian civil war.

THE CONFLICT CONTEXT–CONFLICT ACTUALIZATION NEXUS

Importantly, the conflict context provides the contingent or base factors that precipitate civil conflicts in African states. That is, the conflict context plants and nurtures the seeds of civil conflicts. Generally, the conflict context is not sufficient to occasion a civil conflict on its own; instead, it relies on triggers for the actualization of civil conflicts. There are several triggers, including inequities in the distribution of economic resources, a skewed distribution of political power, ethnic discrimination, and ethnic cleansing. The triggers may act singularly or in combination in order to ignite a civil conflict.

Clearly, the transformation of the context is pivotal to the prevention, containment, and management of civil conflicts. In other words, any effort that is designed to minimize civil conflicts must address the factors that are embedded in the conflict context.

CONCLUSION

This chapter has attempted to examine the crucible in which civil conflicts occur in Africa, and the way in which the crucible contributes to the precipitation of civil conflicts. The crucible contains several elements: the colonial legacy, the authoritarian multiplex, the crisis of economic underdevelopment, the social malaise, and the ethno-cultural conundrum. The colonial legacy includes the repressive nature of the neocolonial state in Africa. The postcolonial authoritarian multiplex involves the centrality of the use of force as the principal device for cowing the population into submission, the vitriolic violation of human rights, and the criminalization and privatization of the state. The crisis of economic underdevelopment revolves around inequities in wealth, increasing deterioration of the living conditions of ordinary citizens, escalating levels of unemployment, reduction in the productive capacity of the economy, and a vicious cycle of debt. In the social realm, the problems include poor and inadequate health services, low life expectancy, mass illiteracy, and mass hunger. On the ethno-cultural front, there is the secessionist refrain from various nationalities within the postcolonial African state and the instrumental use of ethnicity by repressive regimes that have lost their legitimacy. Generally, these features are characteristic of the postcolonial social formation in virtually every African state. They serve as the base or contingent factors that are required for the germination and occurrence of civil conflict.

However, the conflict context is not sufficient to ignite a conflict; it requires a trigger, which may be inequities in the distribution of economic resources, disparities in the distribution of political power, skewedness in the distribution of development activities, and ethnic discrimination or ethnic cleansing.

NOTES

1. Vincent Khapoya, *The African Experience*, 2d ed. (Upper Saddle River, NJ: Prentice Hall, 1998), 94.
2. See George Klay Kieh, Jr., "The Roots of Western Influence in Africa: An Analysis of the Conditioning Processes," *The Social Science Journal* 29, no. 1 (1992): 7.
3. Ibid.

4. Walter Rodney, *How Europe Underdeveloped Africa* (Washington, DC: Howard University Press, 1982), 239.

5. Ibid.

6. Khapoya, *The African Experience*, 61–65.

7. Ibid. 94.

8. John Mbaku, "A Balance Sheet of Structural Adjustment in Africa: Towards a Sustainable Development Agenda," in *Preparing Africa for the Twenty-First Century: Strategies for Peaceful Co-Existence and Sustainable Development* (Brookfield, VT: Ashgate Publishing, 1999), 120.

9. See Michael Crowder, "Whose Dream Was It Anyway? Twenty-Five Years of African Independence," *African Affairs* 86, no. 342 (1987): 11.

10. Julius Ihonvbere, "Africa in the 1990s and Beyond: Alternative Prescriptions and Projections," *Futures* 28, no. 1 (1996): 3.

11. Bade Onimode, *The Political Economy of the African Crisis* (London: Zed Press, 1988), 130.

12. John Mbaku, "Bureaucratic Corruption and Reforms in Africa," in *Multiparty Democracy and Political Change: Constraints to Democratization in Africa*, ed. John Mbaku and Julius Ihonvbere (Brookfield, VT: Ashgate Publishing, 1998), 75.

13. Ibid.

14. Ibid.

15. Ibid.

16. Freedom House, *Freedom in the World: An Annual Survey of Political Rights and Civil Liberties*, 1997–1998 (New York: Freedom House, 1998), 600–602.

17. George Klay Kieh, Jr., "Democratization and Peace in Africa," *Journal of Asian and African Studies* vol XXXI, nos. 1 & 2 (1998): 106.

18. Ibid.

19. John Clark, "National Conferences and Democratization in Francophone Africa," in Mbaku and Ihonvbere, *Multiparty Democracy and Political Change*, 97.

20. Ufo Okeke Uzodike, "Democracy and Economic Reforms: Developing Underdeveloped Political Economies," in *Democracy and Democratization in Africa: Towards the Twenty-First Century*, ed. E. Ike Udogu (Leiden: E. J. Brill, 1997), 21.

21. United Nations Economic Commission for Africa, *African Alternative Framework to Structural Adjustment Programs for Socio-Economic Recovery and Transformation: A Popular Version* (Addis Ababa: ECA Secretariat, 1991), 2.

22. Amilcar Cabral, *Revolution in Guinea* (London: Stage 1, 1969), 5.

23. See Kofi Hadjar, *On Transforming Africa* (Trenton, NJ: Africa World Press, 1987), 9.

24. See Frederick Clairmonte and John Cavanaugh, "Impossible Debt on Road to Global Ruin," *Guardian*, January 9, 1987, 1.

25. See Bread of the World Institute, *Causes of Hunger* (Silver Springs, MD: Communications and Graphics, 1994), 109.

26. Uzodike, "Democracy and Economic Reforms," 22

27. Ibid.

28. Ihonvbere, "Africa in the 1990s and Beyond," 6.

29. Bread of the World Institute, *Causes of Hunger*, 109.

30. Ibid.

31. Food and Agriculture Organization, cited in Kieh, "Democratization and Peace in Africa," 106.

32. Bread of the World Institute, *Causes of Hunger*, 109.

4

Civil Conflicts in Africa: Patterns and Trends

George Klay Kieh, Jr.

INTRODUCTION

Since the dawn of the era of "flag independence," Africa has experienced and continues to experience civil conflicts. Virtually every region of the continent has been affected by the "civil conflict epidemic." Nevertheless, contrary to the dominant view in Western circles, conflict is not peculiar to African societies. As Chris Garuba correctly asserts, "conflict conceived as the incompatibility of goals, interests and objectives is endemic in human relations."[1]

Civil conflicts in Africa have been, and still are, precipitated by many factors—cultural, historical, economic, political, and social. However, each conflict has its own particular precipitant or precipitants. Some of the conflicts have resulted in civil wars, while others have not. Henry Wiseman gives an encapsulating assessment of the conflict conundrum in Africa:

> the "just wars" of national liberation, which have all run their course, have been followed by internal conflicts, secessionism, and interstate wars; and with some notable exceptions, the states of Africa are beset by internal economic and political turmoil. In many states, national cohesion and stability are either precarious or non-existent.[2]

Against this background, this chapter has two objectives. First, it will examine the patterns of civil conflicts in Africa. Second, it will delineate the trends of civil conflict. The overall purpose is to situate the case studies in this book within the broader civil conflict crucible in Africa.

THE PATTERNS OF CIVIL CONFLICTS IN AFRICA

Several major patterns of civil conflicts in Africa can be identified: the secessionist pattern, the struggle over state power pattern, the democratization pattern, the ethnic pattern, and mixed pattern.

The Secessionist Pattern

The actors in the secessionist pattern of civil conflicts are a government and an ethno-national group or groups. The government may be autocratic or democratic. In other words, the form of government is not a major determinant of the occurrence of secessionism.

The centerpiece of the conflict often revolves around secession. That is, the ethno-national group agitates for the establishment of its own sovereign and independent state. Conversely, the government, irrespective of its complexion, attempts to keep the body politic together.

The protagonists may use a variety of methods for pursuing their respective agendas. These may range from the articulation of verbal disagreements to warfare. The latter method is used when efforts at peacefully resolving the conflict fail.

Civil conflicts over secessionism are essentially by-products of the colonial legacy. That is, colonialism reconfigured the geopolitical landscape of Africa by incorporating hitherto independent states into new colonial constructs. In some cases, the politicization of ethnicity, as reflected in the repression and marginalization of some ethnic groups by the regime in power, precipitated the secessionist fervor.

Several cases are instructive. Barely six years after it gained independence from Britain, Nigeria was thrown into civil war. The war pitted the military government against the Ibo-dominated Biafra.[3] The major complaint of the Ibo ethnic group was that it was marginalized in both the configuration of power and the distribution of resources in Nigeria. Accordingly, the Ibos felt that they could improve their lot through the establishment of their own independent country. The reverberations of the civil war transcended the borders of Nigeria: African states were polarized over the conflict, as they aligned with one party or the other. After a bloody two-year civil war, the Biafran secessionists were forced to capitulate militarily. Since then, the Ibos have continued to complain about their marginalization in the Nigerian body politic. In fact, some Ibos are fervent advocates of the "balkanization of Nigeria solution." The belief is that by dividing Nigeria into several mini-ethnic states, the Ibos will then be able to take control of their destiny. In short, the "secessionist Biafran ghost" is still haunting Nigeria. It will be interesting to see the way in which the Obasanjo regime handles the new secessionist clamor that has the potential to cause the disintegration of the Nigerian state.

Another case is the civil war in Senegal; it involves the Senegalese government and the Casamançais. The latter party, which is primarily made up of members of the Diola ethnic group, occupies Casamance, a region in southern Senegal. Physically, Casamance is separated from "mainland Senegal" by the Gambia. This divide has tended to invigorate the secessionist impulse. As Michael Crowder observes, "This separateness was emphasized by the very name Casamance. The people describe themselves to this day as Casamançais rather than Senegalese . . ."[4]

Casamance was initially colonized by the Portuguese in the sixteenth century.[5] It came under French rule as a result of the Franco-Portuguese Convention of 1886.[6] During the colonial era, the French imperialists incorporated Casamance into Senegal. This generated resentment from the Casamançais, and in turn ignited their struggle for secession and independence. The Casamançais organized the Mouvement des Forces Démocratiques Casamance (MFDC), as the principal vehicle for waging an armed struggle against the Senegalese government. In the postcolonial era, the failure of the Senegalese government to address the crisis of economic underdevelopment in the Casamance region has exacerbated the conflict. As Mohammed Faal argues, "Casamance which is termed the 'bread basket of Senegal' has no university, and the infrastructure, apart from those centered on the tourist attractive areas, is chronically underdeveloped."[7]

Unfortunately, the Senegalese government has failed to engage in meaningful discussions with the MFDC and the Casamançais. Instead, the Dakar regime's principal policy has been and continues to be based on the military defeat of the MFDC. Accordingly, in 1995, Senegal signed a Security Accord with neighboring Guinea-Bissau. Under the agreement, Senegal has carte blanche permission to pursue MFDC forces into the territory of Guinea-Bissau. Three years later, Senegal intervened in the civil war in Guinea-Bissau. The ostensible purpose was to disrupt the flow of arms from the renegade Guinea-Bissau soldiers, who were fighting to oust the Vieira regime, to the MFDC forces in Casamance. To date, the Senegalese civil war continues, with the belligerent parties intransigently maintaining their positions.

In Mali, there was a secessionist civil war between the government of military dictator General Moussa Traoré and the Tuaregs, a minority nomadic ethnic group based in the northern part of the country. The Tuaregs' demand for self-determination and independence was precipitated by their repression and peripheralization by the military dictatorship of General Moussa Traoré, who ruled Mali from 1968 until his removal in 1991. The difficult state of affairs forced scores of Tuaregs to flee Mali, in search of safety and security in various neighboring states—Algeria, Libya, Mauritania, and Niger. Those Tuaregs who fled to Libya enlisted the support of the Libyan government for their cause. Accordingly, in 1988, with Libyan support, the Tuaregs organized the Mouvement Populaire de Libération de l'Azaouad (MPLA), as the central instrument for prosecuting their war for self-determination. The MPLA launched an armed rebellion that occasioned, among other things, a refugee crisis that forced over 200,000 civilians to flee for safety.

However, with competing egos and appetites for power, the MPLA degenerated into various factions; this made the civil war multi-frontal. On several fronts, the various factions of the MPLA were fighting one another; on another, the various factions of the MPLA fought the government.

In 1991, a major development occurred. The dictatorial Traoré regime was deposed. This provided an opportunity for the belligerent parties to reassess the civil war. A year later, democratic elections were held, and Alfa Konaré ascended to the presidency. The new regime launched a full-scale peacemaking effort with the various factions of the MPLA. The Konaré regime enlisted the assistance of the United Nations, neighboring states, and domestic actors—elders and the leaders of civil society organizations. The peacemaking crusade paid dividends with the signing of a peace accord in 1992 between the Malian government and the various factions of the MPLA; the accord ended the civil war. In exchange for ending their drive for secession, the Tuaregs were promised autonomy in the conduct of their local affairs.

The Struggle over State Power Pattern

The struggle over state power pattern has several aspects. The players are usually various domestic political groups and the government in power or, in the absence of a government, various domestic political groups. Usually, the various groups are supported by external actors who have a stake in the outcome of the conflict.

The focus of the conflict is control of state power. Characteristically, each actor seeks to promote its own agenda, which embodies its interests. The competing agendas are often portrayed in "zero-sum terms."

The various actors employ an array of methods for promoting their agendas, especially the articulation of their claims to state power. Some use the mobilization of grassroots support. Others use methods such as the organization of demonstrations and the formation of militias. Correspondingly, the form of the conflict swings back and forth like a pendulum: The conflict may move from a crisis to a full-blown civil war.

Several civil conflicts in Africa can be subsumed under this pattern. For example, Angola has been engulfed in a civil war since it gained independence from Portugal in 1975. Originally, the conflict involved three parties: the Popular Movement for the Liberation of Angola (MPLA), a Marxist organization led by Agostinho Neto, the conservative, right-wing, and pro-capitalist National Union for the Total Liberation of Angola (UNITA) headed by the chameleon-like Jonas Savimbi, and the National Front for the Liberation of Angola (FNLA) led by Holden Roberto. When Portugal ended its more than 400 years of colonial control over Angola, it failed to design modalities for facilitating the transfer of power. Hence, the three political factions insisted that each of them was the rightful heir to state power. Given its position of strength and buoyed by its support from the overwhelming majority of the countries in Africa, the MPLA emerged as the temporary victor in the struggle for the control of state power.

Barely a year after it seized state power, the MPLA-led government was faced with a two-sided civil war: On the one hand was UNITA and on the other hand was the FNLA. Subsequently, the civil war drew in the superpowers of the time–the Soviet Union and the United States. The USSR aligned with the MPLA, while the United States supported both UNITA and the FNLA. With money, weapons, and military training from their external patrons, the three factions intensified the civil war. However, later on, the FNLA disbanded, leaving the MPLA and UNITA as the contending parties.

With the end of the Cold War, the chemistry of the Angolan civil war changed in two major ways. First, the MPLA was forced to renounce its Marxist predilections and to adopt a liberal democratic and pro-capitalist complexion. Second, having proven to be an unreliable marauding band of money and power-obsessed individuals with no nationalistic agenda for Angola, UNITA fell out of favor with the United States, its principal patron. The MPLA-led government having renounced its Marxist orientation, the United States rewarded it with recognition as the legitimate government of Angola. Despite that, the United States called for a peaceful resolution of the civil war that included a power sharing arrangement with Savimbi's UNITA. Prior to the change in American policy, the United Nations had undertaken both peacemaking and peacekeeping efforts in Angola. For example, between 1990 and 1992, the United Nations sponsored various peace talks and undertook two peacekeeping operations under the auspices of the United Nations Angolan Verification Mission (UNAVEM I and II). These UN-led initiatives created an atmosphere conducive to settling Angola's leadership conundrum. The kernel of these efforts was the conduct of presidential and legislative elections in 1992, in which various parties including the MPLA and UNITA participated. According to the results of these elections, the MPLA won the presidency and a majority in the new multiparty parliament. However, UNITA refused to end the war and participate in the political process. Jonas Savimbi, the UNITA leader, insisted that the only solution to the protracted Angolan civil war was to make him the president of Angola.

Amidst the continuing carnage, the United Nations continued its conflict resolution efforts. In 1994, the UN brokered the Lusaka Peace Accord, which, inter alia, called for a cease-fire, disarmament, demobilization, the formation of a new and integrated armed force with soldiers from both the MPLA-led government and UNITA, and the holding of new presidential and legislative elections. Again, Savimbi and UNITA lost the elections. Characteristically, Savimbi refused to accept the will of the Angolan people, insisting that he be handed the presidency as the price of peace. In response, the MPLA-led government made concessions to Savimbi, including appointing members of UNITA to positions in the state bureaucracy and giving Savimbi a status comparable to that of a vice president. In order to supervise the Lusaka Accord, on February 9, 1995, the United

Nations established the United Nations Angolan Verification Mission (UNAVEM III) consisting of 6,500 UN soldiers and 500 military observers.[8] Unfortunately, these efforts have not ended the conflict, which has taken a heavy toll on the civilian population. Liz McClintock describes the travails of the Angolan people:

> Limits on civilian freedom of movement, both physical and political, hinder the peace efforts at the grassroots level. Angola remains one of the most heavily mined countries in the world, and, in the provinces, MPLA and UNITA forces still tightly control the interaction of civilians under their authority. The human rights records of both MPLA and UNITA forces are dismal, and despite the presence of a UN human rights mission, very little has been done to curb abuses.[9]

In Mozambique, the circumstances that occasioned the civil war over the struggle for state power were different from those in Angola. Unlike Angola, in Mozambique a single national liberation movement led the struggle for independence against the Portuguese colonialists. FRELIMO (Front for the Liberation of Mozambigue), the nationalist movement, provided a vehicle for all Mozambicans who wanted to end 400 years of Portuguese colonialism. Finally, in 1975, FRELIMO led Mozambique to independence, espousing a Marxist-Leninist ideological orientation.

Alarmed by FRELIMO's Marxist-Leninist Weltanschauung, Portugal acting in concert with South Africa, Rhodesia, and the United States organized the Mozambican National Resistance Movement (MNR or RENAMO) as the opposition group and rival contender for the control of state power. With financial and logistical support from its external patrons, RENAMO plunged Mozambique into a civil war. The war claimed more than 1 million lives. It is further estimated that, out of a total population of 17 million, some 5 million people were internally displaced, and about 2 million others fled to neighboring states.[10]

As in Angola, the end of the Cold War changed the dynamics of the Mozambican civil war. RENAMO, the rebel faction, lost support from its external patrons who viewed the war as inimical to their emerging post–Cold War interests. Consequently, they forced RENAMO to seek a peaceful settlement. Similarly, the FRELIMO-led government was forced to renounce its Marxist-Leninist orientation and adopt liberal democracy and its capitalist economy. Accordingly, as an initial step, a cease-fire was achieved in 1992, under the supervision of a United Nations Peacekeeping Force. Two years later, multiparty presidential and legislative elections were held. FRELIMO won the presidency and the majority of the seats in the new parliament. The elections settled the question of leadership and ended the civil war. Currently, Mozambique is engaged in the Herculean task of peace building.

In the ethnically homogenous southern African state of Lesotho, the struggle over state power erupted after the 1998 parliamentary elections. According to the election results, the Lesotho Congress for Democracy Party (LCD) won a landslide victory, but the Basotho Congress Party and other opposition parties refused to accept the results. Each of the opposition parties was laying claim to the mantle of leadership. Amidst the conflict over leadership, the military intervened. The result was the eruption of chaos that bordered on civil war.

Sensing the danger the struggle over power in Lesotho posed for the entire southern African region, South Africa and Botswana sent troops as part of a peacekeeping force, under the aegis of the Southern African Development Community (SADC), the regional organization. The intervention was resisted by the Royal Lesotho Defense Force (RLDF). Consequently, the SADC Peacekeeping Force and the RLDF engaged in armed hostilities that led to the death of scores of people and the destruction of property.

The parties to the conflict agreed to cease armed hostilities and to settle the leadership impasse through discussions. The arrangement has apparently worked, as evidenced by the non-recurrence of hostilities.

The Third Wave of Democratization Pattern

The third wave of democratization pattern is the newest type. It arose in 1990, following the end of the Cold War. The third wave pattern has several basic features. The actors are usually an authoritarian government and various domestic political parties and other forces. The government may have been elected in either undemocratic or democratic elections.

The conflict usually revolves around political democratization and its attendant characteristics of respect for civil and political rights, free, fair, and regular elections, accountability and transparency in the conduct of governmental affairs, the rule of law, the independence of the judiciary, and the centrality of a viable civil society.

As in the other patterns of civil conflict, the conflicting parties may employ a host of methods including civil wars. Interestingly, even when the parties use civil wars, they rationalize them as vehicles for "establishing democracy."

In the Central African Republic, in May 1996, the military staged a coup d'état against the democratically elected government of Ange-Felix Patasse, who had been elected president in 1993 as part of the process of political democratization that began in 1991. However, France intervened militarily and restored the Patasse regime.

In the Republic of Congo, a Sovereign National Conference was held in 1991 against the background of the autocratic excesses of the military dictatorship of General Denis Sassou-Nguesso, who had ruled the country since 1979. At the end of the conference, President Sassou-Nguesso was stripped of his powers and reduced to a titular head of state. An interim government was established and this government supervised the holding of democratic elections in 1992, the first democratic elections in the history of the country. Pascal Lissouba was elected president and reelected in 1995.

Dissatisfied with their defeat in the two presidential and legislative elections, the political parties of General Sassou-Nguesso and others organized militias—Sassou-Nguesso established the "Cobras." Upheavals began in June 1997, when President Pascal Lissouba attempted to disarm the Cobras.[11] Nineteen weeks of civil war followed.[12] At the end of October, having captured the capital, Brazzaville, and the oil industry center, Pointe Noire, Sassou-Nguesso was inaugurated as the new president.[13] Militias loyal to ousted President Lissouba continued to conduct guerrilla warfare.[14] Although cease-fire accords were signed in November and December 1999, the situation remains fluid.

Niger was affected by the "wave of political democratization" that swept through Congo and several other Francophone African states in 1991 and 1992. A Sovereign National Conference was held in 1991, and it ended more than nineteen years of military rule. Two years later, President Mohamane Ousmane was elected in the first multiparty presidential and legislative elections. Unfortunately, in January 1996, the military aborted the political democratization process, when Col. Ibrahim Bare Mainassara toppled the democratically elected government of President Ousmane. Subsequently, Mainassara consolidated his power and transformed himself into a civilian president, following a bogus presidential election. In 1999, President Mainassara was killed in an airport ambush mounted by some members of his Presidential Guard. After a brief period of continued military rule, elections were held, and a new government was elected.

In Zambia, the great euphoria that greeted the dawn of the "third wave of democratization" in 1991, following the defeat of President Kenneth Kaunda and his United Independence Party (UNIP) in the first multiparty democratic elections, has quickly disappeared. This is because President Frederick Chiluba, the celebrated labor union leader who defeated Kaunda, has reverted to authoritarianism. For example, in 1997, the Chiluba regime implicated former President Kaunda and eighty-five other critics of the government in a bogus coup plot, under the "State of Emergency."

Previously, President Chiluba had used "citizenship" as an instrument for barring former President Kaunda from contesting the presidential election. The Zambian government argued that since former President Kaunda was a Malawian, not a Zambian, he was therefore not eligible to contest the Zambian presidency. This fabricated claim was designed to assure the reelection of President Chiluba, who had lost legitimacy.

The Ethnic Pattern

In the ethnic pattern, the actors are usually a government dominated by an ethnic group and parties representing other ethnic groups. In other words, the players in the civil conflict are the political representatives of various ethnic groups.

The central issue in the conflict is the monopolization of political power by one ethnic group to the exclusion or marginalization of others. That is, the regime in power assigns the important positions in the public bureaucracy to a particular ethnic group, while relegating the other ethnic groups to the periphery.

As in the other patterns of civil conflicts, the actors use a host of methods to articulate and fulfill their agendas. One of the most commonly used methods is warfare. The common justification is that the use of violence becomes necessary upon the failure of peacemaking efforts to resolve the conflict.

The only country in Africa where ethnicity was the only cause of a civil conflict is Djibouti. In cases like Burundi, Chad, Rwanda, and Sudan, while ethnicity was a factor, it was not the sole precipitant of the conflict.

In Djibouti, every sphere of the polity, including the political arena, is based on ethnicity. This has its roots in colonialism: France fanned ethno-cultural polarization between the Afar minority and the Isaa majority. This continued even after independence was granted in 1977. For example, the Isaa ethnic group organized the Popular Rally for Progress Party (RPP) and the Afars established the Front for the Restoration of Unity (FRUD). Conflict between the two ethnic groups and their respective political parties erupted in 1981, when the Afar-based political party was outlawed; thus, the Isaas' political party became the only legal party in the country.

After years of conflict, a compromise was reached in 1992, under which FRUD, the Afars' political party, was "re-legitimized." However, during the national elections a year later, FRUD refused to participate; consequently, a civil war erupted. In 1997, the RPP-led government negotiated a truce with a faction of the military wing of FRUD. The major precondition was the formulation of a power-sharing agreement between the Isaas and the Afars. Internally, political power is divided by means of ethnically balanced cabinets while the prime minister is always an Afar.[15] The presidency has remained in the hands of Aptidon, an Isaa-Somali.[16]

THE MIXED PATTERN

The great majority of the civil conflicts in Africa fall under the mixed pattern. As in the other patterns, the actors in a conflict are a government and various domestic groups.

The causes of a conflict are multiple factors, both contingent and proximate. The former consist of the base factors that are deeply rooted and nurtured over a period of time. The latter comprise the trigger or triggers that aggravate the base factors and ignite a civil conflict. Similarly, the methods used by the various parties vary. As in the other patterns, the utilization of a particular method is dependent upon the state of the conflict.

There are many cases, but only a few will be examined here. In Algeria, a civil war erupted in 1992. Underlying this was a protracted conflict generated by family feuds, personal grievances, class inequities, ethnicity, and religion. The trigger was the military's intervention in politics when it became clear that the winner of Algeria's first multiparty elections would be the Islamic Salvation Front.[17] Consequently, the Islamic Salvation Front was outlawed.[18]

In the aftermath of the military's takeover of the reins of government, various armed militant opposition groups, especially the Islamic Salvation Army (AIS, the armed wing of the Islamic Salvation Front) and the Armed Islamic Group (GIA), initiated an armed rebellion against the military regime.

Despite several peace efforts and the holding of two national elections, the conflict continues. The belligerent parties are causing terror and carnage among the civilian population. By 1999, an estimated 100,000 civilians had been killed.[19]

In Burundi, there has been a cycle of civil conflicts since the country gained independence from Belgium in 1962. At the root of these conflicts has been a synergy of factors including class inequities, ethnicity, militarism, and the struggle for the control of state power. The most recent civil conflict was triggered by the overthrow of the regime of President Sylvestre Ntibantunganya by Pierre Buyoyo, a quintessential putschist, in 1996. Since then, various armed factions have been organized, plunging the country into a violent civil war that has claimed thousands of lives. There is hope that the various mediation efforts launched by external parties will help end the carnage.

Cameroon, since it gained independence from France on January 1, 1960, has been engulfed by a multidimensional civil conflict involving regional, class, and political differences. Jeffres Ramseys explains the depth of the civil conflict:

> In 1994, Cameroonians were united by at least two things: support for their football team's second World Cup appearance and condemnation for neighboring Nigeria's occupation of the disputed Bakassi Peninsula. But, politically, Cameroonians remain deeply divided.[20]

The regional dimension of the conflict pits the French-speaking North against the English-speaking South and West. In economic terms, wealth is concentrated in the hands of a small ruling class consisting of compradors from the various parts of the country. Politically, there are differences between the ruling People's Democratic Party and the opposition, mainly the Social Democratic Front (SDF) and the Democratic Union.

Although the conflict has not degenerated into civil war thus far, there have been occasional acts of violence. For example, in May 1990, the SDF organized a rally in Bamenda, the main town of the Anglophone West, over government objections.[21] Government troops opened fire on school children returning from the demonstration.[22] The government media tried to portray the SDF as a subversive movement of "English speakers," but the movement has attracted significant support in Francophone areas.[23]

In the Democratic Republic of the Congo, there have been three civil wars. The first one was in 1960, shortly after independence. It involved a struggle for control of state power by various political factions. The second civil war pitted the autocratic government of Mobutu Sese Seko against the Alliance of Democratic Forces for Liberation (ADFL) led by Laurent Kabila. Kabila received military support from Rwanda and Uganda in the conduct of the war against the Mobutu regime. By May 1997, Kabila and the ADFL overthrew the Mobutu regime. The dictator fled the country and later died in exile.

However, a little over a year following Mobutu's downfall, a series of conflicts occurred between President Kabila and his domestic supporters and his external supporters, Rwanda and Uganda. The conflicts were precipitated by President Kabila's supporters' dissatisfaction with his performance. According to the supporters, President Kabila's first fourteen months in office were marked by repression, corruption, nepotism, and authoritarianism.[24] Thus, in August 1998, the third civil war began with an army rebellion. Thereafter, the scope of the conflict widened with the formation of various armed factions and the involvement of Rwanda and Uganda as patrons of some of these factions. Various countries supported President Kabila. Godfrey Mutisya provides an excellent summation of the complexities of the "third Congolese Civil War":

> The ongoing civil war in the Democratic Republic of the Congo (DRC) exposed the interplay between interstate and intrastate conflicts. The conflict there has so far drawn in Namibia, Angola, Zimbabwe, Rwanda and Uganda. The Congolese Movement for Democracy (CMD) . . . backed by the Rwandan and Ugandan governments, was seeking to overthrow Laurent Kabila, and military conflict erupted in August 1998. They appeared to be on the verge of success before Angola, Zimbabwe and Namibia intervened militarily to restore the authority of Kabila's government—thereby putting the rebels on the defensive.[25]

Various efforts have been made by the United Nations and the Organization of African Unity to find a peaceful solution to the conflict. The most important is the Lusaka Peace Accord, which among other things calls for a cease-fire and the disengagement of foreign troops from the conflict and the departure of foreign troops from Democratic Republic of the Congo. A United Nations Peacekeeping Force and observers are supposed to supervise the cease-fire and monitor compliance with human rights standards. However, there are still difficulties in the implementation of the accord.

In Sierra Leone, a civil war erupted in 1991 after decades of civil conflicts. The basic factors that contributed to the conflict included class inequities, authoritarianism, wanton corruption, graft, greed, and the wholesale mismanagement of economic resources, particularly during the almost twenty-year reign of the autocratic President Siaka Stevens. The trigger was an armed insurrection launched by the Revolutionary United Front (RUF) led by former Corporal Foday Sankoh, with support from the National Patriotic Front of Liberia headed by Charles Taylor. Since then, Sierra Leone has been plagued with a bloody civil war that has claimed thousands of lives and destroyed the country's already inadequate infrastructure.

Since the commencement of the war, the Economic Community of West African States, the Organization of African Unity, and the United Nations have undertaken various conflict resolution efforts. The Economic Community of West African States sent the Monitoring Group (ECOMOG), the sub-regional peacekeeping force, and brokered the Conakry and Abidjan Accords. Unfortunately, these efforts failed to end the war. In early 2000, the three organizations brokered the Lomé Peace Accord. A United Nations Peacekeeping Force was sent out following this, but these efforts have failed to end the conflict.

CONFLICT TRENDS

Civil conflicts in Africa have followed various trends. In the 1960s, there were three major trends. First, most of the conflicts focused on the decolonization process, with the exception of the conflicts in the Portuguese colonies. Second, there were various conflicts over the control of state power in countries like the Democratic Republic of the Congo, Togo, Burundi, Burkina Faso, the Central African Republic, Ghana, Congo, Mali, Nigeria, Niger, Sierra Leone, Somalia, and Sudan. These conflicts culminated in military coups d'état and the subsequent installation of military regimes. Third, there were secessionist conflicts in Ethiopia, Nigeria, and Senegal.

In the 1970s, the focus was on decolonization in the Portuguese territories, principally Angola, Cape Verde, Guinea-Bissau, and Mozambique. The struggle over control of state power continued, and led to an increase in the incidence of military coups. For example, putschists ousted both civilian and military regimes in various African countries, including Benin, Ghana, Mauritania, Niger, Nigeria, the Central African Republic, Equatorial Guinea, Burundi, Ethiopia, the Comoros, Madagascar, Rwanda, the Seychelles and Uganda.

In the 1980s, three trends were evident: continued struggles over control of state power, secessionism, and mixed. In the struggle over state power, coups occurred in Ghana, Guinea, Guinea-Bissau, Liberia, Nigeria, the Central African Republic, Burundi, the Comoros, the Sudan, Lesotho, and Burkina Faso. The secessionist conflicts continued in Ethiopia and Senegal, and new ones emerged in Mali and Niger. The decade also witnessed an increase in the use of civil wars as methods for waging conflicts. By the end of the decade, there were ten civil wars raging throughout the continent.

In the 1990s, all of the patterns of civil conflict were at play. The "third wave of democratization" pattern was exemplified by conflicts in several Francophone African countries. In some cases, dictatorial regimes were ousted through the use of the Sovereign National Conference, multiparty democratic elections were held, and the "wheels of political democratization" were set in motion. In Malawi and Zambia, two long-time despots, Kamuzu Banda and Kenneth Kaunda, were defeated in those countries' first democratic elections. The struggle over the control of state power caused military interventions and takeovers in Algeria, the Gambia, Côte d'Ivoire, Mali, Niger, Nigeria, Sierra Leone, Republic of

Congo, São Tomé and Principe, and Lesotho. In Niger, Sierra Leone, and the Republic of Congo, the democratically elected governments were overthrown. However, in the case of Sierra Leone, the democratically elected government was restored through the military intervention of the Economic Community of West African States (ECOWAS).

The secessionist pattern declined in importance as a consequence of peacemaking efforts in Ethiopia, Mali, and Senegal. In the case of Ethiopia, peaceful secession was granted to Eritrea, which became a sovereign and independent state. In Mali, the new democratically elected government successfully negotiated an agreement with the Tuareg ethnic group. In Senegal, although peace talks were held between the government and the Casamançais secessionists, there was no breakthrough.

As for the mixed pattern, there was a marked increase evidenced by new civil wars in Algeria, Burundi, the Central African Republic, Congo (Brazzaville), the Democratic Republic of the Congo, Guinea-Bissau, Lesotho, Namibia, and Rwanda. In addition, old conflicts continued to rage in countries like Liberia, Sierra Leone, Somalia, and the Sudan.

Significantly, the 1990s also marked the collapse of apartheid in South Africa through a negotiated settlement between the African National Congress and the Afrikaners, the white minority. One of the major events in South Africa was the rise of the African National Congress to power through the first multiracial democratic elections. Also, the bloody and protracted civil war ended in Mozambique.

CONCLUSION

This chapter has attempted to examine the patterns and trends of civil conflicts in Africa. Five major patterns were identified: the secessionist pattern, the struggle over control of state power pattern, the third wave of democratization, the ethnic pattern, and the mixed pattern. The major feature of the secessionist pattern is the demand by an ethnic group for self-determination and independence. The struggle over state power revolves around competing efforts by various political factions to take control of the state's machinery. The third wave of democratization involves crusades to oust dictatorial regimes through the Sovereign National Conference and democratic elections and efforts by putschists to reverse democratic gains. The ethnic pattern centers on disagreements between and among various ethnic groups over the distribution of political and economic power in a polity. The mixed pattern, the most pervasive in Africa, involves a confluence of contingent and proximate factors leading to civil conflicts.

In terms of trends, each decade beginning with the dawn of the postcolonial era was examined. The purpose was to delineate the directions civil conflicts took during each period. For example, the first half of the 1960s focused on the decolonization process, with the exception of the Portuguese colonies. The second half of the 1960s witnessed secessionist conflicts and struggles over the control of state power. In addition, it was during this decade that military intervention through the coup d'état became a major method for "settling" conflicts over control of state power.

Finally, some of the protracted civil conflicts in places like Mozambique and South Africa ended during the last decade of the twentieth century. However, several old conflicts continued, while several new ones emerged. Clearly, civil conflicts have adversely affected Africa as reflected in deaths, refugee crises, the exploitation of children as soldiers, the gross violation of human rights, traumatization, the destruction of the infrastructure, stagnation in economic activities, capital flight, polarization, and instability. Undoubtedly, democracy and development will not be possible in the continent unless the root causes of these civil conflicts are seriously addressed.

NOTES

1. Chris Garuba, *Capacity Building for Crisis Management in Africa* (Lagos, Nigeria: Gabumo Publishing Company, 1998), xi.
2. Henry Wiseman, "The OAU: Peacekeeping and Conflict Resolution," in *The OAU after Twenty Years*, ed. Yassin El-Ayouty and I. William Zartman (New York: Praeger, 1984), 123.
3. For an excellent discussion of the intricacies that led to the Nigerian civil war, see Dan Agbese, *Fellow Nigerians* (Lagos: Africa NewsWatch Publishing, 2000).
4. Michael Crowder, *Senegal: A Study of French Assimilation Policy* (London: Methuen and Company, 1967), 109.
5. See Mohammed Faal, "Casamance and the Crisis in Guinea-Bissau," *Democracy and Development* 2, no. 3, (1999), 18.
6. Ibid.
7. Ibid.
8. See Liz McClintock, "Angola," in *International Negotiation Network, The State of the World Conflicts Report* (Atlanta: The Carter Presidential Center, 1996), 20.
9. Ibid.
10. F. Jeffress Ramseys, *Global Studies: Africa* (Guilford, CT: Dushkin/McGraw Hill, 1999), 153.
11. Peace Pledge Union Online, "The Republic of Congo," under *Wars and Armed Conflicts*, 2000, 1. (Internet).
12. Ibid.
13. Ibid.
14. Ibid.
15. Ramseys, *Global Studies: Africa*, 104.
16. Ibid.
17. Peace Pledge Union Online, "Algeria," under *Wars and Armed Conflicts*, 1.
18. Ibid.
19. Ibid.
20. Ramseys, *Global Studies: Africa*, 71.
21. Ibid., 72.

22. Ibid.

23. Ibid.

24. See Peace Pledge Union Online, "Democratic Republic of the Congo," under *Wars and Armed Conflicts*, 2.

25. Godfrey Mutisya, *Conflict Watch* Durban, (South Africa: ACCORD, 1999), 2.

PART II

CASE STUDIES

5

Civil Conflicts and Conflict Management in the Great Lakes Region of Africa

Musifiky Mwanasali

INTRODUCTION

The geographic region known in Africa as "the Great Lakes" takes its name from the system of lakes and affluents which drain the Great Rift in east central Africa. They include Lakes Turkana, Rwitanzige (formerly Albert or Mobutu), Rweru (formerly Edward or Idi Amin), Kivu, Tanganyika, and Malawi. This body of water washes the shores of Kenya, Uganda, the Democratic Republic of the Congo (DRC), Rwanda, Burundi, Tanzania, and Malawi.

Together, the countries of the Great Lakes region accounted for approximately 20 percent of the African population in 1998.[1] Although population density varies from low (Democratic Republic of the Congo and Tanzania) to very high (Rwanda, Burundi, and part of Kenya), the area which is directly adjacent to Lakes Rweru, Rwitanzige, Kivu, and Tanganyika is among the most densely populated in the African continent. The population, which contains a slight majority of women, is mainly under twenty-five years old.

The World Bank classifies the countries of the Great Lakes region in the low-income group. All are severely indebted with a very high ratio of debt service to Gross National Product (GNP) and exports.[2] Per capita Gross Domestic Product (GDP) in 1998 remained below U.S. $400 and, overall, growth was negative everywhere. The region's economic performance varies greatly from country to country. So does endowment with natural resources: there is a sharp contrast in this area between, on the one hand, what a Belgian geographer called "the Congo's geological scandal" and, on the other hand, the resource scarcity of landlocked Rwanda or Burundi. The economic miracle that was once hailed in

Kenya has faded away, in contrast to Uganda's steady recovery.[3] Meanwhile, Tanzania continues to search for a way out of its long economic slump.

In their speeches much more than in their deeds, the authorities in the Great Lakes countries have committed themselves to economic cooperation and the joint exploitation of the region's natural resources. Among the most notable sub-regional organizations set up in this regard are the (once dead but now revived) East African Community of Tanzania, Uganda, and Kenya, and the defunct Communauté Économique des Pays des Grands Lacs, (CEPGL), grouping the former Zaire, Rwanda, and Burundi.

Cooperation has not been achieved, as chronic civil strife, personal animosity among neighboring rulers, and the their constant interference in each other's internal affairs have frequently occurred. As a result, for nearly four decades, the countries of the Great Lakes region have been engulfed in a chronic pathology of despotic rule, civil conflicts, and external destabilization schemes with disastrous consequences in the social, economic, and humanitarian spheres.

This chapter focuses chiefly on the internal strife and external interference that have characterized interstate relations in the Great Lakes region. Its aim is to unveil the political dynamics that perpetuate violence in this region, and to show how these dynamics have contributed to the recurrence of armed conflicts and political instability within and among states.[4] First, I describe the general pattern of political violence and military coups in Rwanda, Burundi, Uganda, and the DRC. As the epicenter of the atrocities in the region, the four countries give testimony to the destructive effects of the combination of domestic instability and external interference on the search for security and lasting peace. Second, I highlight the political factors that explain the chronic incapacity of the countries of the Great Lakes region to achieve political stability and sustainable peace. More specifically, I point to the precarious security conditions prevailing in the region as stemming from the failure of the established authorities to address effectively the formidable challenge of citizenship in the context of a highly polarized society. Finally, I survey the response of the international community before sketching a proposal that anchors conflict management in the local communities of this greatly troubled region of the world.

CHRONIC POLITICAL INSTABILITY

Civil conflicts in the Great Lakes are the consequence of what David Singer calls "the multiple pushes of the past [and the] multiple pulls of the future."[5] Aside from the occasional mutinies in the barracks and the frequent stories of aborted coups d'état by the nation's alleged enemies,[6] most of these conflicts qualify as civil wars. All show a recurrent pattern of political violence carried out by repressive regimes against internal opposition or against large segments of their own population. Such regimes, and the politico-military forces that oppose them, frequently resort to deadly weapons as the preferred mode of managing political disagreements. In most cases, countries in the vicinity of the conflict zone become involved in supporting the belligerents, either directly or indirectly, thus worsening the internal troubles of their warring neighbor.

These observations are generally not in dispute. The main disagreement resides in the diagnosis of the nature and character of the conflicts, as well as the best approach to prevent, manage, or resolve them. As is the case for Rwanda and Burundi, the dominant paradigm of conflict analysis is still grounded in the primacy of primordial sentiments and the deep-seated hate such sentiments have generated over time between the majority and minority ethnic groups. For the proponents of this mode of explanation, the root causes of civil wars now raging in the Great Lakes region are to be found in the distant past of Rwanda and Burundi. This is so casually said that the "past" has become an acceptable explanation, as if "the only thing that happened [in the past] was laying the foundations of a present crisis."[7] Despite convincing historical evidence to the contrary, the dominant literature on civil conflicts in mainstream academia, the media, and policy circles continues to blame historical patterns of ethnic exclusion and ethnic polarization.

It is important to continue to challenge academic and policy discourse of this kind. Historical circumstances have assuredly played their part in the onset of conflicts. However, what is much needed is an analysis of how the "past" has continued to act on current political dynamics to feed the need by political adversaries to resort to communal violence as a means for managing or settling differences that are essentially political or economic in nature.

Rwanda's Bloodbath

The Great Lakes region remains one of the bloodiest and most violent regions of the world. The cycle of violence that distinguishes this from the other parts of the continent began in earnest in Rwanda in 1959, and it has continued unabated in Rwanda, Burundi, Uganda, and now the DRC.

Rwanda has been by far the bloodiest theater in the region. The seeds of the recurrent violence were sown in 1959 when Rwanda's Belgian tutors decided to terminate the system of collaboration that had long structured ethnic identities and encouraged the virulent ethnic antagonisms that we deplore today. Moved either by equity considerations or by a mere desire to stave off calls for independence by its former collaborators, the Belgian metropolis instructed the colonial authorities and Roman Catholic missionaries to reverse long-standing discriminatory practices against the Hutu and promote equal opportunity.[8] Subsequent to this change of colonial policy, and in reaction to the mysterious death of the last Rwandan monarch, numerous Tutsi families and a few disgruntled former colonial collaborators opted for exile in neighboring countries. Some even began to threaten their upcoming return to power in Rwanda, by force if necessary.

An unsuccessful attempt was launched from Burundi in 1963, barely a year after the country's independence. In the wake of the aborted military raid, President Grégoire Kayibanda revived the old colonial ideology of Hutu-Tutsi enmity in an attempt to consolidate his fragile power base.[9] He launched a policy of repression against all political opponents and encouraged the persecution of Rwandan Tutsi. The witch-hunt culminated in the 1973 massacre and caused the overthrow of the Kayibanda regime by Major Juvénal Habyarimana.[10]

The collapse of the despotic Habyarimana regime twenty years later was the result of the failure of the Rwandan head of state to keep a tight lid on the ethnic activism of some hardcore members of the ruling party, the Mouvement de Rassemblement National Démocratique, (MRND). The MRND's rise to political prominence had already cost the Habyarimana regime the support of a large segment of the population, including many officers and other soldiers.

Two events deserve special mention as they illustrate the gradual erosion of Habyarimana's despotic rule. The first was the institution of the MRND youth militia in the 1980s, allegedly with the help of French instructors. Recruited mostly among unemployed Hutu youth, these paramilitary forces provided the MRND hawks with an effective weapon with which to take over the country by force. Nicknamed *interahamwe*, that is, those who attack together, Hutu youth militiamen caused widespread fear and created a climate of political terror that in the short term benefited the establishment but ultimately led to its destruction by force.

Then came the government's uncompromising opposition to the return to Rwanda of exiled Banyarwanda (Tutsis and Hutus who traced their ancestry to the Democratic Republic of the Congo) living in neighboring countries. Arguing that the country was already overpopulated, and too small and too poor to welcome back all the refugees and exiles, the Habyarimana regime advised them to apply for citizenship in the country where they were already residing.[11] The exiles included the descendants of the Tutsi families that had fled the country after the death of the last Rwandan monarch in 1959 and the massacres of the civilian population in 1962 and 1972. From 1973 onward, they also included Hutu who fled the country for personal reasons, for fear of political repression, or in support of the Rwandan armed opposition congregating in Uganda.

Although they are not the only group involved, the MRND hawks are clearly largely responsible for the atrocious violence that has rocked Rwanda since 1990. In their desire to exercise dominion over the country, they hijacked state institutions and sought to rid the country of all types of political opposition. The MRND politics of exclusion eventually led to the humiliating military rout of the Rwandan army by the RPF, the Rwandan Patriotic Front, and its military wing, the Rwandan Patriotic Army. Under the command of Fred Rwigyema, a major general in the Ugandan army, the RPF capitalized on the unpopularity of the Habyarimana regime in its drive to recruit fresh troops and launch a military offensive against the Rwandan regime. Overwhelmed militarily, and lacking the will to fight, the Rwandan army was saved from capitulation by Zaire's elite presidential troops.[12]

In retaliation for the RPF's 1990 invasion, and in reaction to its allegedly indiscriminate killing of Hutu civilians, the Rwandan Army and the MRND youth militia attached whomever they suspected of collusion with the RPF *inyenzi* ("cockroaches" in Kinyarwanda).[13] The victims included Hutu of moderate or oppositional political views and, randomly, members of the Tutsi minority not in government. Intensified after General Habyarimana's death in April 1994, these massacres prompted another full-scale RPF military invasion of Rwanda. With the capture of Kigali in July 1994, Paul Kagame and his troops ended the MRND-led genocide, but they have so far failed to bring lasting peace to their country and the region. Instead, since August 1998, the government of Rwanda has been sponsoring an armed insurrection against the government of the DRC in a bid to achieve security. Yet this remains elusive, as the RPF continues to fight against the armed remnants of the MRND militia, the Rwandan army, and a score of armed groups still operating within Rwanda and in the neighboring DRC.

Burundi: Provocation and Retaliations

Like its neighbor, Burundi became independent in 1962. Unlike Rwanda, it remained a monarchy until 1966, when Michel Micombero engineered a coup d'état that ousted the reigning but weak Mwami and turned the country into a republic. Under the banner of the Union pour le Progrès National (UPRONA), Micombero created a ruthless political system that survived him and his two successors, Colonel Jean-Baptiste Bagaza and Major Pierre Buyoya.

In an attempt to halt the persistent cycle of violence and atrocities that had rocked the country since independence, Major Buyoya set in motion a process of political dialogue and national reconciliation. He oversaw the drafting of a charter of national unity and asked the Burundians to adopt it by referendum in 1992. Subsequently, political pluralism was instituted and a dozen parties were officially recognized. In June 1993, candidates competed for the office of head of state and seats in the National Assembly. FRODEBU, a newly created political party headed by Melchior Ndadaye, won a landslide victory in the first round of elections, and its chairman became the first and still the only elected head of the Burundian state. His tenure was not long; he was killed along with much of his cabinet only three months after the elections.[14] The interim head of state, who was appointed by the National Assembly, died in the same plane crash that killed General Habyarimana.

Since 1962, Burundi has been, like Rwanda, the bloody theater of a ruthless civil war. Every Burundian putschist justified his coup d'état by the need to restore law and order, usually in the aftermath of a massacre of the civilian population. Micombero justified his action in this way when he overthrew the monarchy in 1966. Despite his rescue by Zairian soldiers in 1972, Micombero did not survive a new wave of atrocities that rocked the country and brought Colonel Bagaza to power in 1976. Bagaza was in turn toppled in the aftermath of yet another wave of atrocities allegedly instigated by the Palipehutu Party.[15]

Massacres took place once more in the aftermath of the 1987 coup that brought Major Buyoya to the presidency. The 1993 coup d'état, which resulted in the assassination of Ndadaye, unleashed another frenzied massacre of Hutu and Tutsi, particularly in rural areas.

Efforts by the interim government to negotiate new power-sharing arrangements with the main political parties were repudiated by the army and hardcore members of a few smaller parties. Meanwhile, random acts of violence continued unabated, each providing more provocation and inciting more retaliation. It was in these circumstances that the 1996 coup took place and brought Major Buyoya back as the head of a country that was slowly sinking into anarchy. Although the Burundian army has largely averted a Rwanda-like bloodbath after the death of the president ad interim in 1994, it has not been able to defeat several armed factions of the political opposition operating within Burundi and from bordering countries.

Uganda: Coups and Backlash

It is remarkable that just like their colleagues in Rwanda and Burundi, Uganda's presidents have routinely berated their predecessors by accusing them of gross abuse of human rights. But, sooner or later, they all became the perpetrators of the same crimes. Idi Amin justified the overthrow of his despotic predecessor on the ground that he grossly violated political freedom and human rights. On his first return to power, Obote denounced the atrocities committed by his infamous predecessor against the people of Uganda. Even President Yoweri Museveni joined in this chorus by exposing the inhumanity of the Obote and Okello regimes. Now fighting two armed rebellions against his rule, and after deploying a force of nearly 10,000 troops to incite a rebellion in the DRC, President Museveni is also subjected to the same accusation he has used against his predecessors. His political enemies call him "the worst dictator that Uganda has ever known."[16]

Ugandan politics have been dominated by autocrats for so long that scholars like Dan Nabudere do not hesitate to blame the country's political instability on dictatorship, weak political institutions, and external forces.[17] The first serious political crisis occurred in 1966 when Milton Obote, the incumbent prime minister, changed key provisions of the constitution to allow him to become head of state. In the process, he abolished traditional sources of power and sent the Kabaka into exile. Idi Amin Dada, to the general applause of the Ugandan people, got rid of President Obote soon thereafter.[18] Not long after assuming power, Idi Amin proclaimed himself field marshal and president for life, and plunged the country in an uncalculable bloodbath. He was to be toppled a few years later, thanks to the intervention of the Tanzanian army. The memories of Amin's atrocities had not yet faded away when his successor, Mr. Lule, began to show dictatorial impulses. He, too, was immediately ousted, hauled out of

Uganda by the Tanzanian army, and put under house arrest in Dar es Salaam until he was sent into exile in Kenya.

President Binaisa was perhaps the only exception to this long line of tyrants. Upon replacing the short-lived Lule government, Mr. Binaisa undertook to implement the newly agreed institutional provisions. He thus instituted pluralism and attempted to broaden political participation. He was at once thrown out by a group of putschists who opposed his political reforms. Later, the same putschists organized new presidential elections that brought Obote back to power. A member of the opposition at the time, Museveni rejected Mr. Obote's presidency on the ground that the elections that brought him back were rigged. Museveni later took his National Resistance Movement to the bush, and with the help of Burundi, Tanzania, and a few leaders in other countries of the region, routed the Ugandan army in 1987 and toppled President Okello who had just replaced Obote. He has been in power since.

From Zaire to the DRC: Security and Human Rights Concerns

In October 1996, four obscure political parties met in Lemera, South Kivu, to form yet another political grouping that would rise to prominence as the Alliance des Forces Démocratiques pour la Liberation du Congo, (AFDL).[19] Around the time the AFDL directorate was established, a general climate of insecurity prevailed in eastern Zaire, in the Kivu provinces, due to the massive presence of Rwandan refugee camps more or less under the control of the remnants of the *interahamwe* militia and defeated Rwandan soldiers. Meanwhile, a handful of Zairian authorities in South Kivu began to harass Congolese of Tutsi origin, and threaten to confiscate their property and send them by force to Rwanda and Burundi.

Faced with mounting threats to its very existence in North and South Kivu, the RPF attacked Zaire and occupied the town of Uvira and the nearby city of Bukavu. Thus began the odyssey that would lead, in less than a year, to the demise of the dictatorial regime of President Mobutu Sese Seko and the rise of the current strongman, Laurent Désiré Kabila.

In May 1997, "Mzee Kabila," as he likes to be called, appointed himself the new president of the country that he rechristened the Democratic Republic of Congo. On June 30, 1997, surrounded by the heads of state of Rwanda, Burundi, Uganda, Angola, and Zambia, Mzee Kabila took the oath of office and thanked all his friends for their political and military support in his drive to "liberate the Congolese people from years of oppression and crass misery."

The swearing-in ceremony did not go well for the new Congolese strong man, owing largely to a very low attendance by the Kinois (residents of Kinshasa) and to the hecklers who snarled insults at President Museveni. Still, President Kabila and his AFDL comrades deserve praise for succeeding where the Zairian internal opposition had for many years failed, that is, in riding the country of the corrupt regime of President Mobutu. The warm reception that the AFDL received during its epic march and the refusal of many Zairian officers and troops to die for a decrepit political order tell us much about the high hopes of the country and its people for a new era and mentality.

Soon after the establishment of the Kabila government, personal security improved greatly, particularly in urban areas. The sight of military uniforms was no longer causing fear in the population. Former Zairian soldiers were by and large incorporated into the new Forces Armées Congolaises (FAC). Military roadblocks were dismantled, and the war against armed robbery was stepped up. The government employed strenuous efforts to eradicate the endemic corruption, and with the exception of isolated incidents of property confiscation by army officers and individual soldiers, most Congolese were free to move within and outside the country.

Yet the need for many changes remained, particularly in the security, political, and economic domains. To be fair, the authorities inherited a decaying country, and all indications pointed to the fact that it would take them quite a long time and strenuous efforts to satisfactorily solve some of the problems. However, the AFDL, whose priority was to make citizens of a people that for decades had been treated like subjects, appeared to be wearing the old mantle of the single-party state. The future of the democratic process, painstakingly launched by the National Conference in 1990, remained uncertain. The small advances made during the last years of the Mobutu regime toward the creation of a free and open political space were gradually rescinded. Freedom of the press was rapidly vanishing, and when they were not banned, political parties and human rights organizations were closely monitored and their leaders continuously harassed and intimidated. A few party leaders and activists were even imprisoned or banished to their native villages. The masterminds of the wave of ethnic intolerance that swept Katanga Province in 1993 were still roaming free, while security conditions in the eastern part of the country worsened considerably.

The reason for the growing popular discontent with the new political class resided in the arrogant ways in which the newcomers decided to rule the country and manage public affairs. The AFDL's arrogance made it difficult for many Congolese—at least those who chose or were forced to stay out—to establish working channels of communication with the new government. Many members of the new power structure were perceived as self-important and so entrenched in the righteousness of their convictions that they appeared to disdain anybody who did not think or act like them. Despite its genuine efforts to eradicate the roots of insecurity and crime, the Kabila government, perhaps because of its contradictory policies and the political misgivings of some of its officials, reinforced the cynical opinion that politics in the DRC were just the same as in the former Zaire.

At any rate, barely a year after its rise to power, the Kabila government inflicted on itself unnecessary damage to its popularity and authority. The Congolese people needed a coherent and reasonable answer to some of the key issues that concerned their lives. To provide this, the new authorities needed to give a clear indication of the nature of their leadership and their vision for the future of the country. Instead, the country was ruled by presidential decrees; regionalism superseded competence in public sector appointments; and policy inconsistencies and judicial arbitrariness became the norm.

The government abandoned political reconciliation in the name of economic reconstruction, and asked the country to rally behind an incoherent macroeconomic plan.[20] In a move reminiscent of the Mobutu regime, political parties and rallies, except for those organized by the AFDL, were banned to avoid the influence of partisan politics in the mobilization of the resources needed for reconstruction. In deciding to pursue the path of economic reconstruction and skip national reconciliation, the Kabila government ensured its own political failure.[21]

Social justice was another great concern for the Congolese people. Among the Congolese who warmly welcomed the new authorities were the people known as Refoulés. These were the Kasaiens who were forcibly expelled from southern Katanga by militia members of a Katangan political party led by Gabriel Kyungu wa Kumwanza, with the encouragement of some influential members of the Roman Catholic clergy and large businesses in Lubumbashi, Likasi, Kasai, and Kolwezi. During their appalling ordeal, many Kasaiens lost family members, property, and dignity, simply because they were not considered "true," that is, native, Katangais. The advent of the new government raised hopes among the Refoulés and their children that they would regain their rights and a little of what they had lost, and that their oppressors would be prosecuted and punished according to the law. None of this happened. Instead, the Kabila government appointed criminals like Kyungu to high posts in the government and the business world. Non-Katangan professionals continued to be harassed in Katanga Province, while a drive was conducted to recruit (incompetent and sometimes unqualified) Katangans to various senior governmental posts, including posts in the intelligence services and the armed forces.

A similar ordeal faced residents of Bukavu and Goma who had lost their property to the Banyamulenge in the 1996 liberation war.[22] After a preliminary investigation by the government, some property was returned to its rightful owners. President Kabila was accused of delaying justice and retribution because of his close ties with the Katangais and the Banyamulenge. Among the Kasaiens, suspicions of the Kabila government were augmented by the banishment of Mr. Etienne Tshisekedi, a Kasaien and leader of the largest political party in the DRC, to his native village in Kasai. By contrast, Katangan *génocidaires* were living free and undisturbed in their native Katanga, or given top government jobs in the capital. In the Kivu provinces, the deployment of Rwandan troops, the alleged infiltration of Rwandans and Burundians (both civilians and former soldiers) of Tutsi origin among the Banyamulenge, and the predominance of Tutsis among the provincial authorities, created strong suspicions among local residents that President Kabila was in the pay of his Rwandan mentors in the RPF.

Needless to say, such perceptions and suspicions did not improve the climate of insecurity or the lack of trust in the government and among local communities. Security concerns in the Kivu provinces were heightened, as the Kivu provinces became a corridor and an arena of military confrontation for a score of national armies and armed militias in the Great Lakes region. Social harmony was destroyed among the numerous ethnic communities that shared the same geographical space. Ethnic tensions increased over contested occupation of ethnic spaces and the settlement in those spaces of new refugees, immigrants, and victims, and perpetrators of ethnic massacres. All this formed the backdrop for the war that Rwanda, Uganda, and, to some extent, Burundi launched against the Kabila government in August 1998, which has once again attracted the attention of several African countries and foreign interests in the Great Lakes region.

The intensification of armed conflicts in the region, the sharpening of the Tutsi-Hutu divide in Rwanda and Burundi, the occupation of the Kivu provinces by Rwandan soldiers and their protégés in the Rassemblement Congolais pour la Démocratie (RCD) have nurtured wild rumors about the annexation by Rwanda of eastern DRC. The production by some Rwandan politicians of maps of dubious origins, detailing the geographic extent of precolonial Rwanda to include the Kivu provinces has exacerbated fears and ethnic resentments in this already troubled region. And this climate has served well the objectives of the numerous armed groups as well as their arms suppliers and financial backers.

Human rights conditions remain deplorable in the DRC, both in the regions controlled by the forces loyal to the Kabila government and those under the occupation of Congolese rebels and their Rwandan and Ugandan sponsors. Security conditions for women and children are precarious, and the presence of *kadogo* (child-soldiers) is a blatant violation of international law and an example of outright disregard for human rights. Political prisoners are yet to be freed, while public disagreements with the rebellion, its backers, or the Kabila government is severely repressed. Appeals and lobbying efforts by Congolese human rights organizations have fallen on deaf ears. The war in the DRC continues to intensify, despite the recent signing of peace agreements and various international pronouncements intended to end it.

PARTICIPATION AND CONSTITUTIONALISM

The preceding sections have painted a picture of the chronic instability, constant violence, and unspeakable atrocities that have beset the heartland of the Great Lakes region in the past four decades. Notwithstanding the 1993 elections in Burundi and the short-lived government of Uganda's President Binaisa, the established authorities in the region have failed to work out, let alone implement, a clear, agreed-upon, and lasting framework of norms and principles to guide political transactions in their societies. They have kept changing the rules of the political game in the middle of the game just, to paraphrase Wole Soyinka, to grant themselves the discretion to award a goal when the ball had missed the net, according to their judgment about the place where the goalposts should have been in the first place.[23]

Some scholars attribute the recurrence of coups and atrocities in the region to the effect of dictatorship and the influence of Western imperialism. Others blame the lack of viable political institutions. However, all these factors are only manifestations, not the causes, of the problem. During the Cold War, "Western imperialism" played a major role in determining the conditions for acceding to power and the criteria for the distribution of political resources within and among the countries of the region. Regardless of what is meant by this term, "imperialism" alone does not explain why the political elite choose violence as a means to consolidate their fragile power. It cannot serve as a justification for the amount of communal violence in Rwanda or Burundi. Likewise, while in agreement with the thesis of a lack of institutions, I nonetheless uphold the view that in the main, political institutions derive their worth from the political principles that have given life to these institutions and on the basis of which they operate.

In my view, the crucial cause of political instability in the Great Lakes region resides in the mode of rule instituted in these countries and the ways in which the authorities cope (or avoid dealing) with the task of governing their polity. These entail the institution of a viable social order, the creation of a political space and broadening of political participation, and the achievement of sustained economic growth, amidst (and in spite of) social tensions and polarization. At the heart of the matter is the central question of how the authorities can foster a sense of citizenship and uphold a constitutional order that is acceptable to the population at large.

Citizenship in a Polarized Society

At the time of independence, with very few exceptions, the newly established authorities vowed to modernize traditional rule, put an end to social polarization, and develop their economy.[24] Nearly everywhere, however, the first item on the agenda preoccupied the postcolonial elite, with their determination to dismantle, by all means, all political alternatives and competing sources of power. First, they instituted single-party regimes and centralized state power in their hands. Next, they took on the Kabaka, the Mwami, and other influential traditional elite members, on the pretext of the need to modernize traditional societies, which politicians like Obote, Nyerere, Micombero, or Kayibanda invariably considered as the bastion of ethnicity and social divisions.

While disparaging traditional chiefs and issuing decrees that took away whatever authority local chiefs still held, the postcolonial elite could not resist the temptation to wink an eye at ethnicity, regionalism, or clan-ism or dress themselves in the cloth of traditions whenever this appeared convenient. Some went so far as to rely on their own clan members, rather than their broadly defined ethnic or regional allies, in their attempt to monopolize access to state power and the material advantages it conferred. Colonel Jean-Baptiste Bagaza of Burundi dismissed a fellow Tutsi and gathered around him members of his own clan as political advisers. Another Tutsi officer, who happened to belong to the clan previously in power, staged the putsch that sent Bagaza into exile. Examples of this kind abound in the region.

The rise of the single party as the sole ruling institution and the central organ of the state did very little to improve people's sense of citizenship or broaden their opportunities for political participation. In its drive to become "the master of all tribes,"[25] the single party turned citizens into postcolonial subjects and subjected them to the "enlightened leadership" of its chairman. The founding father of the party was the sole authority entrusted with the task of defining the criteria, identity, and role of the key participants in the political "High Mass." As time went by and the state became the main enforcer of the policy lines defined by the party, coercion became the preferred method of governance.

The Constitution: A Unifying Political Instrument?

In general, the countries of the Great Lakes region have not made a serious effort to find a political principle that can unify their people around an agreed social order. Constitutional reforms and debates, national dialogue, and popular consultations have all revolved around the issue of elections and the appropriate institutional formula for the country. In the rush to elections, little attention has been paid to the fact that since the political climate is highly charged and polarized, there is clearly a danger in organizing quick multiparty elections and setting in motion the process of political transition.

If democracy means a free and open political system that respects individual rights and protects the material and security needs of its citizens, then the authorities in the Great Lakes region should avoid a rush to elections or constitutional reform. They should first seek to create an open political space and define a political principle that can unify their peoples in a free and open social order. Constitutional reform will later come to give official approval to this principle, and only then will general elections make sense.

Very seldom have the leaders of the countries in the Great Lakes region paused long enough to define the nature of the social order and the identity of its beneficiaries. In his analysis of several constitutional reforms in Africa, Sam Nolutshungu makes a useful distinction between constitutional moment and constitutional function.[26] Most constitutional reforms on the continent, he observes, fall into the category he labels constitutional moment. They deal exclusively with the question of the transfer of power from an old political order to a new, and avoid addressing the fundamental issue of constitutional function, namely, the political goal that the new constitution is designed to achieve. Whenever this question is raised, says Nolutshungu, it is usually dealt with in a fragmentary and superficial manner.

The 1993 elections in Burundi are a case in point. They were held after fast-track negotiations and a superficial political dialogue. Furthermore, in the effort to complete the process of national reconciliation set in motion two years earlier, the Charter of National Unity and the ensuing referendum gave the impression that Burundi was moving steadily in the direction of pluralism. As it later turned out, all that was too soon, too fast, but not too inclusive. The major forces that were left out or excluded themselves from this process strongly opposed its outcome and caused the experiment to fail. Vital questions about the nature and role of the military in a civilian regime were only superficially addressed. The spiteful and divisive electoral campaigns did little to heal Burundi's deep wounds. In the end, the fear of many was confirmed a few months later when the president-elect was killed.

Nolutshungu claims that, in general, constitutional reforms have failed to define clearly the political objectives of the new constitution. According to Issa Shivji, Africa's fifty-one constitutions serve only the incidence of the transference of power without even having the function of legitimating it.[27] If this is the case, one can wonder with Shivji, "Why [have] constitutions at all?"[28] Why take the trouble to draft a constitution and submit it to a referendum when everyone knows that there is no need for "a constitution to transfer power, [since] most of the time [power] is transferred through extra-constitutional means, whether through a military take-over or a civilian usurpation, and the constitution only appears *ex post facto*?"[29]

The emphasis by the authorities on the constitutional moment ultimately reinforces the popular belief that politics is not about the broadening of the political space but about the elite's concern and struggle for what Wole Soyinka terms "the spoils of power." Little is done to convince ordinary citizens that, in reforming the constitution, the authorities are first and foremost concerned with the legitimacy of their power in the eyes of their own people, rather than with their international acceptability. This skepticism probably explains why, from Idi Amin to Kabila, the perpetrators of coups d'état seem at first to enjoy some popularity among their compatriots.

To return to the example of Burundi, what might have happened if President Buyoya had slowed down the process of national reconciliation? What if he had decided to delay the general elections until some broadly based agreement could be reached about the nature of the new social order? What if he had not (been) rushed into a fast-track process that eventually ripped society open?

The failure of the authorities in the countries of the Great Lakes region to foster a sense of citizenship among their people contributes significantly to the current instability. To paraphrase Alain Touraine, a citizen is s/he who sees to it that political institutions work properly, respect individual rights, and promote equal representation to the diversity of social interests. In the DRC, just as elsewhere in this troubled region, fostering a sense of citizenship has rarely been among the political priorities of the authorities. And unfortunately, it has not always been the path that these countries have been encouraged to take.[30]

PEACE IN THE GREAT LAKES REGION: WHICH WAY FORWARD?

Three types of conflict management initiatives have taken place in the Great Lakes region. The first consists of humanitarian and military responses by the international community under the auspices of the United Nations and its specialized agencies. The second includes individual and institutional mediation conducted under the auspices of the Organization of African Unity (OAU), alone or in partnership with the United Nations. The third includes ad hoc military and/or economic responses initiated by neighboring countries.

Consistent with the patterns observed in other African countries, the reaction of the United Nations Security Council to the debilitating violence in the countries of the Great Lakes region has generally been dismal. With the exception of the peacekeeping/enforcement mission against the 1960 Katanga secession in the former Zaire, the United Nations Security Council, by its reluctance to intervene and restore the necessary conditions for lasting peace and security in this region, has failed to fulfill its mandate to ensure global peace and security. When the deteriorating political situation in Rwanda required a strong UN presence, the Security Council ordered the withdrawal of UN troops, except for a small contingent composed mainly of ill-equipped Ghanaian soldiers, just as the genocide got underway.[31] When the UN finally got its act together and decided to return to Rwanda, it took fully six months to deploy a peacekeeping force effectively. While the UN Security Council could not raise U.S. $50 million to finance the repatriation of Rwandan refugees from eastern Zaire, roughly U.S. $2 million were spent daily (and for two consecutive years) by the UN and various humanitarian agencies on assistance to the same Rwandan refugees in eastern Zaire. More recently, the UN Security Council decided that it would deploy a peacekeeping force in the war-torn DRC only when it had received guarantees that the safety of peacekeepers would be effectively ensured.

The OAU has directed strenuous efforts toward peace and security in this region. Several meetings have been held at the ambassadorial level, while OAU members have undertaken several initiatives, either individually or collectively, to mediate or facilitate a peaceful end to various conflicts. President Ali Hassan Mwinyi of Tanzania led a team of heads of state and government who, between 1992 and 1994, facilitated and mediated a peace agreement between the government of Rwanda and the Rwandan Patriotic Front. President Daniel arap Moi of Kenya convened two regional summits in 1996, while the former President Pascal Lissouba of Congo-Brazzaville and President Omar Bongo of Gabon convened a summit of the UN Standing Advisory Committee on Security Questions in Central Africa in an attempt to end the anti-Mobutu rebellion in Zaire. The OAU secretary general was consistently and actively engaged in facilitating peace agreements in Rwanda before the genocide and in Burundi between 1993 and 1996. In 1997, the pan-African body convened the Fourth Regional Summit on Burundi in Arusha, Tanzania, which was attended by the presidents of

Rwanda, Burundi, Zambia, Tanzania, Kenya, and Uganda, and the Ethiopian prime minister. Moreover, while the United Nations forces were pulling out of Rwanda during the 1994 genocide, the OAU was desperately trying to assemble in Kenya an African peacekeeping force to be deployed in Rwanda. Owing to a lack of logistical support and funds, and in the absence of a clear mandate, the OAU was unable to mount that peacekeeping operation. In the case of the current war in the DRC, the OAU has deployed an observer mission and set up joint political and military commissions to monitor the implementation of the Lusaka cease-fire agreement signed by the Congolese belligerents and the countries that sponsor them in July and August 1999. These commissions comprise representatives of all the belligerents, under the guidance of the pan-African organization.

The absence of a strong commitment by the UN Security Council to ensure peace and security in Africa and the OAU's perennial lack of resources have left to regional and neighboring countries the task of managing security in the Great Lakes region. This is done through ad hoc policy or military initiatives as well as odd political alliances. Thus, Tanzania got entangled in Uganda's internal affairs, before joining others in support of Yoweri Museveni. Bagaza of Burundi and a few other regional leaders also offered assistance to Yoweri Museveni in his drive to take office by force. Mobutu of Zaire flew to the rescue of Habyarimana and Micombero. Uganda was involved in the RPF rout of the Rwandan armed forces and, two years later, in the overthrow of President Mobutu's regime. Rwanda under Kagame, Angola, Uganda, and a few other countries assisted the AFDL in the war to overthrow President Mobutu. Recently, provocation and military threats were briefly exchanged between Burundi and Tanzania, while Rwanda and Uganda are each occupying portions of the DRC's territory. Meanwhile, the Arusha Talks on Burundi, suspended after the death of the mediator Mwalimu Nyerere, resumed in late February 2000, under the guidance of former president Nelson Mandela of South Africa. After several setbacks, the warring factions in Burundi have agreed to a peace plan; however, the peace is tenuous.

With so much personal animosity and suspicion among the political rulers in the Great Lakes, one is right to wonder about the prospects for lasting peace and political stability in the region. Will political mediation, cease-fire agreements, and governments of national unity succeed when in the past, they have proved to be a failure, as was the case when President Mobutu served among the mediators between Habyarimana and the Rwandan Patriotic Front in 1993, and when the Government of Burundi expressed strong and relentless objections to the late Mwalimu Nyerere's facilitation of the inter-Burundian factional dialogue in Arusha?

It is obvious that mediations and facilitations can and should be continued, but in combination with other well thought out peace initiatives, like arbitration and other conflict management tools. Mediators and venues ought to be carefully selected so as to exclude personal controversies and locations too close to the conflict zone. A new mediation strategy ought to be adopted, including the broadening of the circle of concerned parties. Furthermore, islands of peace ought to be created or identified and enhanced. All too often, inordinate amounts of time, energy, and resources are wasted in an attempt to reconcile individuals holding extreme positions. In such cases, scarce resources are squandered on useless efforts to bring together factional leaders who have little interest in reconciliation. Such resources should be used to strengthen the silent majority, that is, the constituency of respectable and respected individuals or groups longing or actively working to promote lasting peace.

CONCLUSION

To conclude this chapter, I wish to emphasize my conviction that military options can and will never bring a lasting settlement of problems that are essentially political. The moment may be opportune to shift the focus away from the current obsession with reconciling warring factions toward the setting up of conditions for peaceful cohabitation at the community level. This is a promising approach to sustainable peace, at a time when unending civil conflicts have torn apart communities and entire families.

This community-based approach to conflict management has been tried, with the minimum amounts of resources and mixed results, by a network of peace-oriented nongovernmental organizations (NGOs) in Rwanda, Burundi, Uganda, and the DRC. NGOs and civil society leaders in the four countries are assiduously working to rebuild trust and confidence through the opening of open channels of communication between the military and the civilian population, and among feuding community leaders. A human rights organization based in Burundi, called Ligue Iteka, began in 1995 to work in the northwestern part of the country, which was inhabited by a majority of Hutu villagers. This region has been the theater of intense military operations in which Burundian rebels fought against the so-called "mono-ethnic Tutsi army." Civilians got caught in the vortex of violence perpetrated by both regular and rebel troops.

Initiatives of this kind deserve much support from the international community, because they may help rebuild the social fabric which has been torn by decades of military destruction. Let us now hope that the international community will pay heed to the call for peace and local efforts toward peaceful coexistence. The time has come to try another peace strategy in the Great Lakes region.

NOTES

1. Compiled from United Nations Economic Commission for Africa (UNECA), *Economic Report on Africa 1999*, E/ECA/CM.24/3 (Addis Ababa, Ethiopia: UNECA, May 1999), 72.
2. See World Bank, *Trends in Developing Economies 1995* (Washington, D.C.:

World Bank, 1995). The figures for the Democratic Republic of the Congo since 1990 and for Rwanda and Burundi from 1993 to 1997 are unreliable.

3. A comparison of the sectoral distribution of GDP (percent) in Kenya in 1980 and 1997, for example, shows a relative decline in agriculture, industry, and manufacturing but a growth in the services sector. See UNECA, *Economic Report on Africa 1999*, 73.

4. The focus of this chapter is on armed conflicts. According to Peter Wallensteen and Karen Axell, a situation of armed conflict exists when there is use of armed force by two parties, of which one at least is the government of a state, and which results in at least twenty-five battle-related deaths per year. See "Conflict Resolution and the End of the Cold War, 1989–1993," *Journal of Peace Research* 31, no. 3 (1994).

5. David Singer, "Armed Conflicts in the Former Colonial Regions: From Classification to Explanation," in *Between Development and Destruction: An Inquiry into the Causes of Conflict in Postcolonial States*, ed. L. van de Goor, K. Rupesinghe, and P. Sciarone (New York: St Martin's Press, 1996), 39.

6. President Nyerere of Tanzania once accused the United States of masterminding a coup against his regime. See his *Freedom and Socialism* (Dar es Salaam: Oxford University Press, 1968), 200.

7. Mahmud Mamdani, *Citizen and Subject: Contemporary Africa and the Legacy of Late Colonialism* (London: Heinemann, 1976).

8. Guy Logiest, *Mission au Rwanda* (Brussels: Didier Hatier, 1988.)

9. Ethnologists such as Baumann, Speke, and Gotzen first developed this ideology. It was later adopted as a policy by the Belgian administration and Roman Catholic missions in Burundi between 1885 and 1931. The ideology rested on a dubious premise about the existence in precolonial Rwanda of a feudal system in which "white-negroes," Tutsi monarchs and lords, held dominion over a tribe of "Bantu negroes," namely the Hutu people, who were made to serve the lords. This ethnology was reflected in the first political manifestos in Rwanda. For example, the *Manifeste des Bahutu* strongly attacked the Rwandan feudal system for systematic violations of the rights of the Bahutu. The first political parties, created in 1959, also drew inspiration from this feudal theory. Thus, the Union Nationale Rwandaise recruited mainly among the Tutsi, while Parmehutu drew its membership largely from among the Hutu. A republican state was proclaimed at independence with a Hutu as president.

10. Juvénal Habyarimana was the first Hutu officer trained in the Rwandan army under the new colonial political arrangements. He seized power in 1973 on the pretext of restoring law and order, and in the main, the Rwandan population applauded the decision.

11. The RPF successfully capitalized on this decision to justify its recourse to military means to overthrow the Habyarimana regime.

12. After the death of "General Fred," killed during this expedition, Paul Kagame, another officer in the Ugandan army, took command of the RPF. See Karrim Essack, *Civil War in Rwanda* (Dar es Salaam: Newman Publishers, 1991).

13. Théoneste Hategekimana, "Le Mouvement Terroriste 'Inyenzi' dans la Région du Bugesera" (undergraduate thesis, École Supérieure Militaire, Kigali, Rwanda, 1987).

14. Pursuing the reconciliation agenda of his predecessor, Ndadaye formed an inclusive cabinet of national unity. He was joined in his efforts by a number of Tutsi, and was opposed by Tutsi elements in the army and Hutu in such extremist parties as Palipehutu. See Gaetan Sebudandi and Pierre-Olivier Richard, *Le Drame burundais: Hantise du pouvoir ou tentation suicidaire* (Paris: Karthala, 1996); André Guichaoua, *Les Crises politiques au Burundi et au Rwanda, 1993–1994: Analyses, faits et documents* (Ville-

neuve d'Ascq, France: Université des Sciences et Technologies de Lille, Faculté des Sciences Économiques et Sociales, 1995).

15. Palipehutu is one of several political parties fighting the Buyoya regime. It predates Mr. Ndadaye's FRODEBU. Like the MRND in Rwanda, its ideology is reportedly based on the notion that the majority exclusively should hold power. Palipehutu has opposed efforts toward reconciliation, and has referred to all those who advocate it as enemies. Its combatants received training alongside the Rwandan militia during the Habyarimana regime and benefited from the support of the MRND by using the Rwandan territory as a base for military incursions into Burundi.

16. One argument claims that even though Museveni has not been elected, his regime does not qualify as a dictatorship since there is freedom of the press to a large extent. One may openly criticize ministers and government policies, but not the president or his regime. See Mahmud Mamdani, *Politics and Class Formation in Uganda* (London: Heinemann, 1976); and Dan Nabudere, *Imperialism and Revolution in Uganda* (Dar es Salaam: Tanzania Publishing House, 1980). Not surprisingly, the Lord's Resistance Army (LRA), which leads a brutal anti-Museveni war in northern Uganda, has a different opinion of Ugandan politics and its leader.

17. Nabudere, *Imperialism and Revolution in Uganda.*

18. Mamdani, *Politics and Class Formation in Uganda*, and Nabudere, *Imperialism and Revolution in Uganda*, have inspired this chronological sketch.

19. The AFDL emerged from obscurity after the onset of Rwandan military attacks in Kivu. At its creation, it included four political groupings, namely, the Parti Révolutionnaire du Peuple (PRP) headed by Laurent-Désiré Kabila, the Alliance Démocratique des Peuples chaired by Déogratias Bugera, the Mouvement pour la Libération du Zaire of Masasu Ningaba, and the Conseil Régional de Résistance pour la Démocratie, a political grouping with a military wing headed by Kisasse Ngandu. With the exception of Laurent Kabila, whose career dates back to the 1960 Simba rebellion, all the other parties and their chairmen were previously unknown outside the small circle of their members and sympathizers.

20. In 1997, the government decided to set up the Commission de Pacification au Nord et Sud Kivu (the Pacification Commission in North and South Kivu). The open and frank discussions of the commission, the integrity of its members, the issues it covered, and the spontaneous participation of local people in the debate constituted a courageous step toward making the Congolese house a home for all. Another national forum on reconstruction was to take place in early 1998. But these forums were abruptly canceled without an explanation.

21. After Laurent-Désiré Kabila had proclaimed himself head of state in Congo and following intense repression directed against political opponents, Congolese voices expressed their discontent with the new government and urged it to free all political prisoners, respect human rights, and democratize society. The overwhelming reaction of the international community to Congolese demands was to ask the Congolese "to give President Kabila time."

22. Nearly all the houses and then contents in the Quartier des Biens Mal-Acquis (a neighborhood nicknamed "ill-acquired-goods") in Uvira, South Kivu, were confiscated by the Banyamulenge. To justify their possession of stolen property, some Banyamulenge leaders argued that the confiscation was carried out in retaliation for the goods that their own people had lost to various looters during the time of the Mobutu regime.

23. Wole Soyinka, *The Open Sore of a Continent: A Personal Narrative of the Nigerian Crisis* (New York: Oxford University Press, 1996).

24. See Mamdani, *Politics and Class Formation in Uganda*, and Issa Shivji, ed., *State and Constitutionalism: An African Debate on Democracy* (Harare, Zimbabwe: SAPES Trust, 1991).

25. Mamdani, *Politics and Class Formation in Uganda*, 289.

26. Sam C. Nolutshungu, "The Constitutional Question in South Africa," in Issa Shivji, ed., *State and Constitutionalism*, 92.

27. Issa Shivji, "Contradictory Class Perspectives in the Debate on Democracy," in Issa Shivji, ed., *State and Constitutionalism: An African Debate on Democracy* (Harare, Zimbabwe: SAPES Trust, 1991), 254.

28. Ibid.

29. Ibid.

30. See Henry K. Anyidoho, *Guns over Kigali* (Accra, Ghana: Woeli Publishing Services, 1997).

31. See Organization of African Unity, *Rwanda Conflict: Basic Documents—Arusha Peace Agreement and Kinihira Agreement* (Addis Ababa, Ethiopia: OAU Conflict Management Center, n.d.).

6

Understanding the Liberian Civil War

Augustine Konneh

INTRODUCTION

Civil wars have raged in a number of countries: Sudan, Ethiopia, Angola, Mozambique, the Democratic Republic of the Congo, Burundi, Somalia, and Liberia, to name some of the more prominent. Although these wars are usually portrayed in the Western media as caused by "tribalism," this portrayal is often a simplification of complex realities. Regionalism, inequalities in the provision of services, political demands by those without power, and outside intervention (especially encouragement from the superpower blocs during the days of the Cold War) have frequently contributed to the outbreak of civil war.

Western press accounts of African civil wars routinely emphasize tribal or ethnic divisions and ignore the broader problems dividing African peoples. Thus, for example, in Rwanda the absolute emphasis on the conflict between Hutu and Tutsi "tribes" ignores the political background of the imperial legacies of division between groups, and the recent attempts to moderate the political domination of one group over others. This move toward cooperation was halted by the 1994 slaughter, in which ethnic division was used as a tool against the forces for political change. In Somalia, again, the Western picture of competing clan-based warlords not only ignores historical experiences and the consequences of distortions, inadequate articulation, domination, and dependence, but also obscures the more long-term failure of the Western model of the nation-state to take hold in the region.[1] These examples of the distortion arising from an exclusively "tribal" view of African conflict could be multiplied.

At the structural level, discussions of conflicts often overlook or underestimate the state's role in the generation and reproduction of contradictions and coalitions that culminate in conflicts. The construction of a violent, undemocratic, and highly interventionist state under colonialism suffocated civil society, underdeveloped indigenous entrepreneurship, and divided the people. This oppressive state was transferred intact to the new leaders upon independence. Lacking economic power, they exercised only limited control over their territories. They could not promote growth (much less development) and were thus unable to fulfill the rosy promises of the nationalist struggle. Within a few years (or months in some cases) the neocolonial state was confronted with challenges from peasants, women, workers, and the unemployed. Finding itself in a defensive position, it easily resorted to the manipulative, exploitative, and repressive tactics, institutions, and politics of the colonial state. It became badly delegitimized and drove opponents into exile, into jail, or underground. Many recent political upheavals in Africa are mere manifestations of this long-standing contradiction between the states and civil society.

The Liberian civil war presents a useful case study of the limitations of Western perspectives on African civil conflicts. In the Liberian case, as in others in Africa, the civil war has been presented as a tribal struggle. A deeper examination, however, shows that what the West calls "tribalism," in fact, includes a range of other issues: the relationship between the elite and other groups, the differential impact of economic development, conflict over changing religious practices, and microeconomic crisis. Therefore, a closer examination of the onset of Liberia's civil war reveals the way in which tribal conflict converges with other points of tension in African society. In this chapter, I argue that the Liberian civil war was caused by a multiplicity of interrelated factors.

HISTORICAL PERSPECTIVE

Liberians are quick to point out that their country is the oldest African republic and the only country on the continent never to have fallen under European control during the colonial period. (Although Ethiopia makes the same claim, it was under Italian colonial rule for a short time.) Liberia has long been allied with the United States of America, with which it has had close historical and financial ties for over a hundred years.

The Settler establishment in Liberia began in 1821 when freed Americans of African ancestry, under the protection of the United States and the private sponsorship of the American Colonization Society, settled in the country. These settlers followed American models and strategies as they expanded their territory on the coast through outright conquest, the purchase of land not subject to sale, and the conversion of treaties of friendship into deeds of ownership. A Settler elite monopolized political power and economic resources, although they numbered less than 5 percent of the population.[2] The indigenous majority population was controlled by force and by the co-optation of local leaders into a system of colonial administration based on indirect rule. The interior did not come under real control by the Liberian government, however, until the end of the nineteenth century and beginning of the twentieth, when areas were brought under government control mainly to prevent the British and French from claiming the entire hinterland.[3]

By 1871, the Liberian government had become entangled in debt due to loans it had taken from the British and the French, and had to negotiate with respect to their debts by making concessions to these powers, which laid claim to the country. Eventually, the United States (which had a paternalistic interest in Liberian affairs because of its role in the state's founding) prevented European incursion into Liberia, assumed the loans, and provided a general receiver to the Liberian government, while plans were made to reschedule loan payments. Liberia had to make major economic concessions to foreigners, particularly the Firestone Plantation Company.[4] This indebtedness made Liberia dependent on foreign capital for its maintenance. At the same time, it exacerbated the relationship between the government and the interior, because in order to serve foreign capital interests the government spearheaded the labor mobilization of interior groups. Also, a flight of people from towns and villages resulted from the state's attempts to bring interior groups into a cash system and wage economy.[5]

A single party, the True Whig Party (TWP), which ruled continuously from 1877 to 1980, dominated the political system.[6] The system remained relatively static until William V.S. Tubman was elected president in 1944. He addressed for the first time the issue of the gradual integration of the indigenous people into a national society that would continue to be fashioned according to Settler norms. In addition, he further opened Liberia to overseas investment and trade in an effort to move beyond small-scale agriculture and reliance on a single product, rubber. For example, Tubman promoted the exploitation of high-grade iron ore deposits by American, Swedish, and German interests. These actions set in motion major changes in the Liberian economy in the postwar period, including a vast expansion of interior roads.[7]

President Tubman's devotion to national integration was nominal at best, however. The benefits of the new economic developments continued to be distributed unequally. These conditions of growth without development continued under William R. Tolbert, who succeeded Tubman upon the latter's death in 1971. During the period of Settler rule, Liberia's economy was under the control of European and American expatriates, Lebanese traders, and Settler politicians; these conditions thus fit the terms of dependency theory. The United States had widespread economic investments in Liberia, especially in rubber and iron ore, a major Voice of America transmitter, an OMEGA navigational station, and a major communications installation for State Department messages going to and coming from sub-Saharan Africa.[8]

Despite improvements in power sharing, non-Settlers continued to operate at a disadvantage in the Liberian economy and social order. By the 1970s, more indigenous Africans were being educated at the University of Liberia, Cuttington

University College, and abroad; and the government employed them, although they received lower pay and fewer perquisites than the members of the elite. The indigenes could be admitted into the ruling elite, however, by marriage, by adapting Settler ways, or by becoming wards.[9] Similar hierarchical relationships developed within the military; officers were almost always Settlers, while enlisted men were drawn from the indigenous population. These conditions played a major role in fostering the 1980 coup.

Seven causes contributed directly to the coup. First, there were deteriorating economic conditions including rising inflation, declining food self-sufficiency, and increased migration from the rural areas to the urban centers in search of nonexistent jobs.[10]

Second, flagrant nepotism existed in public and private employment. For example, President Tolbert's son, A.B. Tolbert, was a lawyer, an ambassador at large, and a member of the House of Representatives. Christine Norman, a daughter of President Tolbert, was deputy minister of education and held a monopoly on the importation and sale of all textbooks for the public schools. Frank Tolbert, a brother of the president, was president pro tem of the Senate; Stephen Tolbert, another brother, was minister of finance; and Burleigh Holder, a son-in-law of President Tolbert, was minister of defense. The list goes on and on.[11]

Third, student protests and labor strikes contributed to growing levels of unrest. Student dissent over the political and economic systems reached a crescendo during the final year of the Tolbert regime. The "straw that broke the camel's back" occurred in 1979 when the government planned to increase the price of rice, the staple food of the Liberian diet. Students, workers, the unemployed, and others took to the streets protesting the plan and used the event as an opportunity to protest more than a century of injustices. In early 1980, the Tolbert government arrested and jailed several political activists. In response, various groups in civil society called for their immediate release.[12]

In addition to student strikes, there were labor union strikes. Twelve such strikes occurred in 1976 alone. The unions' demand for better salaries and better working conditions was paramount in their protests. The growing number of strikes prompted the legislature to give President Tolbert emergency powers on an annual basis to deal with unions and strikes, to mobilize for defense, and to take other extraordinary measures. Nevertheless, the unions continued to protest working conditions until 1980 when Tolbert was ousted from power.[13]

Fourth, two new opposition political groups—the Movement for Justice in Africa (MOJA) and the Progressive Alliance of Liberia (PAL)—emerged in the late 1970s to challenge the elite. No such action had occurred under Tubman. Amos Sawyer, an independent candidate for mayor of Monrovia, was to run against a TWP hack in 1979. Sawyer's candidacy was supported by various groups seeking reforms and disgruntled élites—PAL, MOJA, and student movements. Sawyer was such a popular candidate that President Tolbert postponed the election. In early 1980, a new opposition party, the Progressive Peoples

Party (PPP), emerged, headed by Bacchus Mathews.[14] A few months later, however, the PPP was banned by the Tolbert regime and its leaders were arrested and imprisoned on the charge of treason.

Fifth, the society began to open up to hinterland people; they became better educated. More professional people began to enter political life. Against a rising tide of expectations, change was not rapid enough. While President Tolbert made superficial liberal changes in the political system, they did not lead to the equitable distribution of power between the Settlers and the indigenous peoples. For example, members of Settler stock were still occupying the major positions in the government. Even in those instances where the liberal reforms instituted by the Tolbert regime attempted to redistribute political power, the effect was to strengthen the patron-client relationship between the Settlers and the indigenous people. For example, positions such as those of First and Second Deputy Speaker of the House of Representatives were established in order to narrow the political power gap between the indigenous people and the Settlers. However, because the position of First Deputy Speaker was assigned to the old counties, the base of the Settler stock, and that of the Second Deputy Speaker to the new counties, the home of the indigenous people, more power was concentrated in the hands of the Settler stock while the superficial appearance of empowering the indigenous people was given.[15]

Sixth, economic changes left a large group of people behind, and their economic position declined in absolute terms. Such changes included a drop in exchange rates and delayed payment or nonpayment of salaries. These conditions mainly affected the dispossessed lower classes. Discontent came to a head in April 1979, when the government abruptly raised the price of a 100-pound bag of rice from $22 to $30. This price hike led to major street demonstrations, to which the government brutally overreacted. Hundreds of Liberians were left dead or wounded in the wake of police gunfire, and a year of ferment began.[16]

Seventh, President Tolbert nearly drove the country into bankruptcy with the preparations for hosting the Organisation of African Unity (OAU) Summit Meeting in July 1979. Approximately $200 million were used to build a resort hotel, fifty-three elegant villas—one for each head of state—adjacent to it, and other structures. In addition, each of the fifty-three delegations was furnished with seven cars, color television sets, and other "amenities." Although the villas and hotel were supposed to be used by tourists after the OAU meeting, Liberia was not ready for tourism. For example, the common tourist action of taking out a camera on the streets in Monrovia could result in an arrest.[17]

THE COUP OF APRIL 12, 1980

On the night of April 12, 1980, seventeen enlisted men, all from indigenous ethnic groups, broke into the Executive Mansion and murdered President Tolbert in his bedroom. There was general rejoicing in the country and fewer than a hundred people were killed as Settler power fell in one loud bang. Shops were looted, property was confiscated, and homes were vandalized. Many of the Settler elite fled to the United States.[18]

A military government under the leadership of Master Sergeant Samuel K. Doe assumed leadership of the country. The new government was named the People's Redemption Council (PRC) and the commanding general was Thomas Quiwonkpa (who later came into conflict with Doe). Many indigenous civilians served in the military government. Several members of the cabinet were opposition political leaders holding Ph.D. degrees from American universities. For example, Boima Fahnbulleh (Ph.D., George Washington University) was minister of education and foreign affairs.[19]

In the first two years of the military regime, Sergeant Doe was popular. This was evidenced in the support his junta enjoyed from students, newspapers, labor unions, clergymen, and opposition political leaders. However, they all became disillusioned eventually as the perception spread that the only people in Liberia benefiting from the new order were the military and their families. Sergeant Doe became increasingly agitated about the dissent and closed down newspapers. Other African countries, at first, refused to accept him. The United States, initially uncertain, supported him. The PRC failed in its attempts to maintain stability or achieve economic development.[20]

While the military claimed that it could foster stability better than the civilians could, in fact it became the main source of instability. The PRC confiscated property, executed thirteen leaders of the old regime, and imposed curfews and restrictions on movement as military leaders came to rely on their monopoly of force.[21]

No measures were taken against the Settlers; and eventually Doe welcomed them back and even urged them to return home, with some becoming prominent in his government. Ernest Eastman, for example, was minister of foreign affairs and Emmanuel Shaw was minister of finance. However, Doe's inner circle consisted overwhelmingly of members of his own ethnic group, the Krahn, who had been denigrated in the past. His policies created ethnic strains that had not been present prior to his rise to power.[22] Prior to Doe's regime, intermarriages and harmonious relationships existed among the indigenous groups. Clearly, it was his intent to politicize ethnicity that created the antagonistic situation, particularly between his Krahn and the Gio and Mano ethnic groups.

Economic policy and practice were a complete disaster. Sergeant Doe and his regime had no ideas, let alone programs, that might have benefited the Liberian economy. Deterioration occurred in almost every Liberian economic index during Doe's ten years in power—inflation higher than under Tolbert; vast layoffs in the iron ore concessions (1,300 in 1984 alone); and no new economic projects. Finally, only United States aid and assistance prevented the Liberian economy from completely collapsing. Nearly $100 million a year in financial aid came to Liberia from the United States. This was more than double the total amount received during the nine years of Tolbert's rule.[23]

TRANSITION TO "CIVILIAN" RULE

Most military governments maintain that they are committed to returning to civilian rule, and the same was true with the Doe junta. Doe soon proved, however, to be a lawless and brutal tyrant who had no intention of disengaging himself or the military from politics. In October 1985, he brazenly stole the election that was to have ushered in civilian rule. A new constitution had been approved in advance. During the general elections of 1985, three political parties, the Liberian Action Party, the Liberian Unification Party, and the Unity Party, were permitted to oppose Sergeant Doe, the candidate of the state-sponsored National Democratic Party of Liberia. Neither the United People's Party nor the Liberian People's Party (LPP) was allowed to participate. Those were the two most popular political parties at the time. Many people were harassed, but they braved the threats and intimidation to attend the rallies of opposition parties during the campaign.

Sergeant Doe restricted opposition political parties from organizing as he formed his own party, the National Democratic Party of Liberia (NDPL).[24] In August 1984, he jailed Amos Sawyer, dean of the College of Humanities and Social Sciences, and George Kieh, Jr., lecturer in Political Science at the University of Liberia, both leaders of LPP. These arrests inspired the students at the University of Liberia to organize protest gatherings. Sergeant Doe sent approximately 200 soldiers from his mansion guards to storm the campus, injuring over 100 people and killing an undetermined number. Many beatings, rapes, and assaults occurred; records, books, machinery, and laboratories were destroyed. Millions of dollars in damage resulted from this chaotic three-hour attack.[25]

After the vote in the 1985 presidential election, as it became clear in early counting that Sergeant Doe was losing badly, he ordered the ballot boxes collected and taken to a secret location in Monrovia. There, his handpicked people did the counting and announced that Doe had won 51 percent of the vote, with Jackson Doe of the Liberian Action Party (no relation) coming in second. With the perpetration of this fraud, Doe's little remaining credibility completely disappeared.[26]

THE SECOND REPUBLIC

The fraudulent election was immediately followed by an attempted coup in November 1985, led by Thomas Quiwonkpa, one of the most prominent leaders of the 1980 coup. It almost succeeded, but eventually failed. Quiwonkpa was murdered and 500 to 2,000 people died in the reprisals that followed. These reprisals were particularly severe in Nimba County, Thomas Quiwonkpa's home area. Many Mano and Gio were killed, and hundreds of people were detained, starved, and otherwise mistreated, until Doe declared a general amnesty in June 1986. Hundreds of Mano and Gio soldiers were summarily executed on the grounds of the Executive Mansion. Ethnic violence had begun, although ethnic tensions had been minimal prior to 1980.[27]

With Doe's regime, ethnicity and "tribe" began to define the central principle of the Liberian government. This new development specifically connects to the drastically altered circumstances caused Doe's overthrow of the long-standing Settler dominance. It should be emphasized that even though Doe made ethnicity central in his policymaking, most Liberians did not view ethnicity as the defining core of society. Many Krahn, for instance, did not benefit from Doe's rule and complained about it like everyone else.[28]

Doe's regime, known as the Second Republic, was completely dominated by Doe. He hired and fired ministers without explanation and surrounded himself with members of his own ethnic group, placing them in important positions. For example, Edward Taye was commissioner of immigration; John Ramsey was minister of state; George Boley was minister of education; and Harry Nayou was minister of state for presidential affairs. Doe's signature innovation was to ethnicize the armed forces of Liberia, packing the officer corps and key units with Krahn. In the multiple upheavals of his decade-long rule, Krahn soldiers responded to repeated protests, plots, and failed coups by murdering, raping, and pillaging on a huge scale.[29]

Sergeant Doe also controlled the Liberian economy. It is estimated that during his reign, he and his advisors received approximately $300 million from the public treasury, an amount roughly equal to half the anemic gross domestic product for the regime's final year in power. Doe amassed a personal fortune of approximately $250 million that he kept in a Bank for Commerce and Credit International (BCCI) account in London and in other banks overseas. Liberia's distinctive American connection (the United States dollar remains legal tender) helped him establish a lucrative money-laundering racket. Prices continued to soar while schools, hospitals, and other institutions faced collapse as Doe and his government depended almost entirely on aid from the United States to stay afloat.[30]

REACTIONS OF ETHNIC GROUPS TO POLITICAL AND ECONOMIC CHANGES

Economic changes and political conflict have had different effects on different ethnic groups. The specific place a group occupies within the Liberian polity and within the Liberian economy determines where it stands in relation to the changes. By examining the particular cases of major ethnic groups in Liberia, the differential impact of change can be specified.

Krahn

A few members of the Krahn ethnic group benefited from the economic and political largesse of the Doe regime. For example, Edward Slangar owned a private corporation which held contracts for government equipment and supplies, and John Beh made away with millions of government dollars, never to return to Liberia. However, the majority of Krahn remain impoverished and poverty stricken. Even in Doe's hometown of Tuzon, the modest development that took place was concentrated in Doe's family's area, while the rest of the town remained basically underdeveloped. In the larger context of Grand Gedeh County, therefore, the people received very few economic benefits from the Doe regime.[31]

The entire Krahn ethnic group, however, was held responsible for the Doe regime's "reign of terror." This led to the death of thousands of Krahn group members. This example demonstrates how civil conflicts (the roots of which are to be found in deeper socioeconomic and political factors) can be turned into simplistic ethnic conflicts.

Mano and Gio

In the aftermath of the 1980 coup, General Quiwonkpa of the Gio ethnic group became commander-in-general of the Liberian Armed Forces and a senior member of the PRC. He recruited some members of the Gio and Mano groups into the new government. For instance, Harry Yuan was managing director of the Liberian Electricity Corporation (LEC), Moses Duopu was minister of labor, and J. S. Guannu was ambassador to the United States. Accordingly, the perception was created that the political fortunes of the Gio and Mano groups were tied to Quiwonkpa. In 1983 Doe demoted General Quiwonkpa to the largely administrative position of secretary general of the PRC. He took this step with the intention of minimizing Quiwonkpa's power because he saw Quiwonkpa as his principal rival in the ruling military council. However, under pressure from some intellectuals from Nimba and from other Nimba citizens in the armed forces, Quiwonkpa refused to accept the demotion. Angered by Quiwonkpa's defiance, Doe concocted a coup in which he implicated Quiwonkpa and several members of the Gio and Mano ethnic groups. Quiwonkpa and his close associates fled Liberia.

After the fraudulent election in which Doe declared himself president, Quiwonkpa organized a coup attempt in November 1985. However, it was foiled and Quiwonkpa and some of his associates were killed. Doe used the opportunity to heighten the conflict he had manufactured between his own Krahn group and the Gio and Mano ethnic groups. His regime embarked on a campaign of terror in Quiwonkpa's own region of Nimba. Thousands of innocent civilians were killed, and villages, towns, and farms were burned.[32]

When Charles Taylor while in the Ivory Coast decided to launch his rebellion against Doe's regime, he appealed to the Gio and Mano associates of the late Quiwonkpa. He assured them that if they joined ranks with him they would have the opportunity to take revenge on Doe and his Krahn ethnic group.

Clearly, this is another indication of how ethnicity has been manipulated to achieve the goals and objectives of various armed factions.[33]

In terms of the impact of the civil war on the Gio and Mano ethnic groups, the results have been mixed. On the one hand, the Taylor-led National Patriotic Front of Liberia (NPFL) has executed some prominent members of the Gio and Mano ethnic groups who were perceived as posing threats to Taylor's political ambitions. On the other hand, their own kin who are fighters in the NPFL have spared some ordinary members of these groups. Interestingly, the NPFL destroyed villages and towns in the Nimba area.[34]

Mandingo

The members of this group are merchants in such commodities as cattle and kola, as well as shopkeepers and sellers in the open-air markets. During the Doe regime, many of them began to diversify into more profitable high-demand business areas, mainly transportation and energy (gasoline and kerosene). In the 1980s, they also began to enter the mainstream of Liberian life by running for political office. Mamadie Sirleaf, for instance, became a senator from Bong County in the Second Republic.[35]

Doe allied with the Mandingo as a way of building support for his regime. However, only a few members of the group's elite reaped economic and political benefits, while the majority remained marginalized. Despite this fact, Doe succeeded in creating the perception of an alliance between the Krahn ethnic group and the Mandingo against the Mano and Gio.[36]

The support that the Mandingos were perceived as providing to the Doe regime made them targets for revenge by victimized groups. During the rebel invasion of Liberia on December 24, 1989, a prominent Mandingo, Alhaji Daramy, went on television and declared Mandingo support for Doe in repelling the rebels. His action caused many people to turn against the Mandingos because of their alignment with Doe, whom many people hated, especially the Gios and Manos.[37]

Political antagonism toward the Mandingos combined with long-festering conflicts and tensions. One practice that caused such tensions is the Mandingos' "one-way street" marriage. Muslim Mandingo men may marry non-Mandingo women, but Mandingo women may not marry non-Muslim men. As a consequence of this practice, the children of ethnically mixed families are raised as Muslims. The reason why Mandingo men refuse to permit their women to be married to men of other ethnic groups is that, while women of other ethnic groups convert from traditional religion to Islam if married to Mandingo men, the reverse happens in the case of Mandingo women. In intermarriage between local women and Mandingo men, it is the identity of the male that prevails, thus leading to the establishment of Mandingo communities, especially along trade routes.[38]

Also, traditional Liberian leaders and men in positions of authority in traditional secret societies felt threatened by the growing power of Muslim leaders and clerics. Instead of going to traditional healers to cure problems, both psychological and physical, many Liberians began seeking the Muslim imams because they felt that the imams were more effective in providing protection and in meeting other needs. This practice served to increase resentment toward Muslims.[39]

In addition, many Liberians resented what they felt was a Mandingo monopoly of certain aspects of the economy. For instance, Mandingo traders introduced domesticated animals and plants, garments and styles of dress, numerous material goods (such as iron, guns, and money), and utensils (such as plates, spoons, and knives). They used trade paths connecting indigenous Liberian populations to link the coast with the savanna and traded for kola, ivory, camwood, pottery, rice, and slaves. In return they bought tobacco, cattle, European manufactured goods, and salt. The Mandingo were also skilled craftsmen who introduced new types of agricultural tools and were excellent blacksmiths and weavers.[40]

On the eve of the civil war, all of the grievances of other Liberian ethnic groups against the Mandingo were manifested in killings and the destruction of Mandingo properties. Many Mandingos fled to exile in Sierra Leone and Guinea.

The other thirteen ethnic groups in Liberia were not included in the conflict that Doe manufactured and the NPFL and others exploited. Many of those killed were identified as government officials or individuals who had material possessions such as cars and houses that Doe's army sergeants wanted. Only in a few instances did fighters ask for the ethnic affiliation of civilians. Even if one hailed from "the correct ethnic group," it did not ensure one's safety.

THE CIVIL WAR

From the Ivory Coast, Charles Taylor (a Settler who claims to be a Gola), a former official in Doe's government, led Liberian exiles and dissidents in an incursion into Nimba County beginning on December 24, 1989. Under the leadership of Taylor, the NPFL committed numerous murders and destroyed property in Nimba, causing thousands of Liberians to flee to the nearby Ivory Coast. The NPFL had taken control of most Nimba and Bassa counties by May, thus cutting the country in two. At the iron ore mine at Lamco, the death and destruction was enormous. Ethnic strife was further provoked as the Mano and Gio formed the basis of Taylor's support. By the end of May, various West African countries had called for an end to hostilities. The United Nations, which had brought in large amounts of food and medical supplies during the worst periods of fighting, announced a withdrawal of its personnel after Doe's soldiers attacked one of its refugee compounds, killing four refugees and abducting forty.[41]

Doe's government began to lose control as the NPFL forces advanced toward Monrovia. Gbarnga fell to Taylor and the rebels shut down the international airport. By the middle of July 1990, Doe had barricaded himself in the Executive Mansion while Taylor controlled almost all of the country, declaring himself president of a government of "reconstruction."[42]

From the beginning, all sides made war against civilians with tragic results. Thousands were murdered and hundreds of thousands fled into nearby countries. Eventually, as many as 700,000 Liberians (out of a population of 2.5 million) sought refuge elsewhere, primarily in Sierra Leone, Guinea, and the Ivory Coast. Approximately 600,000 more—over half of the population—were displaced from their homes but remained in various areas of Liberia.[43]

On July 30, 1990, troops alleged to belong to President Doe's army murdered over 600 men, women, and children who had sought refuge in St. Peter's Lutheran Church in Monrovia. The rationale given for their murders was that they were not members of Doe's ethnic group. However, the Doe government denied allegations that Krahn troops had committed the murders.[44]

On August 24, 1990, a West African peacekeeping force, initially consisting of 3,500 members, arrived in Monrovia to help put an end to the killing of civilians. West African states through their organization, the Economic Community of West African States (ECOWAS), sought to establish a framework for a cease-fire and an interim government in Liberia. However, after peace talks failed, ECOWAS decided to send a peacekeeping force called the Economic Community of West Africa Monitoring Group (ECOMOG). Soldiers mainly from Nigeria, Ghana, Guinea, Sierra Leone, and the Gambia made up ECOMOG. They were sent to Liberia to bring about a cease-fire. In August 1990, ECOWAS held an All-Liberian Conference in the Gambia at which Amos Sawyer was appointed head of an interim government, to remain in power until the time for elections.[45]

In September 1990, Prince Johnson, leader of a group that had broken away from the NPFL, captured Doe and murdered him. Doe's death temporarily weakened and disorganized his supporters. The conflict was now mainly between Taylor's and Johnson's armies. Taylor accused ECOMOG forces of supporting Johnson. This belief led his forces to attack ECOMOG forces, resulting in Taylor's forces having to fight two groups at the same time.[46]

In March 1991, Taylor's forces and the Revolutionary United Front (RUF) attacked Sierra Leone, thus beginning the destabilization of that country's government. The reason for the attack was that the Sierra Leone government had supplied soldiers to the ECOMOG forces in Monrovia, thus preventing Taylor's group from taking over the city. Attacking Sierra Leone would redirect the attention of the West African countries, and Taylor would have a chance to seize power and declare himself president. Also, his support for the RUF was a way of gaining access to Sierra Leone's diamond reserves, a critical source of funding for his rebel faction in Liberia. The remnants of Doe's old army regrouped as the United Liberation Movement for Democracy in Liberia (ULIMO) and reentered the fray in September 1991, attacking Taylor's territory from Sierra Leone. This group served the government of Sierra Leone with the hope of receiving financial and other support in the attempt to conquer and capture Taylor.[47]

Through the remainder of 1991 and the first half of 1992, relative calm prevailed as Taylor's forces continued to control most of the country, with ULIMO in charge of parts of Western Liberia near the Sierra Leonean border. In July 1992, fighting between the NPFL and ULIMO intensified in Western Liberia with ULIMO enjoying surprising success; the NPFL's forces advanced to the outskirts of Monrovia. Later ECOMOG drove Taylor's forces away from Monrovia into the interior.[48]

ECOMOG finally and completely drove the NPFL troops from central Monrovia in October 1994. Eventually, a sort of cease-fire was reached with Taylor controlling most of the country, ECOMOG in charge of Monrovia, and the interim government under Amos Sawyer completely dependent on the ECOMOG forces.[49]

Several previous cease-fire efforts had failed. The various parties blamed Taylor and his group. An agreement (signed by Sawyer's interim government, Taylor of the NPFL, Hezekiah Bowen, chief of staff of the Armed Forces of Liberia, and Alhaji Kromah, head of ULIMO) reached in 1993 in Cotonou, Benin, had seemed to have the best chance of ending the fighting and beginning the long reconciliation and rebuilding process. A new interim government was set up to replace the former interim government of Amos Sawyer; and each of the main parties was to appoint a member of the five-member council of state which was to run the country until elections were held. Problems arose, however, when Sawyer refused to step down; and there were major disagreements over the composition of the council.[50] However, after mediation and negotiation, a new transitional government was established, which was followed by two others. Nevertheless, none of these arrangements resulted in peace.

In July 1996, heads of state of ECOWAS met again (this time in Abuja, the new capital of Nigeria), to further attempt to make arrangements for restoring peace to Liberia. They developed an aggressive timetable that included deadlines for disarmament, encampment, and repatriation. These activities were scheduled for completion before the election that was tentatively scheduled to be held in May 1997. However, certain challenges to this timetable had to be overcome: Taylor had to be willing to comply; financial and logistical resources had to be made available; and the repatriation and registration of Liberians scattered throughout the world needed to be accomplished. Without a resolution of these problems, valid elections would not be possible. The development and enforcement of the timetable was the most serious effort made toward ending the civil war.

PRESIDENTIAL ELECTIONS OF 1997

The activities of disarmament and encampment were partially completed before the elections, which were held on July 19, 1997. Thirteen parties participated. However, only two, "the National Patriotic Party of Taylor and the Unity Party of Ellen Johnson-Sirleaf," were serious contenders.[51] Taylor's party had more money and better campaign communications techniques designed to reach the Liberian people. In addition, Taylor distributed bags of rice and money. As a result, he won the election in a landslide, gaining approximately 75 percent of the vote.

Observer teams were sent from several countries to monitor the elections. Some European and U.S. monitors returning from the countryside said the vote there appeared to be even more lopsided in Taylor's favor. However, according to former U.S. President Jimmy Carter, who led a forty-member team from the United States, "There were a number of small irregularities, which is normal in any election. It was obvious that inadequate voter education was completed prior to the election."[52] The voting regulations restricted participation to Liberians who were residing in the country at the time of the elections. No refugees or non-refugees living in other countries were allowed to vote.

Why did Liberians vote so overwhelmingly for Taylor? Three primary responses are often given: (1) the people were tired of war; (2) the people felt that it was Taylor's responsibility to rebuild the country since he was responsible for destroying it; and (3) many people saw no viable alternative to him.[53]

PROSPECTS FOR PEACEBUILDING

What do the election results indicate for the future of Liberia? After Taylor's election as president, there was a sense of general goodwill among the Liberian people. Their collective hope was that the Taylor regime would usher in a new era of peace, reconciliation, prosperity, and democracy. Disappointingly, however, the Taylor regime has squandered the Liberian people's goodwill. Several cases are illustrative of this. First, the Taylor regime has a horrendous human rights record. For example, it has killed political opponents and imprisoned journalists and other civil society activists. Second, there is growing poverty, while President Taylor and his cronies live in opulence. Third, the social infrastructure is in disrepair. Public hospitals lack drugs, equipment, and supplies. Taiwan is now funding the operation of the J.F.K. Medical Center, the largest public hospital in the country.

Where does Liberia go from here? Clearly, genuine changes need to be made by the Taylor regime. Paramount among the many actions that must be taken to minimize the risk of another civil war in Liberia are political and economic changes. The national reconstruction efforts must include both political and economic components. In his *Political Economy of Democratization in Africa*, Claude Ake asserts that the key to the recovery of civil war ravaged countries is the political and economic empowerment of the people.[54] To avoid replanting the seeds of conflict, there must be a concerted effort to solve Liberia's chronic political problems. Critical issues in the postcivil war era must include (1) constitutional engineering—the constitution must be the supreme law of the land, both in theory and in practice, which requires the subordination of all institutions and individuals to its various provisions; (2) respect for the judiciary—there must be an independent judiciary, devoid of the usual presidential manipulation, which will serve as the guarantor of civil liberties; (3) respect for fundamental human rights—the exercise of basic human rights must be protected within the parameters of the constitution; (4) a multi-party system—a viable and visible competitive system must be instituted to ensure checks and balances with regard to the powers of the ruling party and its government; and (5) sharing of power—there must be a redistribution of power between the central and local governments.

Economic soundness is critical to the survival of any political system. A poorly functioning economy undermines or undercuts political gains. Thus, Liberia must consider these economic issues as a part of its reconstruction strategy: (1) inflation control—the Liberian economy must be stabilized and strengthened, and price controls must be established to halt inflation; (2) employment—more jobs must be created to decrease unemployment, because increased employment opportunities will help reduce crime and other subversive activities that pose serious problems in Liberia; (3) resuscitate industry—factories that were closed because of the war must be encouraged to reopen, and investors' confidence must be regained by ensuring them a secure environment for business; (4) promotion of trade—trade must be promoted nationally and internationally with the local business sector playing a critical role: the state must create a favorable business environment by providing opportunities for access to loans and other sources of credit, and provide tax incentives that will help facilitate the creation of a strong and viable indigenous business sector, which ultimately must aid in the creation of jobs; and (5) development of agriculture—a major agricultural agenda must be designed to reclaim the land and encourage farmers to return to it. The government must provide agricultural incentives, especially for rural people, guarantee fair prices for products, and assure the people that they are safe from unwarranted government intervention.

SUMMARY AND CONCLUSION

This chapter has presented an overview of the major factors that contributed to the eruption of the civil war in Liberia and the prospects for restoring peace in its aftermath. While ethnicity was the most frequently emphasized reason for the genesis of the war, as portrayed in the Western media, the chapter has examined other factors that played a much more significant role. These factors included political, economic, religious, and external influences. The future of the country is contingent upon how, or whether, these influences can be reconciled within the context of the present administration.

The analysis presented in this case study of the Liberian civil war shows that the discontent reflects the economic and political positions of peoples. It is not tribal alliances as such that matter, but inequity of political and economic opportunities. Only within the context of social and economic discontent can the emergence of ethnic antagonism be explained; only with the anger fueled by such social and economic discontent can governments mobilize ethnic tensions and use scapegoating. Thus, "tribal" violence depends on nontribal discontent. Just as tribalism is not the only issue in Liberia, it is highly probable that it is not the only issue in other African conflicts.

NOTES

1. Julius O. Ihonvbere, "Beyond Warlords and Clans: The African Crisis and the Somali Situation," *International Third World Studies Journal and Review* 6 (1995): 7–19.
2. Ibid., 21–28.
3. Martin Lowenkopf, *Politics in Liberia* (Stanford, CA: Hoover Institution Press, 1976), 33–37.
4. Ibid.
5. J. Gius Liebenow, *Liberia: The Quest for Democracy*, (Bloomington, IN: Indiana University Press, 1984), 47–57.
6. George Klay Kieh, "Combatants, Patrons, Peacemakers, and the Liberian Civil Conflict," *Studies in Conflict and Terrorism* 15 (1992): 127–128.
7. Augustine Konneh, "Mandingo Integration in the Liberian Political Economy," *Liberian Studies Journal* 18, no. 1 (1993): 49; and Lowenkopf, *Politics in Liberia*, 75–77.
8. Liebenow, *Liberia: The Quest*, 137–138.
9. George Kieh, "Taproots of the Liberian Civil War," paper presented at the Third World Studies Association Conference, Omaha, Nebraska, 1991, 6–8; and Liebenow, *Liberia: The Quest*, 23.
10. Kieh, "Combatants, Patrons, Peacemakers," 128.
11. Liebenow, *Liberia: The Quest*, 107–110, 123–124; and G.E.S. Boley, *Liberia: The Rise and Fall of the First Republic* (London: Macmillan Press, 1983), 96.
12. Ibid., 84–87.
13. Ibid., 74–87.
14. George Kieh, "Causes of Liberia's Coup," *TransAfrica Forum* (Winter 1989): 45.
15. Boley, *Liberia: The Rise and Fall*, 88–95.
16. Ibid., 101–105.
17. Liebenow, *Liberia: The Quest*, 170.
18. Ibid., 185–192.
19. Ibid.
20. Ibid.
21. Ibid.
22. Interview with Dr. Christian Baker, now deceased, former president of Cuttington University College, October 1994.
23. Kieh, "Taproots of the Liberian Civil War," 8–11; Patrick Seyon, "Liberia's Second Republic: Superpower Geopolitics in Africa," *Liberian Studies Journal* 12, no. 1 (1987): 64; and Liebenow, *Liberia: The Quest*, 303.
24. Liebenow, *Liberia: The Quest*, 264–290.
25. Ibid.

26. Ibid., 293–296.
27. Ibid., 300–302.
28. Interview with Mark Gibson, a graduate of the University of Liberia.
29. Kieh, "Taproots of the Liberian Civil War," 13–15.
30. Ibid., 15–18.
31. Ibid.
32. Ibid., 19.
33. Kieh, "Combatants, Patrons, Peacemakers,"129–130.
34. Interview with John Saye, Kenema, August 1990.
35. Konneh, "Mandingo Integration," 54–56.
36. Ibid., 56–57.
37. Ibid.
38. Ibid., 57.
39. Konneh, "Indigenous Entrepreneurs and Capitalists: The Role of the Mandingo in the Economic Development of Modern-Day Liberia" (Ph.D. dissertation, Indiana University, 1992), 68–72.
40. Konneh, "Mandingo Integration," 55–57.
41. Kieh, "Combatants, Patrons, Peacemakers," 129–131.
42. Ibid.
43. Kieh, "Combatants, Patrons, Peacemakers," 138.
44. Ibid.
45. "Current Affairs: Liberia—A Farewell to Arms," *West Africa Magazine*, September 23–29, 1996, 1506–1507.
46. *West Africa*, November 1991, 1230.
47. *West Africa*, November 1991, 1365.
48. Carolyn M. Shaw, "Hegemonic Participation in Peacekeeping Operations: The Case of Nigeria and ECOMOG," paper presented at the 27th Annual Liberian Studies Conference, Dayton, Ohio, April 19–22, 1995, 9–11.
49. Ibid.
50. There was evidence that Taylor was not ready for peace and was not ready to honor the Abuja agreement. Ultimately, however, he had to be forced to accept peace.
51. *Heritage* (Special Election Edition), Monrovia, Liberia, June 15–24, 1997; and *Daily Observer*, Monrovia, Liberia, June 19, 1997, 4–6.
52. The Associated Press (press release), July 21, 1997, p. 1.
53. The Associated Press (press release), July 22, 1997, pp. 2–4.
54. For a detailed discussion of how peoples are empowered, see Claude Ake's *Political Economy of Democratization in Africa* (London: Longman, 1995).

7

Military Rule and Sociopolitical Crises in Nigeria

Pita Ogaba Agbese

INTRODUCTION

June 12, 1993 has acquired a near-mythical status in the annals of Nigerian politics, for the date has come to symbolize the determination by Nigerian pro-democracy groups to force the nation's military to relinquish political power. Ironically, June 1993 also represents the most brazen attempt by the military to perpetuate military rule. Specifically, the date has been seen as a focal point in the epic struggle between autocratic military officers and pro-democracy groups. The genesis of the political crisis symbolized by June 12 began in 1986 with the decision by the military, under the leadership of General Ibrahim Babangida, to use the electoral system as a mechanism for restoring civilian rule in 1990. Under this arrangement, the military would, through a series of elections conducted over several years, voluntarily relinquish power to civilian politicians.

After a series of postponements, the military's final disengagement from politics was fixed for August 27, 1993. Thus, a presidential election that was the last in a series of elections designed to usher in the new democratic system was duly held on June 12, 1993. It soon became apparent, however, that the presidential election would not mark an end to military rule. Shortly after the National Electoral Commission (NEC) began announcing the results of the election, it was ordered by the government to stop forthwith. Accordingly, the results of the election were suspended. However, before the abrupt suspension of the results, Moshood Abiola of the Social Democratic Party (SDP) had built a commanding lead and was heading for a decisive victory. In place of transferring power to civilians as the military had promised, General Babangida scuttled the transition program entirely. On June 23, 1993, he told the nation that he had annulled the presidential election. He also disqualified the two presidential candidates, Abiola of the SDP and Bashir Tofa of the National Republican Convention (NRC), from contesting a new presidential election that was supposed to be held a few months after the annulment.

President Babangida claimed that he had been compelled to cancel the election because political controversies associated with the suspension of the election results had threatened the integrity of the country's judiciary. He also claimed that the two candidates, Tofa and Abiola, had used money to corrupt the electoral process. Interestingly, five years after he aborted the transition program, General Babangida adduced new rationales for his action. He now claims that he was compelled, under intense pressure from some high-ranking military officers, to jettison the transition program. While he has accepted full responsibility for his government's annulment of the election, he maintains that he was prevailed upon not to relinquish power by senior officers who did not want Abiola to become president of Nigeria.

Not only did President Babangida annul the election; he also abrogated the decrees under which the election had been conducted. In addition, he removed Henry Nwosu, the chairman of the electoral commission, from office. Babangida also declared all previous actions undertaken by the commission in connection with the presidential election null and void. This was tantamount to saying that the election never took place. Despite the fact that the president had dealt a fatal blow to his own transition program, he tried to reassure Nigerians that the democratization exercise was still on course. He promised to hold a new presidential election and he reiterated his wish to transfer power to civilian politicians by the deadline of August 27, 1993. However, many Nigerians could no longer accept the sincerity of the military's promises to relinquish power. Babangida's annulment of the election and his decision to abrogate the electoral decrees were seen by many Nigerians as solid confirmation that Babangida had a secret agenda: to succeed himself. Nigerians lost faith in Babangida's political credibility. In addition, Nigerians of all political persuasions were convinced that the military could not supervise a genuine transition to democratic rule.

The Babangida regime's unilateral and rather callous annulment of an election that was generally seen as Nigeria's cleanest and least controversial was roundly condemned in all parts of the country. It triggered a series of mass demonstrations in several major cities including Lagos, Benin, Abeokuta, and Ibadan. Many demonstrators were beaten up and the protests were put down violently by the military. Nonetheless, the anger, disappointment, and sense of betrayal that were created by the annulment could not be so easily suppressed. The general resentment of military dictatorship that had been building up in the country before the cancellation of the election reached a critical point after the annulment. Despite the military's heavy-handed treatment of Nigerians who were opposed to the annulment and the apparent unwillingness of the military to relinquish power, the anger against the military could not be easily crushed.

Accordingly, the annulment led to nationwide general strikes by the country's trade unions. Mass-based organizations such as students' unions, market-women's associations, and youth groups demanded an immediate end to military rule and its corrupt practices. Students boycotted classes to press home their demand for the military to relinquish power and for Moshood Abiola, the apparent winner of the election, to be sworn in as president of Nigeria. Internationally, several countries roundly condemned Nigeria. Some of these countries, including the United States, Canada, Britain, and the other countries of the European Union, imposed mild economic sanctions on the country. These were intended as punishment for the military's decision to abort the transition program. Additionally, the annulment and the repressive measures adopted by the successor regime of General Sani Abacha led to the diplomatic isolation of Nigeria by the entire international community. Senior Nigerian government officials were denied entry to foreign countries. International human rights and environmental protection groups including Human Rights Watch, Amnesty International, and Greenpeace demanded the imposition of stringent sanctions, including an oil embargo, on Nigeria for the military regime's wanton violation of human rights in the country.

With the annulment, Nigeria became embroiled in an acute political and economic crisis. As Rotimi Suberu has noted, the annulment "plunged Nigeria into its worst political crisis since the 1967–1970 civil war."[1] The weekly magazine, *West Africa*, commenting on the aftermath of the annulment, noted that it left Nigerians "wading through troubled waters and, to make matters doubly worse, the waters are at high tide."[2] Political tensions arising from the annulment exacerbated and/or triggered intercommunal conflicts that killed many people in various parts of the country. In addition, the sociopolitical tensions created in the wake of the annulment aggravated existing political problems. For instance, regional, cultural, and ethnic polarizations in the country were all heightened as a result of the climate of suspicion and acrimony generated by the annulment. The annulment also created deep and bitter animosity within the military establishment itself. Some soldiers openly supported the annulment, while others saw it as a manifestation of the growing perfidy of the military under the Babangida regime. Soldiers in this latter category felt that the honorable thing for the military to do was to relinquish power and retreat to the barracks. They recognized the reality that military rule had polarized the military. They were also convinced that this polarization of the armed forces was detrimental to professionalism and military morale. The principal manifestation of the depth of the internal wrangling in the military from the fallout of the annulment was the military coup of November 1993 and the alleged coup plots in 1995 and 1997.[3]

Six years after the annulment, the political crisis created in its wake remained largely unresolved. Worse, the climate of uncertainty unleashed by the crisis had had a devastating impact on the Nigerian economy and society. In the first half of 1998, inflation was estimated at over 60 percent. Most factories that had not shut down for lack of raw materials and spare parts were producing at a very low rate. Unemployment was extremely high with most university graduates being unable to find employment even several years after graduation. Poverty accelerated and per capita income fell from a high of $1,000 (in 1980) to a meager $340 by 1996. In 1996, debt servicing of dubious external debts took up over 25 percent of scarce foreign-exchange earnings. Political instability, political uncertainty, and massive corruption combined in a vicious cycle to discourage new foreign investments. What was worse, the political crisis gave new momentum to capital flight, including billions of dollars which top government officials stole from the central bank. Much of this stolen money was deposited in banks in Europe and North America.

Poor leadership, massive corruption, and sheer criminality combined to create abysmal economic and political conditions in the country. One of the biggest manifestations of the economic and political direction which the affairs of Nigeria were taking under military rule was the acute shortage of petroleum which lasted from 1995 until the military left office in May 1999. The petroleum shortage had a major debilitating impact on the economy, which was already in a parlous state. What was so tragic about the petroleum shortage was the fact that Nigeria is the world's eighth largest producer of crude oil, but while it sells crude oil to the rest of the world, Nigeria finds it difficult to supply itself with enough refined oil. The economic mismanagement of Nigeria as symbolized by the petroleum shortage constitutes one of the biggest indictments of military rule. The shortage was not simply a reflection of poor leadership. It was something worse than that. It demonstrated an attitude, pervasive among Nigerian leaders, that their personal and group interests superseded the national interest. The fuel shortage partly resulted from a deliberate practice in which top government officials corruptly amassed wealth through kickbacks from oil imports. Senior military and government officials owned petroleum stations and thus profited immensely from artificially induced fuel shortages. Thus, one of the tragedies of contemporary Nigeria was that its government deliberately aggravated the misery of its citizens to facilitate the criminal enrichment of its top officials.

General Sani Abacha, who came to power in the wake of the political crisis generated by the annulment, ruled Nigeria with an iron hand and planned to succeed himself through a bogus election in August 1998. However, he died of an apparent heart attack in June 1998. Moshood Abiola, the apparent winner of the 1993 election, was arrested in June 1994 and accused of treason for declaring himself the president of Nigeria. He was held in detention until July 1998 when he, too, died of a heart attack. The two deaths gave Abacha's successor, General Abdulsalam Abubakar, an opportunity to design a more credible political transition program. He jettisoned some of the more obnoxious aspects of the Abacha transition program. He dissolved the political parties set up by Abacha. A new electoral body under a respected judge, Justice E. Akpata, was established to conduct fresh elections for the presidency and state and national assemblies.

As tragic as the annulment and the resultant political crises were, the response of many Nigerians to the annulment marks a major watershed in the nation's struggle against autocracy, political chicanery, and massive repression. For the first time in the nation's history, Nigerians from all walks of life and from every part of the country raised a collective voice against military dictatorship and the military's usurpation of political power. The annulment not only galvanized opposition to military rule; it also strengthened the role of civil society in the Nigerian political process. Several new organizations committed to advancing democratic space and to working against autocratic rule emerged in its wake. Similarly, the annulment gave new relevance and a new sense of urgency to the work of older pro-democracy organizations. It also brought a new militancy to labor unions in Nigeria. As Julius Ihonvbere has argued, the annulment convinced many Nigerian intellectual elites to descend from the rarified air of the ivory tower to join the masses of the Nigerian people in the struggle against autocratic governance.[4]

This chapter has a threefold objective. First, it examines how military rule created political and economic crises in Nigeria. It uses the annulment of the 1993 presidential election and the crises triggered by the annulment to show how the military deliberately instigated sociopolitical crises in the country. It is argued that such crises were used from 1993 through 1999 as an excuse for prolonging military rule. Second, the chapter analyzes Nigerians' responses to the annulment. The tactics and strategies adopted by pro-democracy forces to combat military rule in Nigeria are the primary focus of the analysis in this section of the chapter. Third, the chapter highlights important lessons that can be learned from the Nigerian experience in struggling against military autocracy.

DEMOCRACY UNDER MILITARY TUTELAGE?

Despite its early start in the current wave of democratization in Africa, it took Nigeria much longer to get to civilian rule than most other African countries. The process of transferring power to elected politicians which was to have culminated with the June 1993 presidential election began shortly after General Muhammadu Buhari was overthrown in a palace coup in August 1985. Buhari had come to power a year and a half earlier by overthrowing the government of President Shehu Shagari. While the Buhari regime did not articulate any particular program of political transition, it was determined to stamp out "corruption" and "indiscipline." General Ibrahim Babangida, who succeeded Buhari as head of state, promised to relinquish power to democratically elected politicians as swiftly as possible.[5] To this end, his government set up an elaborate program of political transition that entailed the writing of a new constitution, the creation of new political parties, and the establishment of a new national assembly. As part of the transition program, the country's federal structure was further decentralized with the creation of new states and new local governments. A new economic system under which the Nigerian state would play a less decisive role was also supposed to be put in place as part of the transition program.

Above all, the Babangida regime hoped that the linchpin of the succeeding civilian government would be a set of "new breed" politicians. These were expected to be less corrupt than the politicians whom the military had twice removed from office. In addition to the expectation that they would be less venal than the "old breed" politicians, the new breed politicians were also expected to be more "disciplined." The transition was expected to be anchored on new politicians who had not been tainted by the corruption or other moral deficiencies that were blamed for the fall of the two previous civilian governments in 1966 and 1983 respectively.

As the Babangida regime saw it, the military had a duty to fundamentally transform the nature of politics in Nigeria. It had hoped that a new set of politicians practicing politics on a wholesome moral basis would emerge through direct military tutelage. Using decrees, imprisonment, outright disqualification, and other heavy-handed strategies, the Babangida government tried to ensure that "bad" politicians were kept out of the political process. In the military's view, such "bad" Nigerians had constituted an obstacle to the country's progress. Therefore, they had to be prohibited from participating in politics during the transition from military rule. Their exclusion was seen both as a punishment for their nefarious past and as a mechanism for creating political opportunities for the new set of politicians. In addition, the Babangida regime was convinced that the chaotic nature of party politics would be minimized through the direct sponsorship of political parties by the military government itself. To this end, the number of political parties was limited to two. An additional strategy designed to limit political party competitiveness was the decision by the military government to dictate the ideologies and political manifestos of the two parties.

In theory, the military was supposed to be a neutral arbiter in the transition process. In reality, its heavy-handed involvement in the process betrayed its real material interests. As part of the ideological justification for staging coups, the Nigerian military had consistently claimed that it was forced to intervene in politics to throw out corrupt and inept civilian politicians whose corrupt and immoral practices threatened the nation. Accordingly, once the military had corrected the ills of civilian governments, it was obliged to relinquish power and return to the barracks. From this perspective, military rule was designed as a short but necessary interregnum in which the political process could be normalized. As such, military officers could not be permanent governors of the country. They could remain in power only long enough to right all the wrongs created by the ousted civilian rulers. However, given the possibility that the new set of civilian politicians could also engage in nefarious activities, the military had to stand guard permanently to ensure that any set of "bad" politicians was promptly shown the door. Thus, ironically, the supposed higher calling of the military that makes it a guardian of democracy creates a permanent role for the armed forces in the political process. Interestingly, however, the Babangida transition program was supposed to break this vicious cycle. Babangida himself once boasted that his government would be the last military regime in Nigeria.

It soon became apparent that the Babangida regime was not really interested in relinquishing power. Political perquisites that included vast opportunities for private enrichment soon convinced many in the top echelons of the military of the foolhardiness of relinquishing power. Thus, the military began to take various measures designed to sabotage its own transition program. These measures included several postponements of the date for the final retreat of the military from politics, the cancellation of elections, and the creation of additional states and local governments on the eve of elections. Primarily, the objective of these measures was to delay the disengagement program as long as possible. Ironically, while these measures ensured the continuation of General Babangida in office, they contributed to serious doubts about the military's sincerity in its promise to relinquish power. Moreover, they posed serious threats to both the military itself and the Nigerian nation at large.

MILITARY RULE AND SOCIO-POLITICAL CRISES IN NIGERIA

Numerous African countries have experienced devastating crises of one sort or the other in the past decade. Among the most horrendous of these were the civil wars in Somalia, Rwanda, Angola, Liberia, Mozambique, and Sierra Leone. Cumulatively, these wars resulted in the death of millions of Africans. Huge economic and social costs were also imposed by the wars. Additionally, most African countries have experienced appalling economic conditions within the decade. High unemployment, hyperinflation, and huge external debts have become the hallmarks of African economies. In addition, roads, schools, telecommunications, and hospitals have virtually collapsed in many African countries. Hunger, poverty, and high crime rates are some of the more visible symptoms of the contemporary crisis of African states.

Nigeria is no exception to the economic and political crisis confronting the African continent. However, in the Nigerian case, it is clear that neither the economic nor the political crisis arose from a lack of natural resources or a dearth of well-trained personnel. Rather, the economic and political difficulties sprang largely from decades of corruption and maladministration. Kleptocratic military regimes looted the national treasury and in the process caused economic and social havoc for the country. It became increasingly apparent that the military's control of political power posed a threat not only to the armed forces but also to the very survival of the country as a viable single political entity. The naked quest for power among military officers which military rule tends to engender has decimated the ranks of the military. Numerous coups, coup attempts, and even "rumors" of coups led to numerous killings and executions of unsuccessful and alleged coup plotters. In addition, coups destroyed the hierarchical chain of command in the Nigerian armed forces. Junior officers who succeeded in staging coups automatically promoted themselves over their erstwhile superior officers. This practice not only damaged the chain of command;

it also resulted in deep resentment with its attendant negative consequences for discipline.

Military rule was also detrimental to the corporate existence of the military because it created two sets of military personnel: officers with and officers without political appointments. Those officers who held political appointments used their political positions as a means to enrich themselves. On the other hand, officers without political appointments continued to perform purely military duties. Without access to state power, they did not get much opportunity to enrich themselves. This, too, bred deep resentment with negative consequences for military discipline. The resentment felt by officers without political positions was deepened by the tendency of officers who corruptly enriched themselves to openly flaunt their ill-gotten riches.

Military rule created wide polarization and factionalization in the Nigerian armed forces. Senior officers dreaded junior officers for fear that the latter would one day carry out their long-expected bloody coup. On their part, junior officers lived in constant fear of their senior officers. They were apprehensive that they could become victims of witch-hunts designed to wipe out potential coup plotters. Several years ago, General Ibrahim Babangida, then the head of state, raised an alarm over this state of affairs in the armed forces. He reminded his fellow officers that the Nigerian military once had "good old days" when officers "really cared for their men."[6] As he put it: "It was the days of dedicated and committed senior officers who saw their primary [duty] . . . as one of producing honorable, disciplined, healthy and loyal officers and men." General Babangida lamented that the "good old days" had disappeared from military barracks. He noted that instead of common interests between senior and junior officers, a wide "communication gap" had developed between the two sets of officers. Continuing, Babangida pointed out:

> [there] seems to be a lack of commitment on the part of some of our officers and NCOs to the military profession. . . . Many of us as senior officers hardly relate to our juniors. Often the gap between senior and junior officers has widened, thus making dangerously manifest generational cleavages. I expect that the military involvement in politics has had a hand in this. Also I think that the threat of witch-hunting under the guise of plotting to overthrow government is responsible for this.[7]

Military officers have not been able to effectively combine governance and military preparedness. Governance has come at the expense of training and military readiness. High-ranking officers' failure to look after their men forced some soldiers to take up armed robbery on the side. Landlords hired other soldiers on a private basis to collect rents from recalcitrant tenants. Still other soldiers set up illegal tollbooths on highways to extort money and valuable goods from motorists. Illegal and sordid activities such as these further discredited the military in the eyes of many Nigerians. Consequently, many soldiers became demoralized and lost confidence in the military profession. President Babangida and other military officers openly admitted that military rule had a debilitating impact on professionalism and morale. For instance, in an address to senior military officers, he noted that

> The morale of our men is sometimes at a discount. Welfarism is in the doldrums. Those facilities that will enable the men to function and which include medical care, accommodation, clothing, feeding and mobility are in acute short supply. We all must stand to blame for not ordering our priorities to assure that the man is well looked after and sufficiently motivated to utilize the resource available to him to achieve our final objective.[8]

Military rule fundamentally transformed the sociopolitical dynamics of Nigeria. Among other things, the incursion of the military into the political process in January 1966 led to the increasing politicization of the military and the militarization of politics. It has also changed the nature of civil-military relations in Nigeria. Military intervention has abrogated the doctrine of civilian supremacy. In place of the doctrine that civilian political leaders have supremacy over the military and over security policy, military rule in Nigeria helped to entrench a strong belief among military officers that they were supreme. After all, virtually every major political decision in Nigeria over the past thirty years was made by the military or those closely associated with the institution. Thus, the military took it upon itself to determine the form, nature, and contents of political participation. It arrogated to itself not only the power to decide who could rule Nigeria, but also the terms and circumstances of such governance. Military rule not only facilitated military supremacy over state and society in Nigeria; it also allowed the military to appropriate an ever-widening array of roles and responsibilities for itself–often with disastrous consequences. General Ibrahim Babangida listed a wide range of roles and responsibilities that the military assumed in the last two decades. According to Babangida,

> We [military officers] are the government of the day and, as such, are responsible for the normal day-to-day running of the affairs of the nation. We are the defenders of our territorial integrity. We are the planners and implementers of the political program of transition from military to civil rule. We are the reformers of the institutions and organizations of power in the polity as evidenced by the exercise of creating new states and local governments. We are the reformers of the existing battered economy through the Structural Adjustment Program. We are the re-directors of the political process and the architect of the institutions of civil political power. We are the planners and implementers of the process of social reorientation of the civil values in the polity as illustrated in the activities of MAMSER [Mass Movement for Social and Economic Recovery] and DFRRI [Directorate for Food Roads and Rural Infrastructure] . . . These responsibilities define a collective system; they present an institution that organizes every facet of the societal life of the Nigerian nation. They leave no room for a contesting authority or power group; they reduce all non-military leadership groups to pressure groups whose efficacy depends upon influencing but not dictating the course of decisions by the military.[9]

The military's control of state power facilitated its ability to devise new roles for itself. The tragedy for Nigeria was that the more roles the military appropriated for itself, the greater the degree of its ruination of state and society. Thus, the more roles the military appropriated, the less successful its overall management of Nigeria became. Its spirited attempt to carve out new responsibilities for itself was particularly significant in the Babangida and Abacha years (1985–98) when the military embarked upon a wholesale program of frontal transformation of both the economy and the political system.

One of the most pernicious legacies of military rule is the culture of violence that it has created in the country. Autocratic governance as personified by military rule placed premium on force and violence. Dialogue, bargaining, compromise—all essential elements of an effective governing style—were de-emphasized by military officers. Instead, Nigerians were asked to submit to military whims and caprices. Even speech patterns in Nigeria seemed to have been militarized. In the absence of dialogue and compromise, interethnic and intraethnic conflicts were exacerbated in many parts of the country. The military officers did not seem to have any answer to intraethnic and interethnic conflicts. In fact, the perception that the military took sides in these conflicts made their resolution more problematic. In general, military rule increased the level of regional, ethnic, and religious polarization in the country.

Nigeria cannot have a stable and democratic political system without solving the problems that frequent military interventions in the political system engender. Even the 1994 Constitutional Conference set up by the military government identified the military as the basic obstacle to democracy in Nigeria. The conference's Committee on Power-Sharing noted that the military "had aborted all attempts at developing a democratic culture in the country. Their encouragement of sectional interests rather than national interest has divided the country."

Several decades of military rule have demonstrated that the military has no viable solution to any of the national ills afflicting Nigeria. In fact, the military has shown quite conclusively that it is, itself, one of Nigeria's biggest problems. As Adebayo Olukoshi and Osita Agbu have argued, "the military have become the single most important obstacle to the prospect for the realization of a democratic path to national development and to the resolution of the crisis of Nigerian federalism."[10] Not only did military rule constitute a major obstacle to democratization but it also threatened the very existence of Nigeria as a viable, single political entity. It should be remembered that one of the goals of Major Gideon Orkar's attempted coup in April 1990 was the dismemberment of the constituent units of the Nigerian federation.[11] Similarly, the foundations of Nigeria's national unity were rocked by the crisis manufactured by the deliberate annulment of the June 1993 presidential election. As Olukoshi and Agbu have noted, "Nigeria appears to be less united politically than ever before and the specter of disintegration continues to haunt the country with dire consequences for its developmental prospects."[12] Attahiru Jega has argued that one of the consequences of military rule in Nigeria has been the militarization of the country.[13] Jega notes that the militarization of state and society that resulted from decades of military governance has complicated the struggle against autocratic rule.

Military rule also created a criminalized economy in Nigeria. Virtually all segments of the national economy have been rendered comatose by corruption, shady deals, and gross fraudulent practices. Fraud and corruption have escalated as a direct result of state policy, lack of accountability, and unwillingness to enforce laws against criminal and unsavory activities. Military rule legitimized the belief that the reason for acquiring political power is to use it as an instrument for the private plunder of public resources.[14] Soldiers lobbied for political appointments not for the sake of selfless public service but as avenues to private enrichment. The ceaseless use of state power for private capital accumulation by military officers and their civilian supporters generated deep political apathy and a cynical attitude to public affairs among the vast majority of Nigerians.

NIGERIA AND MILITARY DISENGAGEMENT FROM POLITICS

While the last several years represent the boldest attempt by the military to directly and totally dominate Nigeria, at the same time, it has been in precisely those years that the most comprehensive challenge to military rule in Nigeria has been mounted by Nigeria's civil society. President Babangida's program of transition to civilian rule marked the second time in seven years that Nigeria was undergoing such a transition. The first transition was ended in 1979 when the then head of state, General Olusegun Obasanjo, relinquished power to the popularly elected candidate of the National Party of Nigeria (NPN), Shehu Shagari. However, the resultant civilian government did not last long. It was overthrown by the military four years later, in December 1983.[15]

Why did the Babangida regime decide to relinquish power to elected civilians? How can this decision be situated within the theoretical literature on military disengagement from politics? Various theories have been advanced on military relinquishment of political power in the Third World.[16] Of these, the one that has the greatest relevance to the Nigerian experience contends that the military relinquishes power after it accomplishes the political objectives which precipitate its intervention in politics in the first place. According to this theory, the military comes to power not with the intention of holding on to power permanently, but with a limited political agenda—usually to correct anomalies created by the ousted civilian politicians. As soon as the military feels that the anomalies have been corrected, it relinquishes power to civilian politicians. In this context, the primary impetus for military withdrawal comes from the military itself. Similarly, the initiative for military disengagement and the modalities and mechanics of withdrawal are firmly in the hands of military officers. In other words, the military leaves politics of its own volition and on its own terms.

Military officers who are carrying out a transition program on the basis of this theory take it for granted that civilian politicians can make only a minimal contribution to the disengagement program since it is military officers themselves who exercise all political power over the transition. Accordingly, civilian politicians have to assume that the military will leave when it says it will leave. They have to trust in the sincerity of the implementers of the transition program. They must accept all the conditions that the military may impose on their participation in the program. This type of transition is conducted under very rigid conditions set by the military rulers. They control the timetable, the political agenda, and the modalities of the transition exercise, including the power to decide who can contest elections under the transition program.

The 1979 and 1993 programs of military disengagement from politics seem to have been shaped by the above theory and assumptions. Both programs were structured on the belief that the Nigerian military is often compelled to intervene in politics to correct the ills of civilian rule. Once those ills have been properly corrected, the military abandons politics, retreats to the barracks, and leaves the chastised civilian politicians once again to govern the country. Nigerian military leaders tend to believe that while the military may often be compelled to intervene in politics, it has no desire to hold on to power indefinitely. Once it has accomplished the goal of "sanitizing" the political process, it promptly returns to its primary role as the defender of the territorial integrity of the country. To buttress this claim, General Babangida tried to reassure Nigerians in 1986 that "this Administration will not stay a day longer than is absolutely necessary."[17] Each of the military regimes that preceded the Babangida regime had expressed similar sentiments. The two military rulers after Babangida (Abacha and Abubakar) also restated the same promise.

The Babangida transition program was premised on the assumption that the military knew what was wrong with Nigeria, understood the crisis of Nigerian democracy, and had the remedy needed to cure Nigeria of all that ails its politics and its economics. The regime's analysis of the political ills of Nigeria was anchored on the belief that unscrupulous Nigerian politicians, through waste, corruption, and mismanagement, constitute obstacles to the nation's progress. Accordingly, the solution to the crisis precipitated by "bad" politicians was to create a new political system that would prevent such "bad" politicians from ever again acquiring state power. In place of the "bad" politicians, a new set of politicians who were morally wholesome, ethically outstanding, and politically astute would emerge to inherit power from the departing corrective military government. To ensure that Nigeria was no longer threatened by the activities of unscrupulous politicians, President Babangida announced that he would relinquish power only to a new breed of visionary Nigerian politicians with a high sense of moral probity.

Interestingly, the Babangida regime arrogated to itself the power to decide who those Nigerians were. General Babangida believed that it was incumbent on his government to take concrete measures to facilitate the rapid emergence of the new breed of politicians. The first action undertaken to this end was to ban "old breed" politicians from participating in the transition program. The government asserted that such politicians had forfeited their right to rule Nigeria through their earlier involvement in corruption or other unsavory practices. Their exclusion from politics was therefore designed both as a punishment and as a precautionary measure to prevent them from infecting the "new breed" politicians with their moral virus.[18] A second measure taken to facilitate wholesome political behavior entailed the direct government funding of political campaigns and political parties. This was designed to reduce the influence of rich Nigerians on the political process. The government believed that wealthy Nigerians use their money to corrupt politics and the political process. It also believed that private funding of political campaigns allowed rich Nigerians to dominate the political process. It asserted that state funding of political parties and election campaigns would allow more Nigerians to participate in political affairs. It also argued that state funding of the two political parties would open their membership to every Nigerian and thus put an end to the practice whereby wealthy Nigerians who established political parties viewed such parties as their personal property.

Other tasks were also carried out in the ostensible attempt to create the "new" Nigerian political system. For instance, agencies such as the Mass Mobilization for Social and Economic Recovery (MAMSER) and the National Institute for Democratic Studies were set up to inculcate democratic attitudes among Nigerians. Secondly, the government undertook to closely monitor and supervise all elections to ensure transparency in voting behavior. Another strategy aimed at making elections transparent and free of rigging was the adoption of the open ballot system. As originally designed, under the open voting system, voters queued up openly behind the pictures or symbols of the candidates of their choice. The government's intention to keep a close watch on electoral behavior was articulated by General Babangida's warning to politicians that the military would "watch every step, monitor every move and follow every action to ensure that everything is done according to the rules of the game."[19]

All the measures (many of them clearly antidemocratic) adopted by the Babangida government as part of the transition program were rationalized on the grounds that by the end of the transition program, the regime would have created both a new set of morally untainted visionary politicians and a decidedly new Nigerian society. But it soon became apparent to many Nigerians that the transition would never end. First, the date for final military withdrawal kept changing. It was first changed from 1990 to 1992. The 1992 date was later changed to January 1993. January 1993 was subsequently altered to read August 1993. Each postponement was rationalized on two grounds: that the transition program was a learning experience and that the potential civilian inheritors of power had not yet shown themselves sufficiently worthy of receiving the mantle of leadership.

Second, the Babangida regime frequently introduced major changes in the transition program. It refused legal recognition to political parties created by civilian politicians. Instead, it created two political parties by administrative fiat. It took it upon itself to write the constitutions and the political manifestos of the two parties. Twice, it annulled primary elections that were designed to select the two presidential candidates. It then disqualified all the twenty-three candidates who had contested the first presidential primary election. These and many other changes either undermined the transition or introduced serious obstacles to it. Accordingly, President Babangida was accused of deliberately undermining the transition program to perpetuate himself in power. This was popularly termed the hidden agenda. Babangida's seemingly artful political juggling was likened to the mesmerizing dribbling of Argentina's super-star soccer player, Diego Maradona. Babangida was thus dubbed Nigeria's Maradona.

The military government's actions belied its claims that it was using the transition to civil rule to institutionalize democratic governance for Nigeria. Several of its political actions betrayed its true intentions. In place of freedom of expression, freedom of assembly, and freedom of association, the regime muzzled the press, clamped down on labor unions and pro-democracy forces, and prevented people from organizing their own political parties or even discussing alternatives to the regime's political and economic programs. Mass organizations such as the Academic Staff Union of the Universities (ASUU), the Nigerian Labor Congress (NLC), and the Campaign for Democracy were proscribed or their leaders were arrested and detained without trial. Prominent human rights advocates or crusaders for democracy such as Balarabe Musa, Femi Falana, Gani Fawehinmi, and Beko Ransome-Kuti were frequently harassed or put in detention. The regime refused to brook any political opposition. It was particularly intolerant of groups or organizations espousing ideas that were deemed inimical to the military regime's economic and political agenda. Only groups and individuals singing the regime's praises were allowed a free hand to publicly articulate their viewpoints. All this set the stage for the annulment of the June 1993 presidential election.

ANNULMENT OF THE JUNE 1993 PRESIDENTIAL ELECTION

Abiola and Tofa contested the June 1993 presidential election as flag-bearers of the Social Democratic Party (SDP) and the National Republican Convention (NRC) respectively. Two days before the election, a shadowy but pro-military organization called the Association for Better Nigeria (ABN), went to court seeking the postponement of the election. The association charged that several irregularities had occurred during the primary elections in which Abiola and Tofa had emerged as presidential contenders. It accused some state governors of corruptly influencing the outcome of the primary elections. The association asked the high court in Lagos to compel the National Electoral Commission (NEC) not to hold the presidential election as scheduled.

The court action was part of the ABN's calculated design, which Abimbola Davis, an executive of the ABN, called "organized confusion" to disrupt the transition program. Officials of the ABN, claiming to be speaking on behalf of "25 million members," had, even before going to court to stop the election from taking place, written petitions urging President Babangida not to relinquish power. They wanted military rule extended to at least 1997. The NEC argued, correctly, that only it had the power, under the electoral law, to decide the timetable of elections. It therefore went ahead and conducted the election. When it began to announce the results of the election, the ABN went back to court. This time, the ABN urged the court to prevail on the NEC not to announce the results. The court ruled in favor of ABN and issued an injunction against any further announcement of election results. Surprisingly, the NEC decided to accept the court's injunction, but the results that had already been announced showed Abiola with a commanding lead over Tofa.

A few days after the Abuja high court issued its injunction, the Babangida regime annulled the election and suspended the decrees under which the election was conducted. The Babangida regime tried to justify the annulment on several grounds. First, it asserted that it had annulled the election to preserve the integrity of the judiciary. Next, it charged that both candidates, Abiola and Tofa, had committed a series of electoral irregularities during both the primary election and the presidential election. Specifically, it claimed that

> There were proofs as well as documented evidence of widespread use of money during the party primaries as well as the presidential election. . . . Evidence available to the government put the total amount of money spent by the presidential candidates at over two billion, one hundred million naira. The use of money was again the main source of undermining the electoral process.[20]

Third, General Babangida charged that both candidates had "confirmed conflicts of interests which would compromise their position and responsibilities were they to become president."[21] Finally, the government claimed that while the election was itself generally thought to be free, fair, and peaceful, there was

> An array of election malpractice activities in virtually all the states of the federation before the actual voting began. There were authenticated reports of election malpractice against party agents, officials of the National Electoral Commission and also some members of the electorate. If all these were not clear violations of electoral laws, there were proofs of manipulations through offer and acceptance of money and other forms of inducement against officials of the National Electoral Commission and members of the electorate. . . . The conduct of the election, the behavior of the candidates, and post-election response continued to elicit signals which the nation can only ignore at its peril.[22]

General Babangida announced that in view of all the above reasons, his government decided that it was

> [in the] supreme interest of law and order, political stability and peace that the presidential election be annulled. . . . To continue action on the basis of the June 12, 1993, election, and to proclaim and swear in a president who encouraged a campaign of divide and rule amongst our various ethnic groups, would have been detrimental to the survival of the Third Republic.[23]

There are several reasons that raise serious doubts about the government's sincerity in its claims that the election was annulled on these grounds. In the first place, Babangida's claim that his regime had annulled the election to preserve judicial integrity is palpably false. The regime had shown no respect for the judiciary. On the contrary, on several occasions, the government had disobeyed court injunctions compelling it to release critics who had been illegally detained. It even violated many of its own laws and decrees. Contradictory rulings made by several high courts over the election controversy did not represent a serious threat to the integrity of the judiciary. They certainly did not warrant the annulment of the presidential election. The claim that money was used to corruptly influence the election may be true. It was certainly true that much money changed hands before and during the presidential primary election. The fact that the government chose to ignore clear cases of bribery and corrupt inducements during the primary election shows that it had an ulterior motive in allowing the June presidential election to be held. It is difficult to explain this otherwise, given how swiftly the government had dealt with the twenty-three presidential candidates who were accused of offering bribes or of engaging in other types of electoral malpractice in 1992. Moreover, if the government was truly intent on preserving the integrity of the judiciary, why were Abiola and Tofa not prosecuted under the battery of existing electoral laws?

Some Nigerians have tried to explain the annulment in ethno-regional terms. In their view, the election was annulled because a "northern oligarchy" that had allegedly dominated political power in Nigeria since political independence did not want Abiola, a "southerner," to assume the mantle of leadership.[24] No evidence is proffered for this thesis other than the oft-repeated claim that the "northern oligarchy" believes that it has a right to rule Nigeria. While there is certainly a "northern" faction of the Nigerian dominant class, it is simplistic to view the annulment in purely ethno-regional or sectional terms. The forces opposed to democracy in Nigeria, then and now, are national in scope rather than geo-ethnically sectional in their origin, composition, or objectives. Secondly, Abiola apparently beat Tofa in many states in the "north" including Tofa's own birthplace of Kano. Thirdly, the election did not pit a "northern" candidate against a "southern" candidate. Tofa was not viewed as a candidate representing "northern" interests. Abiola was not regarded as a "southern" candidate championing "southern" causes. Abiola had very cordial business and personal relationships with many of the leading politicians from northern Nigeria.[25] Neither candidate espoused a regional or ethnic agenda during the electioneering campaigns. In fact, the two candidates and their parties were kept on a short leash by the military regime.

The claim that the election was annulled because the military felt threatened by the prospect of an Abiola presidency seems far-fetched. Abiola was very close to many of the top military officers, including General Babangida himself. If Abiola had been in any way seen as a threat by the military, he would not have advanced as far as he did. His presidential ambition would have been scuttled just as General Shehu Yar'Adua's was dashed when the twenty-three presidential candidates were disqualified after the first presidential primary elections.

Ideologically, nothing distinguished Tofa from Abiola. The military government created the two parties under which both candidates contested the election, and both parties had a degree of political appeal in all parts of the country. For instance, while the SDP had a majority in both houses of the national assembly, the NRC won a majority of the contests for state governors. Abiola won because in the absence of programmatic differences between him and Tofa, the election boiled down to which of the two candidates was better known. Tofa was relatively unknown even in Kano where he was born. In fact, in the presidential election, Tofa lost even in his own ward in Kano. On the other hand, Abiola was well known throughout the country as a fabulously wealthy businessman, philanthropist, and sports patron. As a "chief launcher," at various fund-raising ceremonies for numerous causes ranging from community development projects to the building of churches and mosques, he had endeared himself to many communities in all parts of the country with his generous donations. Moreover, he owned a chain of national and community newspapers that kept him in the limelight. He had received hundreds of honorary chieftaincy titles from virtually every part of the country. Although Abiola was an ardent Muslim, he had wide support even among Christians.

Another thesis posited that the election was annulled because the military feared that if Abiola became president, he would probe military officers, many of whom were believed to have amassed private fortunes by corrupt means. There is no scintilla of evidence that Abiola intended to probe anybody. Moreover, Abiola's close personal and/or business relationships with several military officers, including President Babangida himself, made it highly unlikely that he would have instituted judicial probes against the Babangida regime. There is no evidence of any ideological or other differences between Abiola and the top echelons of the military. Abiola was quite comfortable with the ideological precepts of the Babangida regime. He committed himself to the regime's structural adjustment program. Thus, it seems quite unlikely that the election was annulled because of ideological or personal differences between Abiola and some top military officers.

Most probably, the election was annulled because President Babangida and many senior military officers simply did not wish to relinquish power. Babangida's determination to remain in power was buttressed by the pressures exerted on him by various groups whose material and other interests were best served by the continuation of military rule. He was urged to remain in power by certain factions/cliques, both inside and outside the military, that were opposed to the democratization program.[26] Some members of these factions/cliques wanted the continuation of military rule so that they could retain their access to state power. State power was crucial to their accumulation of private fortunes. Others, including Arthur Nzeribe of the ABN, did not want Babangida to relinquish power because they felt that the longer Babangida remained in power, the brighter their own chances of succeeding him as president. To some Nigerians, the transition program had become the most lucrative industry (with over 40 billion naira spent on it). Accordingly, the longer Babangida delayed the transition program or the more drastic the changes he made to it, the greater their opportunity to make money out of the program. Other members of the groups opposed to the transition program philosophically distrusted civilian politicians. The assemblage of various groups and factions opposed to a military withdrawal from politics played on the ego and the personal ambition of General Babangida, who began to believe the sycophantic phrases about his indispensability to Nigeria.

The clearest evidence that Babangida intended to perpetuate himself in office can be seen in the strict conditions which he stipulated for candidates wishing to contest the new presidential election slated for July 1993. According to Babangida, a candidate for that election (which was never held) must "Believe, by act of faith and practice, in the corporate existence of Nigeria; possess records of personal, corporate and business interests which do not conflict with the national interests."[27]

Adding confusion to an already confused and tense situation, President Babangida announced, after he had annulled the June 1993 election, that those candidates whom he had earlier disqualified (in 1992) were eligible to contest the new election. As he put it,

> All those previously banned from participating in the transition process, other than those with criminal records, are hereby unbanned. They can all, henceforth, participate in the election process. This is with a view to enriching the quality of candidature for the election and at the same time tap the leadership resources of our country to the fullest.[28]

President Babangida recognized the weaknesses of the civilian politicians and their inability to effectively challenge his domination of the transition program. He therefore concluded that he could get away with his decision to annul the election. He hoped that several factors would leave his decision to annul the election largely unchallenged. First, he counted on the fractiousness and the deep animosity among the politicians. He knew that the politicians wanted state power only for private aggrandizement and would do anything to acquire power. Thus, he figured that the losers would enthusiastically support the annulment. In this, he was not disappointed. All the National Republican Party (NRC) state governors met and issued a statement supporting the annulment and the proposal to hold a fresh presidential election. They threatened fire and brimstone if the June election was de-annulled. Second, some politicians who saw in the annulment an opportunity to bolster their presidential ambitions supported the annulment. Even the SDP, whose candidate had apparently won the presidential election, supported the establishment of the Interim National Government (ING). Rotimi Suberu contends that

> Babangida's elaborate political charade appears to have been constructed on the premise that the excesses of civilian politicians would always provide him with an excuse for extending, modifying, or stalling the democratization project. They never really disappointed him.[29]

Third, Babangida apparently thought that he could depend on political support from some factions of the military which did not want to see the military in general, and Babangida in particular, relinquish power. Babangida had cultivated a popular following among some senior military officers, some of whom, like Colonel Abubakar Umar, had declared publicly that they would do anything, including laying down their lives, for the president.[30] These officers were known as "Babangida Boys" and they occupied strategic positions in the armed forces.

Fourth, the president was well aware that the mass of the Nigerian population had been alienated from the political process. Politicians, including Abiola and Tofa, were not speaking to the needs of most Nigerians. Abiola and Tofa, like other candidates for public office, were highly restricted in the agendas that they had offered the electorate. Moreover, the two candidates lacked political credibility and were seen largely as tools designed by Babangida to frustrate the transition program. Given all these factors, the president thought that most Nigerians would be indifferent to the annulment. The military regime figured that without a mass base, neither Abiola nor Tofa could challenge the decision to annul the election. Even though the election appeared free and fair, the military regime knew that only about 30 percent of the eligible voters had bothered to cast their votes during the election. The military apparently took this figure as a measure of Nigerians' disenchantment with the transition program and their possible indifference to a decision to annul its results. In addition, the corrupt practices and misgovernance of the civilian state governors who had been in office for about two years before the June election had already soured many Nigerians on civilian rule.

Finally, Babangida thought that he had the weight of history behind him. He had, in the course of the transition, annulled two other elections. As Rotimi Suberu has argued,

> Although amazing in its brazenness, the cancellation of [the June] presidential election was consistent with Babangida's previous assaults on his own program. Almost from its announcement in January 1986, the transition program progressively bogged down deeper in contradictions, manipulations, cancellations and postponements.[31]

Not only had President Babangida been cheered on when he annulled previous elections, but much of the pressure to annul those elections had come from the civilian politicians themselves. Thus, those politicians who sensed that they had lost the 1992 presidential primaries urged Babangida to annul the results of the primary elections. Their insistence on the cancellation of the elections played right into the hands of the military officers who were opposed to the transition in the first place.

Contrary to the Babangida regime's belief that Nigerians would be indifferent to the annulment of the June 1993 election, the annulment convinced most people of the perfidy of military administrations. Accordingly, there were immediate condemnations of the annulment. As mentioned earlier, thousands of people took to the streets in Lagos, Benin, Ibadan, and other cities to protest the annulment. Workers staged strikes, and market-women stayed at home in attempts to compel the regime to de-annul the election. Britain, the United States, and other Western countries exerted external pressure in an attempt to force the government to rescind its decision. Domestic and external pressures forced the regime to back down on its insistence that it would hold a new presidential election. Instead, Babangida installed an Interim National Government (ING) with Ernest Shonekan, a prominent businessman, as its head. On August 26, 1993, President Babangida, who had ruled Nigeria for eight years as the most powerful leader in the nation's history, left office in rather ignominious circumstances.

General Babangida and the military underestimated how disillusioned Nigerians had become with military rule. It was obvious that Babangida had no answer to the mounting economic and political problems of Nigeria. Moreover, he had spent the last two years of his rule devising all sorts of tricks to remain in power. His preoccupation with remaining in power led him to ignore pressing political and economic problems. Government officials, and particularly military officers, became more brazen in corrupt practices and the general looting of the national economy. The President also overestimated the degree of support that he enjoyed within the military. He seemed to have discounted the fact that some factions within the military were concerned that politics had destroyed the professionalism of the armed forces. Such factions were prepared to see Babangida and the military leave politics. They were particularly annoyed that the eight-year rule of Babangida had wreaked havoc with military preparedness. In addition, a faction led by General Sani Abacha wanted Babangida to leave office to make room for Abacha to assume the mantle of leadership.

The hurried departure of Babangida on August 26 did not quell the agitation for democracy. The ING could not function properly. For one thing, it lacked legitimacy. It was seen simply as a trick to perpetuate Babangida's rule. In addition, a Lagos high court ruled that the ING was illegal since General Babangida signed the legal instrument that brought it into being after he had already relinquished power as president. All these factors facilitated the November 1993 coup that ousted the ING. General Abacha, the minister of defense in the

ING and a prime player in the Babangida regime, took over as head of state. He immediately dissolved all the democratic institutions set up under the Babangida transition program.

DEMOCRATIZATION: FLAWS IN STRATEGIES AND RESPONSES

Explaining the ease with which the military returned to power and the failure to force the military to de-annul the election requires a thorough analysis of the mistakes made in the course of the aborted transition by politicians and pro-democracy groups. The most serious error was to cede virtually all power and initiative in the transition exercise to the Babangida regime. Civilian politicians believed that criticisms of the program could lead to the derailment of the transition. They meekly accepted the presumption that Babangida was preparing to hand over power not out of any compulsion to do so but out of the goodness and largeness of his heart. It was felt that Babangida and the military had all the power and would refuse to hand over power if the politicians gave them the slightest excuse. Therefore, the best thing to do, politicians felt, was to humor the military by doing whatever the military decreed on the disengagement program. For instance, after the government refused to register the existing political associations as political parties and ordered instead that they be disbanded immediately, Chief Kola Balogun noted that, "The PFN's [People's Front of Nigeria's] immediate reaction is to remain law-abiding. The deed is done and we cannot reverse it."

While the civilian politicians meekly acceded to all the demands made of them, the pro-democracy forces were suspicious of the intentions of the Babangida regime. They believed that Babangida had a hidden agenda to succeed himself. They therefore concluded that the best thing to do was not to participate in the program but to attempt to expose its shortcomings and to show that it was merely a charade. While the analysis that the transition was a charade turned out to be prophetic, the conclusion that flowed from this analysis was politically impotent. By not participating, the pro-democracy groups maintained their innocence. On the other hand, the strategy of standing outside the door and criticizing the program strengthened the power of the regime over the transition program.

Several pro-democracy organizations were set up in the wake of the annulment. Organizations such as National Democratic Coalition (NADECO) and the Movement for National Reformation (MNR) joined forces with pro-democracy groups such as the Campaign for Democracy (an umbrella organization including several pro-democracy groups), the National Organization for Democratic Lawyers, the Civil Liberties Organization, the Committee for the Defense of Human Rights, and others which had been waging vociferous campaigns against the Babangida regime. These and other organizations urged Nigerians to protest against the annulment of the election and reject further military rule. They helped to coordinate strike actions against the military government. They wrote petitions to foreign leaders asking for the imposition of economic sanctions on Nigeria. The pressures exerted by these groups and other Nigerians helped to precipitate the hurried departure of Babangida on August 26, 1993.

As successful as the pro-democracy groups were in registering the discontent of many Nigerians over the annulment of the election, there were serious flaws that hampered their effectiveness in confronting the forces of repression and autocracy in Nigeria. Sakah Mahmud has aptly noted that the pro-democracy forces were not able to coordinate their activities. As a result of this lack of coordination, Mahmud argues that the Abacha regime was

> able to co-opt leaders of some the organizations and thus split their common goals to resist any undemocratic military regime. Other members of the pro-democracy movements had to take a wait-and-see attitude. Whatever the outcome, this is a setback for the movements. Such attitudes will breed further isolation from the Nigerian people who may become suspicious of such movements and regard their leaders as self-seeking like those in power.[32]

Not only were some of those who campaigned most vociferously against the annulment of the election appointed as members of Abacha's government, but some of them had actually called on Abacha and the military to overthrow the Interim National Government! Even Baba Gana Kingibe, Abiola's running mate as the vice-presidential candidate, accepted a position as a minister in the Abacha government. So did such June 12 stalwarts as Lateef Jakande, Ebenezer Babatope, Abubakar Rimi, and Olu Onagoruwa. As Ray Ekpu lamented,

> the return of the military on November 17 wiped away the lingering hope of an immediate return to democracy as all the democratic structures hitherto installed had been shot down. The greater surprise however, is that many distinguished politicians, pro-democracy activists who a few days earlier would accept either democracy or nothing, have now changed direction. They now find it convenient to lie down with the lion, apparently trying to prove that the lion and the lamb can co-exist in harmony or that they have the uncanny ability to run with the hare and hunt with the hound.[33]

Abiola himself did not help matters when he met with Abacha shortly after the coup that ousted the ING and reportedly agreed to nominate candidates for appointment into the Abacha cabinet. This created the impression that he supported the antidemocratic effort manifested by the Abacha coup. In effect, Abiola contributed to the success of the coup staged against his presidency. Reportedly, Abiola was under the impression that General Abacha would overthrow the ING in order to install Abiola as president of Nigeria.

The call on the military to overthrow the ING was informed by the rather naive assumption that once the military took over it would promptly de-annul the election and install Abiola as president. This assumption was based on a very sloppy analysis of the nature of the Nigerian armed forces and the political ambitions of the leading officers. Some pro-democracy forces not only helped to instigate the November 1993 military coup but gave the regime to which the coup had given birth instant legitimacy by agreeing to participate as members of the cabinet. In their eagerness to bury the ghost of Babangida's betrayal, some pro-democracy forces failed to comprehend the political ambition of General Abacha to rule Nigeria.

A second major error made by politicians and pro-democracy forces was that while they recognized that it was highly probable that Babangida would not relinquish power to civilian politicians as he had promised, they made no plans for what they would do if Babangida actually failed to relinquish power. In other words, even though it was apparent that the transition would be aborted, the pro-democracy groups failed to articulate alternative options and responses to the impending abortion of the democratization process. Instead, they spent much of their time before the annulment calling for a sovereign national conference which would discuss pressing national issues. The Babangida regime simply ignored the call for a national conference.

Third, the pro-democracy groups did not adequately mobilize people to resist military rule. The pro-democracy movement lacked financial and other resources with which to embark on nationwide mobilization programs. Accordingly, it limited most of its activities, particularly street protests, to the Lagos/Ibadan axis. This created the impression that protests against the annulment of the election were confined to one section of the country. In fact, the military used this argument to sow seeds of sectional discord among the pro-democracy forces. Sakah Mahmud has attributed the inability of the pro-democracy forces in Nigeria to mobilize sufficient numbers of people to their lack of a mass base.[34] He contends that the pro-democracy groups "operate as elite groups that only call on the masses to protest" against the undemocratic policies of the government.

A few of the tactics used by the pro-democracy forces to compel the de-annulment of the election were clearly wrong. Protesters set fire to homes and properties of people who were suspected of being supporters of military rule or who showed a lukewarm attitude to June 12. While the frustrations that precipitated such actions are clearly understandable, the resort to violence reduced the moral superiority of the pro-democracy forces. Shops belonging to innocent Nigerians, themselves victims of the political impasse, were looted. Many of the street protesters who demonstrated against the annulment seemed more motivated by the opportunity to loot property or to extort money from motorists than by the quest for democratization. In Lagos, motorists had to display green leaves as a sign of solidarity with the protesters. Some protesting groups insisted on motorists buying the green leaves from them. Some protesters were allegedly induced by money from pro-June 12 organizations to demonstrate against the military regime. Ironically, the fear generated by the hooligans who disrupted some street protests prepared the ground for the generals to return to power. The sense of anarchy and lawlessness created in some cities such as Lagos provided a justification for General Abacha to claim that he had seized power to restore law and order.

After the election was annulled, the pro-democracy forces underestimated the significance of the antidemocratic antecedents of the June 1993 election. The pro-democracy forces suddenly forgot the serious flaws in the electoral process such as the rigid conditions under which the election had been held and the fact that the electoral campaign had been devoid of serious discussions of the major issues confronting Nigeria. They also developed amnesia with regard to the truth that Abiola and Tofa were elected as party flag-bearers largely on the basis of political brokerage among self-anointed political leaders. They now discounted the pernicious influence of money on the electoral process. Ironically, many of the pro-democracy groups had vociferously condemned the antidemocratic measures of the transition program before the annulment. The sudden turn-about on the part of the pro-democracy forces, in which they transformed the election into the greatest thing that had ever happened to Nigeria, created credibility problems for the struggle against autocratic rule.[35] It also led the pro-democracy forces to the awkward position of lionizing Abiola as the symbol of democratic struggles in Nigeria! The pro-democracy groups also created the impression that Nigeria would have been democratized if the election had not been annulled, or that the only route to democracy in Nigeria was through the installation of Abiola as president.

Abiola himself also made several grievous errors. Instead of staying in Nigeria to mobilize grassroots support for the de-annulment of the election, Abiola fled abroad, supposedly to urge foreign governments to impose economic sanctions on Nigeria. His flight immediately after the annulment of the election can be attributed to the fact that Abiola had no real political power base in the Social Democratic Party. He created a separate political campaign organization, outside of the structures of the SDP, during the election. His seemingly ambivalent attitude to the annulment of the election made it more difficult to rally support behind him. For instance, when asked about his reaction to the annulment he said, "Whoever Allah has chosen to be president, nobody can stop him. If he has chosen me, nobody can stop me. If Allah has not chosen me, I cannot do otherwise. I leave everything to Allah."[36]

Second, even though it was evident that Abiola had decisively won the election, it took him about a year before he decided to declare himself president. Even then, he went into hiding for ten days after making the declaration. These and other factors led some Nigerians to question Abiola's suitability as the symbol of the democratic struggles in Nigeria. As the weekly magazine, *The Week*, asked, in a scathing critique,

> Was Abiola the kind of rallying point Nigeria needed to wage the democratic struggle in the context of what is now famously referred to as June 12? The garb doesn't fit. A wheeler-dealer, Abiola has never made even a pretension to revolutionary fervor. Nor has he particularly cared for the ideals of justice and fair play. During the duplicitous

transition program of former President Ibrahim Babangida, it was Abiola who played the ambassador for his friend, traveling from one end of Nigeria to the other, rationalizing the cancellation of the presidential primaries of September 1992 and the ban on the 23 aspirants then. It was on the political grave of these aspirants that Abiola contested and ostensibly won the June 12 election that was annulled.

The magazine also noted that

While Nigerians were fighting and dying in the streets, Abiola was safely abroad seemingly internationalizing the struggle. Upon his return after Babangida's exit, his most notable contribution to the fight for democracy was to call on another of his friends in the military, General Sani Abacha, to take over the government. When Abacha eventually did, sacking all the democratic structures in place, Abiola seemed to have seen no incongruity in what was happening to the democratic dream. . . . not until more than six months later when he saw Mandela, in all his glory, being sworn in as president of a free South Africa did he remember his own mandate.[37]

CRISES IN NIGERIA: WHAT MUST BE DONE?

Several suggestions have been put forward as solutions to the political problems in Nigeria An umbrella political opposition group, the United Democratic Front of Nigeria (UDFN) took a stand before Abiola's death in July 1998, insisting that the mandate of the June 12, 1993, presidential election must be respected. The group contended that the key to the resolution of the political impasse lay the recognition of Abiola's victory, the release of all political prisoners, and the formation of a government of national unity. UDFN noted that the primary task of Government of National Unity (GUNT) was to conduct a sovereign national conference (SNC) under which a new political arrangement for Nigeria would emerge. UDFN also called on the international community to impose an oil embargo and a full economic, cultural, and sporting boycott on Nigeria until democracy was fully restored.

UDFN's position on the Nigerian crisis shares a number of similarities with suggestions made by Human Rights Watch and other international pro-democracy advocacy groups. Human Rights Watch urged the Abacha regime to release outright or at least grant bail to "all individuals who are arbitrarily detained or imprisoned (including but not limited to Chief M.K.O. Abiola, those convicted of involvement in an alleged coup of March 1995, and those Ogonis held in connection with the same facts as those for which Ken Saro-Wiwa and his co-accused were executed)." It also called on the regime to "create and promote a climate for free political participation by replacing the existing National Electoral Commission with a genuinely independent electoral commission and by developing an open and fair process for the registration of political parties and the screening of candidates. Human Rights Watch appealed to the Abacha government to abrogate all military decrees and laws that occasioned the violation of constitutionally guaranteed human rights, including indefinite detention without charge, violating the court's right of judicial review, or making it illegal to criticize the transition program.

On its part, the Abacha regime contended that the June 12 election had been superseded by political events. It argued that the Babangida government that had annulled the 1993 presidential election was no longer in power. It also claimed that even Abiola himself had forfeited his mandate by supporting the overthrow of the Shonekan government. The regime pointed out that it had instituted a new transition program and that it was pointless to insist on restoring Abiola's mandate.

To drive home the point that Abiola's mandate had been overtaken by events, supporters of the Abacha regime urged Abacha to stand in an election to succeed himself. As one of his ardent supporters, Samuel Ogbemudia, noted, "the nation has made wonderful progress under General Abacha. I support the move to have him transformed [into] civilian head of state next year. He is, no doubt, the only answer to Nigeria's [problems of] progress and development."[38] Unfortunately, some politicians did not learn any lesson from the 1993 experience. Arthur Nzeribe of the infamous ABN was back in full force urging General Abacha not to relinquish power to civilian politicians. He claimed that socioeconomic conditions were not propitious for the military to relinquish power. He claimed that

> The optimistic days of a peaceful hand-over seem long ago. The forces of disintegration are prevailing in all spheres: political, economic, social and military. The transition dream looks no more than a staging post on the road into an abyss, if we continue the unbridled rush. Indeed, there is a feeling in many quarters that the Fourth Republic is still-born.[39]

Further, he urged that a political role be created for the armed forces. He claimed that his reading of history had convinced him that the only realistic strategy in a country in which the military has exercised political power is to offer a formal political role to the members of the armed forces. As he said,

> There is nowhere in the history of any country where the military have ruled for many years and then decide to turn their back against politics when they return to the barracks. Examples abound. Look at Ghana, Togo, Benin, Burkina Faso, Sudan, Libya. What happened after every military rule? Haven't they shown interest in politics? Why will Nigeria be different after the military have been politicized at all levels? Is the Nigerian army not a political party?[40]

Nzeribe was joined by several shadowy organizations that claimed they were interested in saving Nigeria from "anarchy, chaos and doom." Such groups claimed the Abacha regime should not be hurried out of office otherwise economic doom and political calamity would befall Nigeria. As Mohammed Akwashiki, an official of one of these organizations, argued,

If we allow ourselves to be stampeded, we may end up with a pseudo-democracy. It is not the duration of a program that is fundamental change. The contents of a program, above all, the peculiar nature of the society it seeks to change [are] what is paramount and important. . . . The undue haste and indisciplined approach to sensitive and fundamental national issues that is characteristic of our political enterprise has been the bane of our political development."[41]

Several shadowy organizations such as Youths Earnestly Ask for Abacha (YEAA) were hastily formed to put pressure on Abacha to run for the presidency. While such organizations were formed to give the appearance that there was popular support behind Abacha's self-succession bid, it was clear that the Abacha regime itself was the brains behind the organizations. They received direct funding from the regime, and persons closely associated with General Abacha directly controlled their activities.

The Abacha transition program lacked credibility. Ardent supporters of Abacha who were profiting enormously from his regime made it clear that the entire purpose of the transition program was for Abacha to succeed himself. Other Nigerians who wanted to contest the presidential election were dissuaded or compelled to shelve their plans. In the end, all five political parties unanimously adopted Abacha as a "consensus" candidate! In other words, Nigeria attained the distinction of having only one candidate running on the platform of five political parties in the same election. Other actions of the Abacha regime that created credibility problems for the transaction included the wholesale disqualification of "enemies" of the government from political participation, the refusal by the electoral commission to register "unfriendly" political parties, and the massive repression carried out against leading opposition figures who were either hounded into jail or forced into exile. Thus, the Abacha transition program, even if it had been faithfully implemented, would not have resolved Nigeria's deep political problems. It was simply a charade designed by Abacha to succeed himself as a civilian president.

After the death of Abacha in June 1998, a U.S.-based organization, the Association of Nigerian Scholars for Dialogue (ANSD), called for a two-stage transition program. It suggested that stage one of the transition should involve a transition from military rule to provisional civil rule. The provisional civil government would consist of a College of Governors drawn from the civilian governors (or those constitutionally in line to succeed them) who were sacked when General Abacha seized power in 1993. These governors would then elect from among their ranks three governors from the south and three from the north. These six governors would form a Joint Presidency for two years, rotating the chairmanship among themselves. The association suggested that the Joint Presidency preside over the affairs of the provisional civil government, including the conducting of national dialogues on state and national constitutions and the holding of local and national elections.

ABUBAKAR'S TRANSITION PROGRAM

In his first speech as head of state, General Abdulsalam Abubakar announced that he would stick to the Abacha transition program and relinquish power in October 1998. However, a few weeks later, he announced that new elections would be held in the "first quarter of 1999" and that the military would relinquish power on May 29, 1999. He disbanded the five political parties created by the Abacha regime and annulled all the elections that had been held under the Abacha transition program.

Abubakar justified the dismantling of the Abacha transition program on the ground that it had created "a defective foundation on which a solid democratic structure can neither be constructed nor sustained. Nigerians want true democracy which must be based on a sound democratic foundation to ensure fulfillment and sustenance."

General Abubakar also rejected the call for a sovereign national conference and the establishment of a government of national unity. While Abubakar insisted that the 1995 draft federal constitution written under the aegis of the Abacha regime would provide the underpinning for his own transition program, he did agree to subject the draft constitution to a national debate.

The international community welcomed Abubakar's release of political prisoners and other apparent concessions made by his regime to some opposition demands. In contrast to the ostracism of Nigeria by the international community when the intransigent Abacha was in power, Nigeria under Abubakar was no longer considered a pariah nation. Abubakar was received in audience by the presidents of the United States and France and by the prime minister of Britain. The Commonwealth of Nations rescinded its decision to suspend Nigeria's membership. Foreign investors showed a willingness to return to Nigeria. Consistent with its pledge, the Abubakar regime held presidential and legislative elections in May 1999 and turned over the reins of government to former General Obasanjo.

CONCLUSION

In his analysis of the aborted Babangida transition, Rotimi Suberu aptly observed that "The politicians' conception of democracy as electoral competition among élites for state power and resources, rather than as a contest over competing principles and policies, eventually contributed to the annihilation of democracy."[42] So long as opposition politicians and pro-democracy forces are unable to articulate concrete alternative political and economic agendas for the country, it will be difficult to dissuade the military from seeking to dominate Nigeria. As the 1993 experience has shown, a focus on removing the president from power without articulating an alternative political vision does not necessarily advance the cause of democracy. Such a strategy may actually make the attainment of democracy even more difficult by facilitating the emergence of another dictator.

Clearly, the Nigerian military has played a pivotal role in occasioning and nurturing the political and socioeconomic crisis in Nigeria. For example, during its thirty-year reign, the conditions of the Nigerian masses worsened. With the birth of the "Fourth Republic" in August 1999 and the concomitant installation of a new civilian regime, it remains to be seen whether the Obasanjo government will take steps to address Nigeria's crises of underdevelopment. Specifically, the regime must address the economic, cultural, political, and social problems facing Nigeria.

NOTES

1. Rotimi T. Suberu, "The Democratic Recession in Nigeria," *Current History* (May 1994): 213.
2. *West Africa*, 4–10 October 1993, 1746.
3. Several senior military officers, including a former head of state, General Olusegun Obasanjo, Major-General Shehu Yar'Adua, and Colonel Lawan Gwadabe, were convicted in the 1995 alleged coup plot. Similarly, several generals, including Lt. General Oladipo Diya, the deputy head of state, were convicted and sentenced to death in the alleged coup plot of 1997.
4. For an excellent analysis of the role of Nigerian intellectuals in the struggle against military rule, see Attahiru M. Jega, *Nigerian Academics under Military Rule* (Stockholm: Department of Political Science, University of Stockholm, 1994).
5. For full descriptions and rationalizations of the transition program, see Ibrahim Babangida, *Portrait of a New Nigeria: Selected Speeches of IBB* (Lagos: Precision Press, n.d.); and Ibrahim Babangida, *For Their Tomorrow We Gave Our Today: Selected Speeches of IBB*, vol. 2 (Ibadan: Safari Books, Ltd., 1991).
6. Babangida, *For Their Tomorrow*, 186.
7. Ibid.
8. Ibid., 187.
9. Ibid., 154.
10. Adebayo Olukoshi and Osita Agbu, "The Deepening Crisis of Nigerian Federalism and the Future of the Nation-State," in *Challenges to the Nation-State in Africa*, ed. Adebayo Olukoshi and Liisa Laakso (Uppsala, Sweden: Nordiska Afrikainstitutet, 1996), 96.
11. For an extensive analysis of Orkar's coup, see Julius Ihonvbere, "Structural Adjustment, the April 1990 Coup and Democratization in Nigeria," paper presented at the 33rd Annual Meeting of the African Studies Association, Baltimore, MD, November 1990.
12. Olukoshi and Agbu, "The Deepening Crisis of Nigerian Federalism," 77.
13. Attahiru Jega, "The Military and Democratization in Nigeria," revised version of a paper presented at the conference on "Dilemmas of Democracy in Nigeria," Madison, WI, University of Wisconsin-Madison, November 10–12, 1995, 2.
14. For a detailed analysis of maladministration by state military governors, see the cover story, "Farewell to Failure," *Tell*, September 2, 1996, 10–16. While many of the

state governors failed to pay the salaries of civil servants, they awarded multimillion naira contracts for dubious projects.

15. For details and analyses of the collapse of the Shagari government, see Toyin Falola and Julius Ihonvbere, *The Rise and Fall of Nigeria's Second Republic* (London: Zed Books, Ltd., 1985); and William Graf, *The Nigerian State: Political Economy, State, Class and Political System in the Post-Colonial Era* (London: James Currey, 1988).

16. For a full review of theories on military relinquishment of political power, see Talukder Maniruzzaman, *Military Withdrawal from Politics: A Comparative Analysis* (Cambridge, MA: Ballinger Press, 1987); Christopher Clapham and George Philip, eds., *The Political Dilemmas of Military Regimes* (Totowa, NJ: Barnes and Noble, 1985); and Constantine Danopoulos, ed., *The Decline of Military Regimes: The Civilian Influence* (Boulder, CO: Westview Press, 1988).

17. Babangida, *Portrait of a New Nigeria*, 33.

18. For a critique of the Babangida transition program, see Pita Ogaba Agbese and George Klay Kieh, "Military Disengagement from African Politics: The Nigerian Experience," *Afrika Spectrum* 27 (1992): 5–23.

19. Babangida, *Portrait of a New Nigeria*, 83.

20. Text of an address by President Ibrahim Babangida to the Nation, Saturday, June 26, 1993.

21. Ibid.

22. Ibid.

23. Ibid.

24. For a fuller analysis of this thesis, see Sakah Mahmud, "The Failed Transition to Civilian Rule in Nigeria: Its Implications for Democracy and Human Rights," *Africa Today* 40, no. 4 (4th Quarter 1993): 87–95.

25. While intra-elite intrigues are rampant within the Nigerian ruling class, to interpret the annulment in ethno-regional terms is to ignore many of the more fundamental political forces and factors that were arrayed against the transition to democracy in Nigeria in 1993.

26. For an excellent analysis of the activities of the pro–military rule groups, see Yinka Tella, "Against Hand-Over," *The News*, June 14, 1993, 9–13. For the relationship between the ABN and the Babangida regime, see "The Grand Strategy," *Newswatch*, December 20, 1993, 9–18; and "On June 12 We Chop," *Newswatch*, December 27, 1993, 30–35.

27. Text of President Babangida's speech to the nation, Saturday, June 26, 1993.

28. Ibid.

29. Suberu, "The Democratic Recession in Nigeria," 216.

30. Ironically, Colonel Abubakar resigned his commission from the army in protest over the annulment.

31. Suberu, "The Democratic Recession in Nigeria," 213–214.

32. Mahmud, "The Failed Transition to Civilian Rule in Nigeria," 93.

33. Ray Ekpu, "Alliance with the Lion," *Newswatch*, December 13, 1993, 9.

34. Ibid.

35. For more on this, see Mahmud, "The Failed Transition to Civilian Rule," 93.

36. *Newswatch*, July 12, 1993.

37. Godwin Agbroko, "From the Editor," *The Week*, March 18, 1996, 3.

38. Samuel Ogbemudia, quoted in *West Africa*, September 29–October 5, 1997, 1543.

39. Arthur Nzeribe, "If I were Abacha," press statement, October 1995.

40. Arthur Nzeribe, *Newswatch*, November 6, 1995, 14.

41. Mohammed Sani Akwashiki, president of a shadowy organization known as the Nigerian Council of Youth Societies, made this statement in a paid advertisement in the *Tribune*, October 25, 1995.

42. Suberu, "The Democratic Recession in Nigeria," 217.

8

The Somali Civil War

George Klay Kieh, Jr.

INTRODUCTION

Characteristically, the long struggle of the Somali people against exploitation and repression, including repression by the Soviet and American-supported authoritarian regime of Siad Barre, received no coverage in the Western press. It was not until the early 1990s, following the end of the "Cold War," that the media published the gruesome pictures of starving children, corpses on the streets, moving skeletons, and sickly children watched over by vultures waiting for them to take the last gasp of air, and the United States, the "only surviving superpower," and the United Nations, now under the unprecedented influence of the United States, responded to the Somali disaster.[1]

The dominant view in the emergent scholarly literature is that the Somali civil war is a product of clan-based primordial antagonisms and animosities.[2] Consequently, the conflict resolution efforts by the international community have focused and continue to focus primarily on "reconciling the differences" among the major clan-based warlords and their respective militias. Clearly, the use of the primordial Weltanschauung both as the analytical compass for navigating the "sea of conflict" and as a road map for conflict resolution misses the point. This is because as Peter Little points out, the fact "that current hostilities and political discourses are expressed in terms of clans and ethnicity sheds little light on the reasons for clan based violence and the continuous reshaping of identities."[3]

Against this background, I argue that the Somali civil war must be situated within the broader context of the social formation and its attendant relations of production and distribution. Accordingly, three major questions can be identified:

1. What political, economic and social forces precipitated the Somali civil war, including the use of clans as the *deus ex machina* for waging war in Somalia?
2. What has been the impact of the various conflict resolution efforts on the Somali civil war?
3. What steps need to be taken in order to help resolve the Somali civil war?

THE TAPROOTS OF THE CIVIL WAR

The Somali civil war is the product of the synergy of contingent and proximate factors. In the case of the former, the factors are the evolution of the Somali state, its incorporation into the global capitalist system, and the failure of the first experiment at state-building by the Somali compradors, who assumed the reigns of power when "flag independence" was granted. The latter factors are the repression, exploitation, economic deprivation, social malaise, and manipulation of primordial identities visited on Somalia by the dictatorial regime of General Mohammed Siad Barre.

The Contingent Factors

The contingent factors were fundamental to the shaping of the Somali social formation, especially the configuration of power. Prior to the intervention of external forces, the Somali political economy was built on a communal mode of production and a decentralized primordially based system of governance. Specifically, the means of production, particularly land, were collectively owned by the clan. At the center of the communal mode of production were agro-pastoral activities—cattle herding and farming. Each household was an autonomous unit that contained an entire economy, forming as it did an independent center of production.[4] Production was primarily for household use. The households were loosely linked—especially in times of need—by clan affiliations.[5] Politically, each of the major clans had a titular head (*ugaas*) who served as the anchor of the structure of governance.

Overall, the clans served as the bulwarks against external enemies and dangerous tendencies. There were inter-clan conflicts over such issues as water rights. On the other hand, there was inter-clan cooperation around a host of activities.

While Somali societies were developing autonomously, the Arabs intervened. The Arabs, inter alia, introduced embryonic capitalism and its attendant relations of production and distribution. For example, efforts were made to commercialize hitherto primordial relations. Central to this shift were Somali middlemen or *abbanns* who played a pivotal role in encouraging the attachment to foreign capital. Also, the Arabs introduced a system of unequal exchange under which Somali cattle herders and farmers received less for their products than they were required to pay for Arab products. In order to support the emergent political economy, the Arabs introduced a bureaucracy into the coastal areas of Somalia. Specifically, the bureaucracy sanctified and maintained the exploitative and predatory system of unequal exchange, and it established political control.

Later, the Arab's embryonic mercantile capitalism was challenged by emerging European industrial capitalism. Having consolidated their economic and cultural stranglehold on Somali societies, the European imperialists moved to establish and exert formal political control. In the late nineteenth century, the colonial powers divided the Somali Peninsula into five zones. The British established the Protectorate of Somaliland in the north and occupied the Northern Frontier District of Kenya (now Kenya's Northern Province); the French took Djibouti; the Ethiopians the Ogaden region; and the Italians the remainder along the southern coast.[6] The incipient social formations built on the exploits of Arab interventionism. The European colonialists formalized the incorporation of Somali societies into the global capitalist system and completed the process of the commodification of social relations by shifting from clan-based to class-based interests. Relatedly, the class system was refined and expanded. Under the new relations of production, the upper class consisted of the colonial agents, the middle stratum consisted of Somali compradors, and the lowest tier comprised the subaltern classes consisting primarily of pastoralists and farmers. Characteristically, the colonial state was used as a vehicle for legitimizing and maintaining the mode of production and its associated relations of production and system of unequal exchange and lopsided power arrangements.

When political independence was granted in the early 1960s, the European imperialists balkanized Somalia. France maintained control over the section that eventually became the independent Republic of Djibouti, and the Ogaden region remained under the firm control of Ethiopia. The remaining sectors of British and Italian Somaliland became the Republic of Somalia.

The postcolonial state and its political economy were faced with several major problems. At the base was the neocolonial state bequeathed by European imperialism and colonialism. Another problem was the fashioning of Somali nationalism out of commercialized, commodified, and manipulated primordial identities. Also, there was the challenge of the formulation of the appropriate modalities to address the various colonial legacies, including the economies of the two parts of the newly independent state—the former British and Italian "Somalias." Similarly, there was the perennial problem of the north-south regional divide and its attendant political, economic, and social inequities. Lastly, there was the sensitive problem of Somali irredentism in the Ogaden region under Ethiopia's control.

Amid these problems, the Somali people were hopeful that indigenous rule would fashion a new, democratic, and prosperous postcolonial order. The first major test came during the first national elections held in 1964. Eighteen political parties contested the elections. The Somali Youth League won the elections, amidst charges of fraud. Five years later, during the second national elections, sixty political parties participated. There were charges that the ruling Somali Youth League used state resources to rig the elections. Despite the two elections, the evolving postcolonial order failed to fulfill the expectations of the Somali people. Principally, no effort was made to deconstruct the neocolonial Somali state. Similarly, no efforts were made to forge Somali nationalism. Another shortcoming was the failure by the compradors to address the serious economic, political, and social problems—employment, poverty, political democratization, health care, and education—afflicting the Somali masses. Also, the government was centralized in Mogadishu, the capital city, along with the meager existing economic and social opportunities. This exacerbated the north-south regional divide. For example, the northern clans, especially the Isaaqs in the former British Somaliland, felt neglected and dominated by the southern Somalis.[7] To make matters worse, the various political parties were parochial; this was reflected in their campaign strategies. To ensure attention and gain a chance of winning, each candidate identified his campaign with sub-clan interests.[8]

With the failure of the "first democratic experiment," as evidenced by the burgeoning increase in the misery index, the Somali military hijacked the process of democratization by intervening and seizing control of state power. Terrence Lyons and Ahmed Samatar provide an excellent summation of the opportunity missed by the compradors who governed Somalia during the early post-independence era:

> Many of the generation that brought independence to Somalia were men who grew up under the shadow of British and Italian colonialism. These leaders of the independence movements construed the enterprise as a rare chance to win a personally profitable place in the new structures (particularly the state) and only secondarily as an opportunity to construct new public institutions worthy of the great challenges ahead.[9]

The Proximate Factors

The 1969 military coup d'état in Somalia brought General Mohammed Siad Barre to power. This set the stage for the germination and nurturing of the factors that subsequently triggered the civil war. Like most putschists, General Siad Barre promised the Somali people that his regime would address the crises of underdevelopment. Toward that end, he launched a "socialist agenda" that focused on deconstructing of the neocolonial state, combating illiteracy, addressing gender inequities, undertaking agricultural and livestock projects, and pursuing land reform. As Ahmed Samatar observes, "by 1972, Somalia seemed to have embarked on a quest for a progressive and socialist-oriented political economy."[10] However, Somalia lacked the resources to implement these projects successfully.[11] Accordingly, the Barre regime made appeals to the international community for help. Given the Barre regime's professed socialist ideological orientation, the United States and its allies did not respond positively to the appeals for assistance. On the other hand, the Soviet Union took advantage of the opportunity by forging an alliance with Somalia through a Treaty of Friendship in 1973. Under the agreement, the Soviet Union promised to give Somalia economic and military assistance as the reward for allowing the establishment of Soviet military facilities in Somalia. In the context of the Cold War, Soviet military facilities in a country strategically located in the Horn of Africa gave Moscow major assets in its global struggle with the United States. One major motive for Somalia's alliance with the Soviet Union was the fact that its rival, Ethiopia, was aligned with the United States. Since the period immediately after independence, Somalia has laid irredentist claims to the Ogaden region of Ethiopia; this has been a source of conflict between the two countries. Hence, the Barre regime saw its alliance with the Soviet Union as a golden opportunity to gain access to weapons and ultimately counter American support for Ethiopia.

By 1973, the Barre regime instituted a dramatic shift. It made its non-democratic nature evident by ushering in an authoritarian system. This was reflected in the creation of a bureaucratic authoritarian state based on the personality cult of Barre. In order to sustain his illegitimate grip on power, General Barre developed an extensive security apparatus ostensibly designed for the suppression of the regime's perceived and real opponents. He also manipulated civic groups through patronage. Furthermore, he fostered internecine polarization among the various clans, as in the old colonial strategy of divide and rule.[12] For example, he manufactured periodic inter-clan conflicts, especially among the Marehan, Ogadeni, and Dulbahante clans.

At the time of the shift from rhetorical socialism to autocratic state capitalism, Somalia was hit by a terrible drought. The drought devastated Somalia's agriculture, the mainstay of the economy, and forced the resettlement of thousands of peasants.[13] Although the drought ended in 1976, the Somalia economy continued to experience serious strains occasioned, inter alia, by escalating foreign debt and burgeoning oil prices.[14] Somalia's economic problems were further exacerbated by the Barre regime's determination to revive the historical claim to the Ogaden territory in neighboring Ethiopia.[15] The Barre regime diverted much-needed economic resources away from addressing pressing domestic economic and social problems to supporting the irredentist insurgency led by the Western Somali Liberation Front (WSLF) in the Ogaden region of Ethiopia. The timing of the Barre regime's support for the insurgency was designed to exploit the internal problems in Ethiopia. Eventually, the feudal-autocratic regime of Emperor Haile Selassie was overthrown by the military. After a series of internal struggles for power within the military junta, Colonel Mengistu Haile Mariam seized power and became the head of state of Ethiopia. Mariam declared himself a Marxist, and committed Ethiopia to the "socialist path of development." In order to establish his regime's socialist credentials, American military facilities, including the Kagnew Air Force Base, were closed, and all U.S. military personnel were expelled. Subsequently, the Mariam regime formed an alliance with

Moscow. The fact that the Soviet Union had client regimes in Ethiopia and Somalia, two strategic states in the Horn of Africa, jolted the United States. Washington was fearful, consistent with its "domino theory," that the rest of Africa would fall under Soviet influence.

With the commencement of the Ethiopian-Somali war in 1977, the United States decided that it was propitious to make overtures to Somalia. The reason was that the war between the two Soviet client states had put Moscow in a quandary. The Soviet Union was forced to align with one of its client regimes; eventually, it tilted its support in favor of Ethiopia. Accordingly, the United States used its trusted client states in the oil-rich Gulf states to seduce the Barre regime. The American strategy paid off when General Barre visited Saudi Arabia. During the visit, he was promised $500 million in economic assistance in exchange for the severance of relations between Somalia and the Soviet Union.[16] In addition, Somalia was given weapons by the United States and its NATO allies; these weapons were vital to the prosecution of the Barre regime's war against Ethiopia.[17] Finally, Somalia severed relations with the Soviet Union. As expected, the United States moved in swiftly to fill the void. In exchange for the establishment of American military facilities on Somali soil, the United States provided the Barre regime with "economic and military oxygen": The Barre regime received an average of about $100 million per annum in economic and military assistance from 1977 till the fall of the regime. Also, Washington defended the Barre regime's appalling human rights record in various international forums.

Interestingly, the trading of one neocolonial patron for another did not fundamentally alter the stark realities embedded in Somalia's crises of underdevelopment. American foreign aid was used primarily to bolster the Barre regime's military capacity, in order to wage the regime's war of terror against domestic opponents. By the late 1970s, Somalia was firmly in the grip of an economic and social malaise. For example, the literacy rate stood at only 24 percent.[18] The infant mortality rate was a dismal 177 per 1,000.[19] Life expectancy was forty-one years.[20] The unemployment rate stood at 30 percent.[21] Amidst the crises of underdevelopment, the Barre regime devoted about 29 percent of the national budget to defense expenditure.[22] Exasperated by this state of affairs, civil society increased its protests against the regime. For example, various antigovernment demonstrations were held, as instruments for forcing the Barre regime to democratize. Using the mass anger, a faction in Barre's military launched a coup attempt; however, the coup failed. Characteristically, the Barre regime executed the coup plotters and accelerated the pace of its "scorch the earth" campaign against civil society. Moreover, the Barre regime resorted to its old tactics of divide and rule, by arming loyal clan-based militias.

Faced with continual repression and social and economic malaise, the Somali masses took varied additional measures. Some of them organized various demonstrations. For example, there were antigovernment demonstrations in 1981, sparked off by the decision to allow U.S. forces access to Somalia's military facilities.[23] On the other hand, various regional and clan-based militias were organized. As Hussein Adams asserts, "Siyad's clan persecutions obliged the opposition to utilize their own clans as organizational bases for armed resistance."[24] For example, the Somali Salvation Democratic Front (SSDF) pioneered the formation of clan-based militias as the basis for organized resistance to the Barre dictatorship. Based in Ethiopia, the SSDF drew the great majority of its fighters from the Majerteen clan, part of the Darod clan family; interestingly, General Barre came from the same clan. Unfortunately, the SSDF atrophied due to several factors. There was internal dictatorship. Also, there was a lack of mass appeal. Another problem was that the SSDF was largely dependent upon Libya's support. Sensing the divisions and problems within the SSDF, General Barre seized the opportunity by co-opting the fighters from the SSDF in the campaign of terror against the Somali masses, especially the Hawiye (south) and Isaaq (north) clans.

THE DYNAMICS OF THE CIVIL WAR

Polarized by the unending "regime repression–civil society resistance chain," Somalia was plunged into a civil war. The Barre regime and its surrogates were on one side and several clan-based insurgency groups were on the other. The latter shared only one goal: unity in their determination to oust the dictatorial Barre regime from power. Among the clan-based insurgency groups were the Somali National Movement (Isaaq Clan), the United Somali Congress (Hawiye Clan), the Somali Patriotic Front (Ogadeni Clan), and the Somali Democratic Movement (Digil-Mirifle Clan). The leaders and members of the various militias were divided by their varied class relations. For example, Mohammed Farah Aidid, the head of the military wing of the United Somali Congress, was a member of the bureaucratic wing of the Somali local ruling class. He served as a general in the Somali armed forces and as ambassador to India, and held several other positions in the Barre regime before the split. Muhammed Ali Mahdi, the leader of the political wing of the United Somali Congress, is a wealthy businessman and entrepreneur, and therefore a member of the commercial wing of the Somali comprador class. The differences between General Barre and most of the warlords did not revolve around issues related to the fundamental transformation of Somali society; instead, they were based on personality differences and competing appetites for the largesse associated with the control of state power.

Interestingly, while the civil war was raging, General Barre again relied on his old bag of tricks, which was based on "talking peace during conflict, and making war during peace." In a superficial way, General Barre offered to liberalize the society and to create much-needed political space. The kernel of his superficial reform was the drafting of a new liberal democratic constitution including provisions upholding human and civil rights and political plurality. But, although the constitution was approved by the People's Assembly, the rubber stamp parliament, it was never submitted to a national referendum. The effort to impose a new constitutional structure on the Somali people clearly reflected the fact that the so-called liberalization process was designed to buy time for the Barre regime in its war with the various insurgency groups.

Unimpressed by General Barre's activities, the insurgency groups decided to press on with the civil war. With its rule hanging in the balance, the Barre regime called upon the United States of America, its neocolonial patron, for assistance. At a critical stage in the conflict, the U.S. Department of Defense on June 28, 1988, delivered $1.4 million in lethal aid to the Somali Armed Forces, including 1,200 M-16 rifles and 2.8 million rounds of ammunition.[25] Sensing that long-term American interests were being jeopardized by the Bush administration's support for the Barre regime, several members of the United States Congress protested. In response, the Bush administration was forced to withhold military aid.

As expected, the immediate consequences of the war were catastrophic. Hundreds of innocent Somali civilians, particularly defenseless women and children, were killed. In one case, the Barre regime murdered over 5,000 members of the Isaaq Clan. There was a serious refugee crisis. Over 500,000 Somalis became refugees in neighboring countries, and another 400,000 were internally displaced. Also, the infrastructure—roads, bridges, hospitals, power plants, and so on—was decimated. Given the prevalence of weapons, criminals were placed in an advantageous position in their quest to steal and plunder the possessions of ordinary Somalis. The incidence of violence increased.

Exhausted by the burden of prosecuting a multi-front war amid the loss of public support, the Barre regime was finally defeated by the avalanche of military pressure from the various armed groups in 1991. Initially, the various anti-Barre warring factions agreed to an interim arrangement as the centerpiece of the transition to the post-Barre era. Under this arrangement, Muhammed Ali Mahdi of the United Somali Congress was chosen as interim president. However, the transitional accord quickly collapsed as the various warlords jockeyed for control of state power. To make matters worse, there was an internal power struggle within the United Somali Congress. As Edward Ricciutti asserts, Ali Mahdi and Mohammed Farah Aidid "argued over power, and fighting broke out among their followers."[26] This development triggered off the second round of the civil war, with the various militias as the belligerents.

While the militias were raining terror and destruction on the people of Somalia, the country was struck by famine. The famine led to suffering and death. For example, according to the U.S. Centers for Disease Control, the mortality rates in the Baidoa region were the highest in the history of famine worldwide.[27] In 1992 alone, over 300,000 Somali died of hunger.

CONFLICT RESOLUTION EFFORTS

While the civil war in Somalia was raging, the international system was undergoing a major transformation: The Cold War, which had provided the arena for the conduct of global affairs, was fading; hence, Somalia was no longer of geo-strategic importance to for the United States. The incipient American policy of "cynical disengagement" stressed the importance of the Somalis dealing with their own civil war, although the United States had played a pivotal role in precipitating it. The power shift created by the end of the Cold War left the resolution of the Somali and other civil wars in Africa to indigenous initiatives and solutions. But unfortunately, the Organization of African Unity (OAU), the pan-continental organization, failed to develop a conflict resolution plan for Somalia. Instead, the OAU delegated the responsibility of helping to resolve the Somalia civil war to the sub-regional organization, the Inter-Governmental Agency on Development (IGAD). The organization was ill prepared for this enormous task, because it is a small-scale economic development–oriented organization that lacks the security apparatus required for conflict resolution. In 1991, the IGAD formulated a peace plan designed to help end the civil war. However, the plan failed because some of the warring factions were bent on winning the civil war through the force of arms. While the regional peace efforts were going on, the Somali National Movement announced the creation of a new secessionist Republic of Somaliland in the northwest portion of the country, where the Dolbahunta and Warsengeli Clans are in the vast majority. However, no other country recognized the new secessionist state.

Pressed by the African Caucus, the United Nations decided to intervene in the civil war. The UN mediated a cease-fire between the Aidid and Mahdi factions of the United Somali Congress in January 1992. But the major drawback of this was that it focused on only two of the warring factions, to the exclusion of the majority. Accordingly, the cease-fire collapsed, and of fighting between the two factions began again. In response, the United Nations Security Council passed Resolution 733 imposing an arms embargo on all of the warring factions. This was followed by an effort to mediate a second cease-fire agreement among the warring factions; this cease-fire lasted for an appreciable length of time.

Encouraged by the second cease-fire agreement, the United Nations Security Council passed Resolution 751 authorizing a peacekeeping force for Somalia. In April 1992, operating under UNOSOM I (United Nations Operations in Somalia), 50 unarmed peacekeepers, mainly from Pakistan, were sent to monitor the cease-fire and to support humanitarian relief efforts. Additionally, the United Nations committed itself to subsequently augmenting the strength of the peacekeeping force with another 500 (armed) personnel. However, the U.S. was initially opposed to the UN plan for financial reasons. This prompted some African diplomats to accuse the United States of having a double standard because the U.S. had backed the sending of 14,000 peacekeepers to Yugoslavia.[28] Eventually, the 500 armed peacekeepers were sent. After three months, it became clear to the United Nations that the task of helping to restore order to Somalia was a Herculean one. Accordingly, the UN expanded the peacekeeping force to 4,200 security personnel. But in December 1992, after witnessing looting, anarchy, and the inadequacy of security, the United Nations Security Council passed Resolution 794. Under the resolution, the Security Council authorized an increase in peacekeeping activities especially to safeguard the routes for the delivery of humanitarian relief to defenseless civilians. Subsequently, the UN authorized the United States to provide a large part of the peacekeeping force. Interestingly, the American contingent was not placed under the central control of the overall commander of the UN peacekeeping force. Instead, the American contingent operated like an independent peacekeeping force.

Operating under the codename "Operation Restore Hope," the United States sent 28,000 peacekeepers to join the UN peacekeeping force in Somalia. According to both American officialdom and the United Nations' leadership, the expanded peacekeeping force had limited objectives. These limited objectives included restoring enough order that the relief operation could be conducted without large-scale loss of relief commodities through theft and restoring food security, so that people could supply their own needs.[29] The peacekeeping force did achieve its limited objectives, as reflected in the fairly smooth delivery of humanitarian relief supplies to defenseless civilians; this won accolades from Somali civilians.

Regrettably, having completed its original mission, the United States decided to transform the UN peacekeeping operation into a *peace building* one. The ultimate goal was to reestablish American neocolonial control over Somalia. In turn, this would have given the United States control over Somalia's newly discovered oil reserves. Also, the U.S. needed to establish a permanent military presence with bases adjacent to the Middle East's vast oil reserves.[30] The Somali people strongly rejected the efforts to reimpose American suzerainty. Taking advantage of the American blunder, the Aidid faction decided to attack the peacekeeping force. One of the Aidid faction's attacks led to the death of twenty-four Pakistani peacekeepers. Against this background, the United States chose to raise the stakes. It made the capture of warlord Mohammed Farah Aidid a new major objective of the peacekeeping mission. In their efforts to capture General Aidid, the American "peacekeepers" demonstrated a callous attitude toward Somali lives. For example, on July 12, 1993, U.S. helicopter gunships attacked Mogadishu and left fifty-four Somali civilians dead.[31] Moreover, in their public pronouncements, some of the American peacekeepers showed their lack of concern for the lives of Somali civilians. As *West Africa* lamented, "US Marines stated that they wanted to go home with their confirmed kill: They wanted to kill a Somali before returning to the US."[32] When confronted with the evidence of the lack of concern for Somali lives, Colonel Fred Peck, the U.S. Marines' spokesman in Somalia, stated that "The compilation of Somali casualties has no military utility."[33] Even some members of the United States Congress strongly denounced the attitude of the American Marines. Military activities led to the capture and subsequent murder of some American soldiers. Having succeeded in its humanitarian mission but failed in its peace building, the United States withdrew its contingent from the UN peacekeeping force. Consequently, the mission was turned over to a new UN force.

The failure of the United Nations' peacemaking and peacekeeping efforts led to the revival of regional initiatives. At the center was the "Ethiopian initiative" supported by both the Inter-governmental Agency on Development and the Organization for African Unity. The initiative led to the Addis Ababa Conference in 1993, involving most of Somalia's warring factions. The conference focused on the cessation of armed hostilities, the creation of a new, stable political order, and economic reconstruction. The parties to the accord agreed to hold elections in Somalia in 1994. Based on the Addis Ababa Accord, the United Nations established UNOSOM II. The focus was on helping to establish local governments in the rural areas. Characteristically, amid strong opposition from some of the warring factions, the Addis Ababa Accord collapsed. Thus, the UN made the determination that the Somali civil war was unresolvable; hence, it ended its mission. John Barraclough provides an apt description of the UN's retreat from Somalia:

> Perhaps no other country has been so publicly abandoned to its fate as Somalia. In 1995 the United Nations intervention force, led originally by gung-ho United States troops, left in humiliation after its failure to stop the civil war. The message was clear. Somalia is a basket case, beyond understanding and beyond hope. The United Nations washed its hands and sailed away, and hasn't offered much help since.[34]

Somalia degenerated into another cycle of violence, death, and destruction, as the various warring factions were locked in intense fighting. Despite the failure of the United Nations' peacemaking and peacekeeping efforts, the search continued for peace. On October 15, 1996, 315 Somali elders under the chairmanship of Sheikh Ibrahim Sheikh Mader initiated a conflict resolution crusade at the Hargeisa Conference. The inter-clan conference brought together a cross-section of elders, religious leaders, politicians, former civil servants, intellectuals, businessmen, and others.[35] Although the initiative was encouraging, it failed to end the civil war. Later, Kenyan President Daniel arap Moi brokered a peace accord including a cease-fire, but after about two weeks, the accord collapsed. This was because some of the warlords opposed the plan on the grounds that it favored some factions at the expense of the others.

In January 1997, Ethiopia launched the "Sodere Process," with the professed goal of ending the civil war. The plan had the following elements:

1. the establishment of a transitional structure of governance;
2. the reopening of the main seaport and airport, which had been closed since 1995;
3. the consolidation of the two separate currencies in Mogadishu; and
4. the joint administration of Mogadishu.

But the plan was opposed by Hussein Aidid, because he claimed that Ethiopia was biased in favor of Ali Mahdi's warring faction, and so the plan collapsed.[36]

In December 1997, Egypt launched the "Cairo Initiative." A Peace Conference on Somalia was held in Cairo, Egypt. It was attended by a sizable number of Somalia's warring factions, including Hussein Aidid and Ali Mahdi Mohammed, the two most powerful warlords. The leaders of Somalia's warring factions agreed to a power sharing accord. The accord, the "Somali Declaration of Principles," was based on several requirements.

1. the holding of a national reconciliation conference on February 15, 1998, to elect a presidential council and a prime minister, and to adopt a transitional charter;
2. an immediate cease-fire; and
3. the disengagement of all opposing forces.[37]

Again, in the context of the "zero sum environment," some of the warlords rejected the plan. As the *Economist* correctly observes, "The Cairo Peace Plan [was] seen by other clan factions as a predominantly Hawiye Clan affair."[38] This was because Hussein Mohammed Aidid and Ali Mahdi Mohammed, leaders of the two major rival Hawiye-Clan based factions, were the dominant players in the Cairo Peace Plan.[39] This made it difficult to hold the National Reconciliation Conference at Baidoa, Central Somalia, since Aidid's faction controlled a substantial amount of territory in the area; the fear was that the delegates' security would be jeopardized. So the conference was postponed several times. In the end, the Cairo Peace Plan collapsed.

While the peacemaking efforts were being pursued, in July 1998, the Somali Salvation Democratic Front (SSDF), a Majerteen and Darod dominated warring faction, announced the secession of northeastern Somalia, and the establishment of the Republic of Puntland. This was a surprise because the SSDF had traditionally advocated a united Somalia.

After the failure of twelve peace accords, neighboring Djibouti initiated a peace process. The centerpiece of the peace initiative was the convening of a Somalia Peace Conference in Djibouti, beginning in May 2000. The conference brought together 2,000 delegates from the various clans, warring factions, civil society, and the population at large. In August 2000, the parties agreed to a peace accord, with the following principles:

1. A transitional parliament with 225 members will be established, drawn mainly from the various clans, with 25 seats allotted to women.
2. The transitional parliament will elect an interim president, who will govern Somalia until the holding of national elections;
3. The warring factions will end their hostilities and effect a cease-fire.

The initiative is supported by the United Nations and the Organization of African Unity. However, some of Somalia's most powerful warlords and the self-proclaimed independent Republics of Puntland and Somaliland are opposed to the plan. Despite the opposition, there is optimism that the Djibouti Peace Plan will end more than a decade of violence, anarchy, death, and destruction in Somalia.

RESOLVING THE SOMALI CIVIL WAR: SOME PRESCRIPTIONS

What steps need to be taken in order to peacefully end Somalia's civil war? Clearly, this is a complicated matter for which easy prescriptions cannot be provided. However, some suggestions are in order. First, the Djibouti Peace Plan should constitute the bedrock of the efforts to resolve the problems. This is because its step by step model is the best approach for tackling the complex web of issues that underpin the civil war.

Second, the international community needs to prevail on the various external players—Eritrea, Ethiopia, and Libya—that are supporting the various warring factions. This is because the intransigence of the warring factions is fueled largely by the belief that their external patrons will continue the supply of weapons.

In a third, and related step, the international community needs to bring pressure to bear on the intransigent warring factions. This could include threatening them with the prospect of being tried by a war crimes tribunal.

Fourth, an internationally supervised national referendum should be held to determine the future of Puntland and Somaliland. Ideally, it would be a good idea to keep Somalia as a single unified state. However, if the self-proclaimed secessionist Republics of Puntland and Somaliland have broad internal support, then the splitting up of Somalia would need to be considered.

Fifth, sustained and continuous efforts need to be made to foster a new culture of nationalism that transcends clans. This could be done, inter alia, by teaching new values that stress nationalism over clan-ism. Also, the formation of broad-based national organizations, including political parties, should be encouraged.

Sixth, the new Somali constitution should prohibit the formation of clan-based political parties. This would help to foster the formation of political relationships, including alliances across clan lines.

Seventh, the new legal system should be impartial. Specifically, the rule of law and the equal application of the law to all citizens should be sacrosanct. This is critical to the development of broad-based national confidence in the criminal justice system. Additionally, it would help obviate the need to resort to violence as a means of seeking redress for grievances.

Eighth, the process of economic reconstruction should be anchored on the prudent use of Somalia's resources for the benefit of all Somalis. This would include the formulation of public policies designed to address the social and economic needs of the Somali people.

CONCLUSION

The chapter has attempted to address three interrelated issues: the root causes of the civil war in Somalia; the impact of the various conflict resolution efforts; and prescriptions for helping to end the civil war. On the first issue, the findings show that both contingent and proximate factors were responsible for Somalia's civil war; in the case of the former, the major precipitant was Somalia's incorporation into the global capitalist system and the vagaries of the resultant peripheral capitalist mode of production and its relations of production and system of distribution. In the case of the latter, the failure of the first democratic experiment and the Barre regime provided the triggers for the civil war.

In terms of the various peace initiatives, the first twelve failed for an assortment of reasons, ranging from the intransigence of the warring factions to the interference of external parties. The Djibouti Peace Plan seems to have promise; but, given the history of the failure of peace initiatives, caution needs to be exercised as the peace plan is being implemented.

The following prescriptions for a peaceful end to the civil war were suggested: the need to establish a transitional architecture; the need for a greater role for the international community in pressuring the various warring factions and their external patrons; the need to create a new culture based on nationalism; the need to encourage the formation of broad-based national organizations, including political parties; and the need for economic reconstruction based on the prudent use of resources and the fair distribution of the proceeds.

NOTES

1. See Julius Ihonvbere, "Beyond Warlords and Clans: The African Crisis and the Somali Situation," *International Third World Studies and Review* 6, no. 7 (1995): 7.

2. For a sample of the literature on the use of the primordial perspective in explaining the causes of the Somali civil war, see Mark Hurband, "The Politics of Violence," *Africa Report* (September/October 1993); Rakiya Omaar, "Somalia: At War with Itself," *Current History* 91 (May 1992): 230–234; Jeffrey Clark, "Debacle in Somalia," *Foreign Affairs* (Spring 1993): 109–123; Fukui Katsuyoshi and John Markakis, eds., *Ethnicity and Conflict in the Horn of Africa* (London: James Currey, 1994).

3. Peter Little, "Conflictive Trade, Contested Identity: The Effects of Export Markets on Pastoralists of Southern Somalia," *African Studies Review* 79, no. 1 (1996): 27.

4. Cited in Ahmed I. Samatar, *Socialist Somalia: Rhetoric or Reality?* (London: Zed Press, 1988), 9.

5. Ibid.

6. Rakiya Omaar, "Somaliland: One Thorn Bush at a Time," *Current History* (May 1994): 232.

7. Ihonvbere, "Beyond Warlords and Clans," 9.

8. Terrence Lyons and Ahmed Samatar, *Somalia: State Collapse, Multinational Intervention and Strategies for Political Reconstruction* (Washington, DC: Brookings Institution, 1995), 3.

9. Ibid. 12.

10. Ibid., 3.

11. George Klay Kieh, Jr., "International Organizations and Peacekeeping in Africa," in *Peacekeeping in Africa: ECOMOG in Liberia*, ed. Karl Magyar and Earl Conteh-Morgan (London: Macmillan Press, 1998), 18.

12. Ibid., 19.

13. Ibid.

14. Ibid.
15. Ibid.
16. I.M. Lewis, *History of Modern Somalia*, cited in *World Forum, U.S. War in Somalia* (New York: World View, 1993), 5.
17. Kieh, "International Organizations and Peacekeeping in Africa," 20.
18. *Information and Resources from Countries around the World*, "Somalia," http://virtualsources.com, 2000, 1.
19. Mary Fox, *Somalia* (New York: Children's Press, 1996), 110.
20. Ibid.
21. *Information and Resources from Countries around the World*, "Somalia," 1.
22. Ibid.
23. Samuel Makinda, *Seeking Peace from Chaos* (Boulder, CO: Lynne Rienner, 1993), 221.
24. Hussein Adams, "Somalia: A Terrible Beauty Being Born?" in *Collapsed States*, ed. I. William Zartman (Boulder, CO: Lynne Rienner, 1995), 76.
25. Peter Schraeder, "The Horn of Africa: U.S. Foreign Policy in an Altered Cold War Environment," *Middle East Journal* 46 (Autumn 1992): 574.
26. Edward R. Ricciuti, *Somalia: A Crisis of Famine and War* (Brookfield, CT: The Millbrook Press, 1993), 28.
27. U.S. Centers for Disease Control, *Morbidity and Mortality Weekly Report* 41 (December 4, 1992): 913–917.
28. Ricciuti, *Somalia: A Crisis*, 35.
29. Andrew S. Natsios, "Humanitarian Relief Intervention in Somalia: The Economics of Chaos," *International Peacekeeping* 3, no.1 (1996): 69.
30. World View Forum, *The US's War in Somalia* (New York: World View Forum, 1993), 7.
31. *West Africa*, "U.S. Brute Force," July 19–25, 1993, 1238.
32. Ibid., 1238–1239.
33. Ibid.
34. John Barraclough, "Somalia-Peace and Reconciliation," *Horizons* no. 20 (1999): 1.
35. Omar Hussein Yusuf, "Somaliland's Isolation," *West Africa*, October 24–30, 1996, 459.
36. See Tamrat Bekele, "Peace and Stability for Somalia," *Addis Tribune*, 1997, 1.
37. Bassem Mroue, "Somalia's Heads OK Power-Sharing Deal," *Sun Herald*, December 22, 1997, 1.
38. The Economist Intelligence Unit, "Ethiopia, Eritrea, Somalia and Djibouti," *The Economist* (London, 1998), 28.
39. Ibid.

9

Democratic Consolidation and Civil Conflict in Zambia

Julius Ihonvbere

> Zambia is trying to consolidate the parameters of a Western-style liberal democracy at a time when the social and economic circumstances are unpropitious, not least because of the traumas involved in moving from statism to a market-based economic regime. . . . [In] many respects, the indications look much less favorable for democratization.[1]

> Defeating the UNIP in 1991 and getting Kaunda out of politics now appear to have been relatively easy, compared to the tasks of building democracy and improving the conditions of our people. To be quite frank, we are not doing a good job, no we are not.[2]

The spate of democratic struggles in Africa in recent times has drastically altered the political landscape in several ways. These struggles have changed the nature of politics, encouraged the emergence of new leaders, movements, and political parties, and reconstituted the demands of popular constituencies and communities.[3] The new struggles, dubbed a "second liberation" or "second revolution" by many scholars, have also culminated in the defeat of first-generation nationalists like Kenneth Kaunda in Zambia and Kamuzu Banda in Malawi and long-ruling military despots like Matthew Kerekou (until his dramatic 1996 return to power), and forced military and civilian dictators like Jerry Rawlings in Ghana and Daniel arap Moi in Kenya to organize open multiparty elections.[4] Even a ruthless military despot like General Ibrahim Babangida of Nigeria was forced in 1993 to hurriedly resign from the presidency and retire from the army by a combined force of pro-democracy movements.

These changes elicited all sorts of euphoric responses from scholars inside and outside (though mostly outside) the African continent. In the self-congratulatory euphoria of the post–Cold War era, while many Western scholars celebrated the victory of the Western capitalist ideology over all other ideologies in the world and declared the arrival of liberal democratic political structures as the "only game in town," others were somewhat cautious. As Larry Diamond put it,

> Democracy has won the great ideological struggle of the Cold War. As a dynamic, coordinated, self-confident international movement, communism is, to quote political scientist Ken Jowitt, "extinct." This extinction has produced a multipolar, fluid, and volatile world in which regimes, ideologies, identities and national boundaries will experience vigorous change and contestation.[5]

In the effort to build universal models to reflect the new victory of democracy (now unequivocally declared to be synonymous with capitalism), the specifics of dependent, underdeveloped, vulnerable, and crisis-ridden economies were overlooked.[6] In fact, there arose a growing impatience with the inability of these poor, unstable, and unsteady political economies to be like the West, especially when the so-called preconditions for democracy were well known to all.[7]

As has become evident, political liberalization does not equal democracy, much less democratization.[8] The efforts of African economies in particular are taking place amidst a plethora of contradictions, coalitions, and conflicts that frequently mediate and/or negate the processes of liberalization. Even the imposition of political conditionalities by donors and lenders (and this worked fairly well in Benin, Kenya, and Malawi) has tended to overlook the specificities of Africa, the deepening crisis of the continent, the character of the regime and state, the nature and politics of the new actors and movements, and the hostility of the global economy to vulnerable African states.[9] As Nicephore Soglo, the recently "defeated" president of the Republic of Benin, has noted in frustration, "People think that once you have got a democracy, everything is going to be free of charge. The danger is impatience."[10] Denis Venter has noted that the "restoration of aid promised by donors on condition of the successful completion of the democratization process has yet to materialize in any significant way."[11] It has also become obvious that most of the new political leaders and movements have not only been outmaneuvered and manipulated by incumbent regimes and old guard politicians (in Togo, Benin, Nigeria, Kenya, Ghana, Malawi), but that they are disorganized, conservative, opportunistic, corrupt, and undemocratic and have not developed an alternative, holistic agenda which would distinguish them from the decadent, repressive, corrupt, irresponsible, and practically visionless leaders and regimes which have bankrupted the continent.[12] Combined with other structural contradictions and constraints, as well as pressures from an increasingly complex and competitive global division of labor and power,

Africa's political liberalization has been rolled back (in Congo, Niger, Benin, Togo, Kenya) or simply stalemated as in the majority of other cases.

ORIGINS OF THE "NEW" LIBERALIZATION

It is not quite accurate to attribute the ongoing changes in Africa to developments in Eastern Europe or to the political conditionalities imposed by donors and lenders in the early 1990s. The opposition to state repression, the suffocation of civil society, the closure of democratic openings, and the domestication and incorporation of the opposition in Africa started in the 1960s with the failure of the nationalist projects. As soon as the nationalists took over the reins of power and failed to execute far-reaching socioeconomic and political changes to empower the people, improve their conditions of living, and terminate neocolonial relations with the forces of imperialism, the elites not only lost the support of the people but they faced massive challenges from students, women, peasants, workers, urban dwellers, and other popular constituencies.[13] Even some of the military coups in the continent were responses to the continuing culture of domination, exploitation, marginalization, and brutalization. The struggles against the neocolonial state, its institutions, and its custodians only deepened with the deteriorating economic conditions, the delegitimization of the state, and the inability of the elites to make a significant difference in the living conditions of the people.[14]

To be sure, the political changes in the continent are also the result of other complex internal and external factors and developments: the delegitimization and weakening of the state; the corruption and demystification of the dominant elites; the decay of infrastructures and basic services; the marginalization of the people from decision-making processes; the suffocation of civil society and the closures of all outlets for independent political expression; the emergence of new political leaders, political movements, and interest groups making open demands for political pluralism; and the unequal distribution of the costs and pains of World Bank and IMF dictated and directed structural adjustment programs. These factors built up the pressures which forced regimes to make concessions to the people, open up the political system, succumb to external pressures, and acknowledge the power of the people and their new (or reinvigorated) organizations.

Developments in the global system were equally important to Africa's initiatives and struggles for democracy: events in Eastern Europe, the end of the Cold War, and the near irrelevance of old allies from the ideological blocs; the commitment of the United States of America to restructuring the global order (with the support of the IMF and the World Bank) to reflect capitalist values; the new emphasis on political pluralism, good governance, accountability, and respect for human rights by donors, lenders, and creditors; the imposition of economic and political conditionalities as preconditions for further aid and trade concessions; and the diversion of investment to other regions of the world at the expense of Africa.[15]

THE CRISIS OF DEMOCRATIC CONSOLIDATION IN AFRICA

What has been going on in Africa since the beginning of the so-called "third wave" is political liberalization, evidenced in the opening up of the political system, the relaxation or elimination of repressive laws and regulations, the introduction of multiparty (procedural) politics, constitutional engineering, and some reintroduction of constitutionally guaranteed rights. [16] Certainly, this amounts to a monumental change in the content and context of Africa. Civilian despots who had openly declared their distaste and distrust for democracy, like Moi in Kenya, have opened the political system to some extent and conducted multiparty elections. There is now, however, almost unanimous agreement that the process of "liberalization" in Africa is not necessarily leading to democratization.[17] Most African dictators, under internal and external pressures, have not found it too daunting to "liberalize" and use multiparty elections to re-legitimize themselves or to divide and disorganize the opposition. Where they have lost elections, they have used such defeats as opportunities to regroup and organize a comeback. Such comebacks, which are currently in vogue in Africa, are largely the result of the inability to move politics beyond the procedural level to the level of consolidation.[18]

Samuel Huntington has argued that democracies "become consolidated when people learn that democracy is a solution to the problem of tyranny but not necessarily to anything else."[19] This is a rather weak "dividend" with which to motivate people to struggle to deepen the democratic process. Defeating tyranny is important but not enough. Democracy certainly must offer more than just the defeat of a despot; it must also guarantee the expansion of the democratic space, the total containment of oppressive rule, an improvement in the modes of governance, opportunities for improving the conditions of living, and the guarantee of an environment encouraging the attainment of the highest levels of the people's creative and productive abilities. Transition governments are often confronted with numerous challenges and constraints which often militate against the move toward consolidation and democratization: these challenges include the powerful legacies of the defeated dictator; deepening socioeconomic crisis; a long-existing culture of mass alienation from the government; and distrust, even hatred, for its institutions, regulations, and custodians; infrastructures and institutions designed to work with despotism rather than with an open and accountable democratic system; and the problems of what to do with the defeated dictator, how to contain and "reform" supporters of the authoritarian system, and how to effectively manage the new freedoms, liberties, and political openings to avoid a general deterioration and descent into anarchy. In addition, under the despot, primordial loyalties were either suppressed or manipulated to give the impression that unity and consensus prevailed. The use of draconian laws, the secret police, other forms of intimidation, and bribes greatly reduced open conflicts.

The new democratic government is often immediately confronted with the resurgence of ethnic, regional, religious, and other primordial challenges, coalitions, and conflicts. If not properly managed, they could immediately distract, divert, and even destroy the democratic process. In the context of problems of poverty, unemployment, inflation, capital flight, pressures from debt and debt-servicing obligations, brain drain, decline in foreign aid and investment, closure of credit lines, inequality in income and opportunities, insecurity and uncertainty, and a tradition of distrust for the government, primordial conflicts can have devastating consequences.[20] If we add conditions of elite factionalization, fractionalization, and opportunism; the weak nature of the political parties; the superficial political and economic programs of the opposition; the limited support the parties enjoy from popular constituencies especially women, students, the working classes, and rural dwellers; and the inability of the new parties and movements to be original in their thinking and politics, the result is often a steady march toward political stalemate, decay, dislocation, and disintegration. In fact, Huntington talks of "authoritarian nostalgia" in which the bad old days suddenly begin to look rather rosy or in comparison to the confused, disorganized, inefficient, unpredictable, and painful present.[21] As we have seen in Nigeria, Benin, Zambia, and even Malawi, "authoritarian nostalgia" is not necessarily an emotional or sentimental feeling as Huntington has asserted.[22] If it is true that the "legitimacy of particular rulers or governments may depend on what they can deliver,"[23] and on "the ability of the principal political elites—party leaders, military leaders, business leaders—to work together to deal with the problems confronting their society and to refrain from exploiting those problems for their own immediate material or political advantage,"[24] then we can expect the yearning for the old regime to be a genuine and serious reflection of frustrations with the present and distrust of the future.[25]

It is now obvious that if the democratic transitions are to survive, the first challenge for the new governments is to sustain the new victories over authoritarianism. Second, they must demonstrate a high degree of cohesion, seriousness, sense of mission, and commitment to the general good. Third, they must immediately initiate processes for bringing the people into the political process, anchoring the future of the democratic process in the consciousness and politics of the people, and advancing it beyond procedural levels by embarking on a genuine process of democratization. Democratization involves the steady and systematic empowerment of the people, their organizations, and their communities in a direction that empowers them to dictate, influence and determine the content and context of politics. Democratization allows the people to incorporate their interests in the institutions and structures of the state, and this makes it possible for public policy to reflect the interests and aspirations of the people. Finally, democratization makes it possible for politics to reflect the issues close to the people: gender equality, human rights, environmental protection, basic needs, participation in decision-making, accountability of the leadership, expansion of democratic spaces, and non-appropriation of the voices of the people. An agenda for democratization makes it possible for democracy to be consolidated largely because it develops and nurtures an environment for collective contribution to projects, collective acknowledgment of problems, and collective acceptance of mistakes. The nature and politics of the contemporary political parties and movements have provided many reasons for skepticism about the future of democracy, especially its consolidation in Africa:

> it seems highly likely that third wave democratic regimes will not handle [their] problems effectively and that they will, in all probability, be no more or less successful in doing this than their authoritarian predecessors. Insurgencies, inflation, poverty, debt, inequality, and/or bloated bureaucracies will continue more or less as they have in previous decades.[26]

In a continent like Africa where the colonial experiences, the neocolonial legacies, the distortions and disarticulations of underdevelopment, vulnerability in the global divisions of labor and power, and the contradictions arising from the balance of forces and character of politics have traditionally militated against the construction of a liberal democratic project, the constraints discussed thus far do not favor the survival of the democratic process much less its consolidation.[27] Below, I focus on some of the points of conflict that have emerged with the democratization process.

DEMOCRATIZATION AND CONFLICTS IN ZAMBIA

With the impressive defeat of the Kaunda dictatorship in the 1991 elections, there were high hopes that the democratic process would be the final solution not just to the one-person, one-party, and corrupt dictatorship of Kenneth Kaunda and the United Independence Party (UNIP), but also to the problems of provincialism, corruption, economic dislocation and decay, ethnic conflicts, and the fragmentation of civil society.[28] The Movement for Multiparty Democracy (MMD), as an agglomeration of disparate opposition elements and interests—alienated businessmen, disgraced and displaced politicians, rural dwellers, religious leaders, students, workers and their unions under the leadership of the Zambian Congress of Trade Unions (ZCTU) and professional politicians—easily mobilized the populace against a highly delegitimized and discredited regime.[29] However, the process of consolidating the victory of the MMD has been constrained by numerous contradictions since 1991. These have steadily eroded its legitimacy, political mandate, and ability to proceed with much-needed reforms. The MMD has had to contend with all sorts of problems no different from those identified earlier. At one level, Zambia is now paying very dearly for almost three decades of despotism.[30] Not only has the government been unable to deepen the democratic process, but it has lost the support of its primary constituency, which is labor; and primordial conflicts, scandals, and a loss of direction have come to characterize MMD politics.[31]

Economic Failure and Conflicts

The MMD's 1991 landslide victory over the UNIP was welcomed as a positive starting point for economic recovery. The multilateral organizations immediately warned the Chiluba government that its record would be evaluated largely on the basis of how much energy it devoted to the implementation of the World Bank–supervised orthodox adjustment program. In his campaigns, Chiluba had stressed the need to vigorously implement the policies of devaluation, deregulation, desubsidization, and tighter fiscal controls. He had made it clear that it would be painful but had also assured the people that the results would be worth the pain and sacrifice. The party's manifesto had also declared its commitment to the creation of an "enabling environment for economic development . . . by implementing a balanced structural adjustment program specifically suited to Zambian conditions."[32] With its nationwide mandate, a comfortable majority in parliament, and the goodwill of the donor countries, which had provided an array of support for the MMD's campaigns, it was assumed that recovery would soon replace decay, deterioration, and crises.

The MMD's record, unfortunately, has been one of failure on all counts. True, it has remained faithful to the adjustment program, but at great cost to its own credibility and its constituency, the labor movement.[33] It has effectively managed two droughts that would otherwise have led to unprecedented disaster. It has reduced inflation (at least officially) from over 100 percent to about 30 percent and has managed to retain the support of donors and some lenders. Investors have not poured into Zambia as the party had hoped and promised the people. Donors have been rather stringent as well. Blaming all the ills on the legacy of the UNIP and the fact that the new government inherited a "battered and tattered" economy and an empty purse is no longer an effective strategy for mediating the anger of non-bourgeois constituencies. Unemployment, inflation, and migration to the urban centers have increased. Those who migrate to the cities find no jobs in the small, weak private sector and most try to get by on petty trade that hardly keeps body and soul together. Crime in the major cities, especially in Lusaka and Ndola, has reached unprecedented proportions.[34] The currency has been devalued to unprecedented levels while salaries have remained depressed or constant.[35] In 1993, Emmanuel Kasonde, the finance minister, warned that inflation remained a major headache and unless it was adequately addressed investors would not return and the economy would remain depressed.[36] The Zambian government therefore introduced a wide range of monetarist responses to promote growth and restore investor and donor confidence in the economy.

A major aspect of the MMD's reform program was in the area of taxation and involved the introduction of an extensive tax review, administration, evaluation, and collection system; the creation of a Special Fund for revenues from the privatization of government companies; and the earmarking of K2 billion for rehabilitating Zambia's terrible road network. In addition, tax relief for the handicapped and low-wage earners was introduced. With various tax measures, the government expected to raise K15 billion in 1993. Proposed expenditure for 1993 was put at K231.9 billion: K197.1 billion was designated as non-drought expenditure, K34.8 billion as drought related. Of the K231.9 billion proposed expenditure, K19.8 billion was expected to come from the sale of donated maize and K212.1 billion from domestic sources. In addition to the vigorous tax reforms, the MMD government set about establishing "favorable macroeconomic policies, political stability, security, the availability of resources and markets, and liberal provisions for the repatriation of profits." As a measure of the degree of openness of the economy and in addition to the "package of tax measures" which was expected to "attract investors and stimulate investment," the MMD government announced that it would "allow the repatriation of 100 percent of after tax profits, with no restrictions, and no bureaucratic screening."[37]

By the middle of 1995, the government had not recorded significant successes in its recovery program. As part of its privatization program, the MMD government liquidated Zambia Airways and sent hundreds of workers into unemployment thus swelling the ranks of the 70,000 public employees already retrenched. Twenty more state companies were listed for liquidation before the end of 1995. This is of course, a very painful choice for a government that derived its legitimacy and support from popular constituencies. Yet the size of the civil service needed to be cut, inefficient parastatals like the Kabwe Mines needed to be gotten rid of, and there was a need to strengthen the productive capacities of Zambians by making them rely less on state subsidies.

However, rather than bringing Zambians together, the government's privatization program seems to be alienating the people, delegitimizing the state and its custodians, and generating widespread opposition. Retrenched workers openly blame the government and join opposition movements to undermine the MMD's credibility.[38] Efforts by the government to expand public participation in the privatization exercise have not benefited workers, whose wages have remained stagnant and whose lifestyles are wracked by inflation and irregular payment of salaries and wages. The 15 firms sold went to "well established businessmen and multinationals who could afford to bid for them."[39] For instance, the 54 million shares sold during the privatization of the Chilanga Cement company were pegged at K65,000 "minimum investment" and the majority of Zambians could not afford such an amount.[40] The opposition press, public campaigns, and commentaries have attacked the biased implementation of the policy and mediated popular support for the MMD's reform agenda.

The infrastructure is still in very bad shape as most roads, public buildings, and bridges remain dilapidated and poorly maintained. Though the government does lack foreign exchange, the corruption within the government makes most

Zambians believe that it "is just like the previous one. It cares for only the rich."[41] About 7 million Zambians out of a population of 9 million live below the poverty line. Copper continues to contribute "more than 90 of the country's export earnings and jobs, directly and indirectly, for some 100,000 Zambians."[42] With copper prices down, frequent talks about privatization in the air, and production falling from 700,000 tons a year in the mid-1970s to less than 400,000 in 1994, the mineworkers and their powerful union have become opponents of the MMD. The state, in spite of vitriolic and suffocating propaganda about privatization, desubsidization, and so on, continues to provide employment for the majority of Zambians in the formal economy. Younger MMD members and the UNIP as well as other opposition parties are capitalizing on the fears of workers, uncertainty among urban dwellers, and frustrations among rural people to campaign for support. In fact, Chiluba had become so frustrated that he openly expressed the view that Zambians were justified in opposing his government. In 1995, following the refusal of Western donors to appreciate the obstacles to his reform programs, Chiluba "openly questioned whether democracy and economic reform are compatible."[43] *Africa Confidential* effectively summarizes the Chiluba reform record:

> The government is an easy target. It has not delivered on its election promises to fight poverty, corruption and drug-trafficking—nor promises of accountability. Chiluba's pragmatic, pro-business team is regarded as corrupt and socially insensitive, even after successive resignations and dismissals. Younger MMD members resent the lax policing that has allowed millions of "hot" dollars (mainly from drug and gem stone smuggling) to be laundered in Zambia. Some US $300 million of drug cash is reckoned to have been funneled through last year [1994], creating more local drug lords.[44]

Growing Corruption and State Delegitimization

Corruption has traditionally been the bane of African politics. Several reasons explain why politicians across the world are corrupt. But in Africa, the weakness of civil society, the corruption of the judiciary, the non-enforceability of laid-down rules and regulations, and at times the cultural rationalization of corruption have contributed to its ever-spreading nature. In Zambia, as in Nigeria, the Democratic Republic of the Congo, and Kenya, it has become an art among politicians and elites in general. Unfortunately, it has also served to erode the credibility of the leaders, waste scarce resources, distort development programs, and compromise the political process. Though the MMD continues to reiterate its full commitment to governmental transparency and to structural adjustment, the problem of corruption within the government has continued to erode the government's credibility and create dangerous political divisions and diversions. This problem is so widespread that it has divided the party, led to the dismissal or resignation of ministers and some founding members of the MMD, forced the donor community to withhold foreign aid, and tainted the good intentions of the government. Since the MMD came to power in November 1991, it has sacked or forced out so many ministers that it is almost impossible to keep count. Some were forced out of office because of allegations of corruption, drug trafficking, abuse of office, and other extralegal activities. This high turnover has not helped with policy consistency and transparency.

Scandals in the cabinet, inefficiency, contradictory pronouncements, and sycophancy à la Kaunda have come to dominate MMD politics in Zambia. Former ministers like Roger Chongwe (Legal Affairs) were alleged to have used their positions to illegally acquire acres of land. Ronald Penza, Derrick Chitala, and Matthew Ngulube have also "grabbed land" illegally.[45] The former vice president, Levi Mwanawasa, resigned in mid-1994 in the midst of accusations about abuse of office and power. A former foreign affairs minister Vernon Mwaanga, who had been arrested in 1984 at Frankfurt International Airport on drug trafficking charges, continued to be accused of running a drug ring. His son, Maliko, was arrested after he was found with high-grade cocaine worth £70,000 sterling.[46] Sikota Wina, another founding member of the MMD, as well as Princess Nakatindi Wina, had to resign from the government following several accusations of drug trafficking. The deputy minister for special duties Edward Chisha, was sacked for beating a lawyer to death in a barroom fight at an exclusive sports club. The list of MMD ministers and prominent officials who are well known for abuse of office, drug trafficking, corruption, indiscipline, and incompetence is long. In spite of Chiluba's personal claim to be "born again," Zambians see him as ineffective and unable to control his ministers, who obviously do not share his visions of a new Zambia.[47] Their acts of corruption have opened up the MMD to bitter attacks from the opposition parties and the public, distracted the government from its goals of adjustment and openness, and limited the ability of the government to call on Zambians to make sacrifices and accept the pains of adjustment. Also, corruption has led to waste, bureaucratic inertia, the privatization of public positions, the development of unproductive patron-client networks, and the erosion of donor and lender support. Pervasive corruption has also promoted widespread skepticism, even among one-time supporters of the MMD, about the party's ability to sustain democracy and the reform programs. Democracy in Zambia has not reduced corruption; if anything, it has made the situation worse.[48]

Ethnicity, Provincialism, and the Redirection of Loyalties

Plural democracy in Zambia has not brought ethnic groups together. Through ethnic balancing, intimidation, co-optation, and other forms of political domestication, Kaunda largely succeeded in papering over ethnic and regional differences and conflicts. The highly complex patron-client strategies of the UNIP succeeded in satisfying the demands of local ethnic leaders and chiefs and gave the impression that all was well, especially as it was not possible to challenge Kaunda or speak openly about community frustrations and dissatisfaction. The rise of the MMD and other opposition parties and the results of the 1991 elections changed all that. Many ethnic groups, provinces that felt neglected, and organizations espousing all forms of autonomous political arrangements surfaced and established their positions in the political landscape of the country. There was an initial honeymoon period in which they tolerated the MMD's excuses and watched its programs. The honeymoon ended less than six months after the 1991 elections. Through political (especially parastatal, ministerial, and ambassadorial) appointments, the location of resources and projects, and statements by leading MMD politicians like Michael Sata, several ethnic communities, provinces, and traditional institutions were alienated. It will be recalled that the "original leadership of MMD was dominated by people from one part of the country: Lozis from Western Province."[49] Of course, as MMD membership grew and political elites defected from the UNIP to join the MMD, its ethnic composition diversified. Yet, regions and major ethnic groups see the Bembas as dominating the government and unduly diverting resources to the northeast.[50] In the original struggle for the leadership of the MMD, Bembas from the Northern Province led by Emmanuel Kasonde (who later became Chiluba's finance minister) had opposed Chiluba, who is also a Bemba from Luapula. When Dean Mun'gomba and Derrick Chitala, also prominent Bembas from the Northern Province, were suspended and later expelled from the party, it created a dangerous rift within the party. When they formed their own party—the Zambia Democratic Congress (ZADECO)—it effectively created stiff competition for Bemba loyalty, support, and votes.

The "scramble for top positions in . . . Chiluba's . . . [MMD] . . . led to further splits in the party along tribal lines" and this in itself posed serious threats to Chiluba's leadership of the party.[51] Scores of critical, even inciting, anonymous leaflets circulate within the bureaucracy, the party, opposition constituencies, and the schools. Some of these have been signed by a group which calls itself the "MMD Progressives," who have dedicated themselves to reforming the party, making it more radical, and ousting Chiluba and his top aides. Chiluba's selection of Vernon Mwaanga, a Tonga from the south who is also well known for his corrupt past and who was sacked by Chiluba in 1994 over drug trafficking allegations, as his running mate for the 1996 election alienated people from Brigadier General Godfrey Miyanda's ethnic group, the Nsenga. The Nsenga are a sub-group of the Bemba and the selection of Mwaanga angered the Bembas. When Chiluba visited the Northern Province in February 1995 on a six-day tour, Bemba Paramount Chief Chitimunkulu not only refused to host Chiluba but also openly declared his support for Kaunda! When the constitution was amended to disqualify Kaunda from the presidential race, other Bemba chiefs like Nkula of Chinsali, Mwamba of Kasama, and Mrepo of Mpika publicly expressed their dissatisfaction with the MMD's desperate strategy.

Loud complaints of marginalization and discrimination are heard from the Southern Province, which had supported the MMD. The Eastern Province, Kaunda's base, has also complained of being punished for supporting and remaining loyal to the UNIP. The UNIP's twenty-five seats in parliament won in the 1991 elections came from the province and the party continues to have influence there. Ethnic and regional identities and loyalties have severely divided Zambian politicians and politics. Today, none of the political parties can strictly be regarded as national in character. The UNIP retains its eastern base. The MMD remains strong in Luapula and the Northern Province. The new party, the Zambia Democratic Congress (ZADECO), is becoming very popular in the north, and the National Party (NP) is strongest in the west. As Elias Nyakutembe has noted, "Flourishing regional politics are part of Chiluba's dilemma and he has still put forward no plan for regional autonomy despite the overwhelming recommendations of the Mwanakatwe Constitutional Review Commission."[52] There are fears that if ethnic and regional problems are left unresolved, in the context of failed social and economic programs, Zambians will come to affiliate themselves simply with their respective ethnic and regional enclaves, with very far-reaching implications for stability, governance, and nation building.

Party indiscipline has also become a major problem. This is evidenced especially in the conflicts between the central MMD government and regional governors who simply refuse to toe party lines, take orders from the center, or reconcile differences with other levels of authority. In the Northern and Northwest Provinces, as well as in the Copperbelt, acts of insubordination, disrespect for party rules and decisions, and power struggles between MMD stalwarts have at various times played into the hands of the opposition and weakened the party. While these struggles and conflicts have often shown that the MMD was yet to see itself as a political party (rather than a movement), they have made it possible for alienated party members to transfer their support to the opposition.

The "Born Again" Syndrome: The Merger of Church and State

The MMD has created a platform for religious tensions and conflicts in Zambia. Conflicts between the state and religious interests are not necessarily new given the experiences with Leshina and Watchtower.[53] The MMD Manifesto declared the country a "Christian country which is tolerant of other religions." Though it also declares a commitment to "freedom of thought, conscience, belief and proclamation of faith," by placing one religion above others which are merely to be "tolerated,"[54] the party seems to be encouraging religious divisions. Chiluba's born again religious position seems to have emboldened the Christians, who now openly make disparaging remarks about other religions. Not only are television programs dominated by religious programs from abroad, but also public functions are full of religious activities. "Religious sycophancy" has become part of Zambian politics as most ministers or politicians, as well as contractors, have become "born again" Christians! However, by refusing to take action against corrupt ministers and politicians, by appointing so many individuals with records of corruption as members of his cabinet, and by taking malicious action against those who oppose him, Chiluba has caused many people to question his born again credentials. More importantly, this public perception erodes the credibility of the leader, the government, and the party. True, major religious confrontations on the Nigerian scale have not erupted yet. However, the tensions are there and, if not adequately managed, could in the future consume the socioeconomic and political agenda of the nation, divide the larger society, and promote unprecedented violence.

THE RISE OF THE OPPOSITION: HEALTHY CIVIL SOCIETY OR POLITICAL OPPORTUNISM?

The emergence of several opposition parties is clearly reflective of a new epoch in Zambian history. Also, it demonstrates a healthy civil society in which political interests and ideas compete freely for support. However, in the case of Zambia, it is doubtful if such claims can be made without some qualification. The opposition can contribute to the strengthening of civil society and the political process only if it does not place itself on the path of self-and national destruction or destabilization. In the first four years of MMD rule, over thirty-four opposition parties and movements emerged on the political terrain. Many of these are led by former leading members, cabinet ministers, and even founding members of the MMD. Derrick Chitala, former minister for presidential affairs and Mbala Central MP and Dean Mungoba, former deputy development minster, formed the Zambian Democratic Congress (ZADECO) after Chiluba dismissed them for corruption and involvement in land deals. The Caucus for National Unity (CNU) was formed by some founding members of the MMD. When Chiluba sacked Emmanuel Kasonde, Arthur Wina, and Humphrey Mulemba as ministers in April 1993, they formed the National Party (NP). They were promptly joined by thirteen other parliamentarians including Akashambwata Lewanika and his sister, Inonge Lewanika. Though none of the opposition parties has the influence, resources, or international visibility of the MMD, their mere existence removes a cadre of leaders from the MMD and prevents the consolidation of party power, unity, and mission.

The opposition parties have succeeded in some by-elections in humiliating the MMD, even in its northern stronghold. Their trenchant attacks against Chiluba and the MMD have contributed to mass distaste for politics and politicians and promoted the alienation of the people. This is evidenced in recent low turnouts at by-elections. Even then, MMD candidates have not fared well in the by-elections. The MMD lost the Chipangali by-election in the Western Province to the UNIP. In Masaiti and Chingola (Copperbelt), and Mwandi (Western Province), Jasiman Chikwaka and Tom Mulele won their by-elections in early 1995 only by very narrow margins in spite of massive support from Chiluba and the MMD machine. Most of the MMD's victory has been facilitated by intimidation, heavy infusion of party funds, direct support from the government, and the distribution of free maize. This strategy has succeeded in getting thousands of hungry villagers to come out to vote.[55] The MMD has also been accused of "vote buying and abuse of voters' certificates" in elections, which enabled it to retain seats in Chilanga and Mandevu (Lusaka), Namwala and Beengwa (Southern Province), Kabompo West (Northwest Province), Chama South (Eastern Province), and Lufwanmyama (Copperbelt-Rural).[56] The focus on personality, character deficiencies, allegations of drug trafficking, and corruption by otherwise respected leaders and ministers has added to the frustration of the people and eroded their interest in politics.

For whatever it is worth, the fear of losing power to the opposition has frightened the MMD and forced Chiluba to become more intolerant of opposition especially as mass defections of cadres and leaders from the MMD, resembling the mass defection of the early 1990s from the then ruling UNIP which contributed to the building of the MMD itself, were beginning to occur. For instance, over eighty MMD cadres from Kabwata and Kanyama constituencies defected and joined ZADECO in July 1995.[57] This was just after prominent parliamentarians such as Roger Chongwe, Chuulu Kalima, and Roshi Santon had defected from the party. In the struggle to rebuild its credibility and regain the political initiative, the MMD has moved from error to error. For instance, it has adopted a strategy of purging critical and militant activists like Derrick Chitala, Dean Mung'omba, Ronald Penza, Simon Mwila, Max Nkole, Paul Tembo, Mathius Mpande, Eric Silwamba, and Roger Chongwe from the party. Rather than addressing the concrete reasons why leading (including founding) MMD members have been defecting to the opposition constituency, Chiluba has tried to bribe potential defectors with political appointments. Five of the new deputy ministers appointed in the July 1995 cabinet reshuffle indicated their intention to join Dean Mung'omba's ZADECO. "More and more, [Chiluba] looks a beleaguered leader presiding over faltering economic reforms and a squabbling party. The improbable alliance of business and trade unions behind his party has long since collapsed, leaving a core of Chiluba loyalists—few of whom command public respect."[58] He is so frustrated that he has lost interest even in his own security agencies. Speaking about the intelligence reports of the Zambian Security Service, Chiluba told reporters: "I read them for five minutes and shred them."[59]

The reemergence of Kenneth Kaunda on the Zambian political scene and the revitalization of UNIP, for example, are sowing the seeds for crisis, instability, even disintegration.[60] As soon as Kaunda declared his ill-advised reentry into politics and was overwhelmingly reelected as party leader by UNIP delegates on June 28, 1995, Chiluba reacted with panic.[61] Rather than allow the new democratic process to define Kaunda's place in contemporary Zambian politics, and against strong warnings from his intelligence services (which he does not respect), Nelson Mandela of South Africa, Robert Mugabe of Zimbabwe, and Sam Nujoma of Namibia, Chiluba began to initiate legal and extralegal mechanisms to contain Kaunda's growing influence. He amended the 1991 constitution through the very controversial role of a twenty-two-man constitutional commission appointed in 1993, whose report was released in June 1995 and included among other prescriptions, redefining the qualifications for running as a candidate for the presidency. According to the new rules, "A person shall be qualified to be a candidate for elections if he or she is a citizen of Zambia born in Zambia [and] his parents are Zambian citizens born in Zambia."[62] Clearly aimed at Kenneth Kaunda, whose parents were Malawians, it has been received with a lot of opposition and unfavorable reactions from inside and outside Zambia.[63]

Chiluba's most embarrassing move was his attempt to have Kaunda deported to Malawi. When the deportation plan was revealed and Chiluba's ministers were making contradictory statements, the unemployed, students, and workers in Lusaka led by UNIP officials embarked on protests which culminated in large scale violence and looting. Kaunda fought for Zambia's independence and ruled the country for twenty-seven years. To amend the constitution on the eve of the 1996 elections, only after Kaunda announced his interest in the presidency and in the light of UNIP victories in by-elections in Mbala, Mpulungu, and Mkushi where MMD candidates were defeated, has been seen as nothing short of victimization. To further humiliate Kaunda, Chiluba threw open to public view Yugoslav-constructed security tunnels under the state house in Lusaka. Chiluba argued that Kaunda used the tunnels to torture political opponents, though he "failed to prove that torture did take place."[64] Kaunda argued that the tunnels and bunkers "were gifts from friendly nations to protect liberation leaders and the presidency from South African aggression. Among those who used the tunnels were Nelson Mandela and Sam Nujoma of Namibia."[65] Rather than attracting sympathy, Chiluba was widely criticized for exposing Zambian state security to the entire world and he was accused of intolerance, opportunism, and disrespecting an elder statesman. Also, the illegal and desperate move "made the opposition more determined to unseat him [Chiluba] and allowed Kaunda to claim the moral high ground."[66]

Within the MMD, Chiluba has not shown any more any accommodation to opposing views and opposing interests. When Dean Mung'omba announced his intention in early 1995 to challenge Chiluba in the presidential race because "Chiluba's government had failed to meet the needs of the poor" and had mismanaged the economic reform program while neglecting agriculture and the rural areas, he was promptly relieved of his positions first as deputy finance minister and later as MMD deputy treasurer.[67] It was convenient for conspiracy theorists in Zambia to link Mung'omba's "two road accidents in less than four months" to attempts by some forces (Chiluba's government?) to eliminate him and terminate his political ambitions. Ironically, Mung'omba's views about Chiluba's record are widely known and no different from those of Kaunda who leads the UNIP opposition: "The nation is now badly divided. . . . The gap between rich and poor is growing bigger and bigger, and that is extremely dangerous. I cannot pretend that an explosion will not be inevitable from angry people from the grassroots level."[68]

Human Rights Abuses in MMD Zambia

The first subsection in the MMD Manifesto under "Political Perspectives" is human rights. In it, the party declared its total commitment to "the protection of fundamental rights and freedoms for the benefit of all Zambians; the promotion of justice and equality among all the people without distinction; the maintenance of the rule of law and the independence of the judiciary." It promised to extend the "Bill of Rights to embrace categories such as the rights of the Press and Children and rights against all forms of discrimination against women."[69] Unfortunately, the party has not been able to translate its rhetoric into action, largely because many of the leaders of the party were fully and visibly associated with Kaunda's one-party repressive rule for years, but also because the party discovered that it lacked the internal cohesion, institutions, and capacities to guarantee basic freedoms and liberties in the context of mounting challenges. Its failed economic programs have generated open criticism and opposition from popular constituencies. Just like Kenneth Kaunda, the Chiluba government has been unable to tolerate open criticism. Demonstrating students have been shot, arrested, and detained without trial and workers have been harassed. Many opposition politicians have been involved in "strange" accidents which they have promptly blamed on the government and the Israeli trainers in the army and airforce: Baldwin Nkumbula, formerly of the NP (who had just defected to the MMD in return for a vice-presidential appointment), died in a road accident in the "company of Chiluba's controversial son, Castro."[70] Also, Kaunda, Mulemba, and Mung'omba, presidential candidates of UNIP, NP, and ZADECO respectively, have all managed to survive "strange" road accidents. Politicians within the MMD who planned to challenge Chiluba in the 1996 presidential elections, and who were conducting preliminary consultations to determine the national spread and strength of their support, were checked when the government banned "all MMD MPs from holding meetings outside their constituencies without express permission."[71]

The press, which the manifesto promised to respect and protect, has also fallen victim to the MMD's intolerant disposition. Not only are the official media controlled and manipulated, but the opposition is frequently harassed for publishing stories of inefficiency, scandals, and failure to live up to campaign promises. The *Weekly Post* has suffered more than any other opposition publication in the country as its editor-in-chief and two colleagues were detained for twenty-four days for writing articles considered to be insulting to Parliament. Prior to this detention, the Chiluba government had manipulated Parliament to pass legislation that allowed the government to detain journalists on a so-called "contempt of Parliament" charge should they publish materials considered by the government and/or Parliament to be in bad taste. There were no time limits or terms attached to such detentions.

Such repressive and intolerant tendencies work directly against democratic consolidation. Such panic-stricken measures simply buy sympathy for the opposition; they have been directly responsible for increasing the support that Kaunda is enjoying. More importantly, they give the impression that the government is unable to build legitimacy or mobilize the people behind an agenda, and that the people can be manipulated and/or convinced to support an alternative political platform. This perception is exactly what convinced certain elements within UNIP, led by Kaunda's son, Wezi Kaunda, to initiate the controversial "Zero Option" in 1993 as a strategy to oust the Chiluba government from power through extralegal means.[72] This episode forced Chiluba, through the MMD-dominated Parliament, to impose a state of emergency, arrest numerous UNIP leaders and activists, and charge them to court. This did not go down well with the international community or with Zambians who had suffered under Kaunda's state of emergency. Nevertheless, it did show the fragility of Zambian democracy and the declining popularity of the incumbent government.[73]

Popular Resistance to the MMD

Democratic consolidation is not possible with regimes or governments that do not possess a strong, reliable, and active constituency. Chiluba rode to power on the back of the Zambian labor movement that he led until he was elected president in 1991. However, the failure of the MMD's reform program and the lack of improvement in the lives of non-bourgeois forces have culminated in strikes, riots, and demonstrations by peasants, workers, and students. As Nyakutemba notes, the main problems of Chiluba "remain poverty, high taxes, soaring unemployment and continually falling living standards. There is also the failure of medical and educational care and corruption in the cabinet."[74] This is the basis of alienation from the MMD and the state as "discontent festers as people see the cities thronged with street vendors selling everything from mounds of gravel to imported Asian consumer goods. Inflation and soaring interest rates discourage investment. High taxes fall on a narrow tax base."[75] These conditions simply increase support for the opposition, especially the UNIP, the NP, and ZADECO, and frequent confrontations between the state and the forces of civil society.

The ZCTU that Chiluba headed for almost two decades is openly opposed to his structural adjustment, especially his privatization program. Teachers have organized strikes against the government, as have taxi drivers, local authority workers, and civil servants. Workers located in MMD strongholds in the major cities of Kitwe, Lusaka, Solwezi, Kasama, and Kabwe have organized strikes against the government. Peasants are smuggling their products across the border to neighboring countries for better prices. Chiluba has relied on the security forces to put down peaceful demonstrations and some Zambians have been shot or killed by the police. At the very least, Chiluba has lost the support of his own constituency and moving the democratic project to the consolidation stage is currently not on the agenda. It will take enormous efforts to sustain the liberal content and context of the current initiatives in the country. Though observers and analysts had believed that "Chiluba will be hard put to convince voters that he can deliver the fruits of democracy in his second term of office, as he failed in the first,"[76] he did win a very controversial second term in the 1996 election.

CONCLUSION: TOWARD CONFLICT MANAGEMENT AND DEMOCRATIC CONSOLIDATION

Zambia is a typical example of the problems, even failure, of the liberal democratic enterprise in a distorted, underdeveloped, dependent, vulnerable, and crisis-ridden political economy. True, the political terrain has been liberalized and basic freedoms are greater than under the defeated UNIP. However, this is not enough. The people are much worse off than before liberalization and this has posed problems for the democratic enterprise. Of course, donors and lenders have not provided sufficient support or given Zambia any breathing space. Yet, even if billions of dollars had been poured into the country, the factionalization and fractionalization of the elite, the opportunism, indiscipline, corruption and decadence, and irresponsibility, and unproductive character of the Zambian bourgeois class would have meant that the aid and support were squandered. The MMD has not tried to deepen the political process, mobilize the people, empower popular communities and constituencies, dismantle the neocolonial state and construct a popular national state, strengthen civil society, or construct a national project.

The government has been more concerned with paying political debts, containing all forms of opposition, guaranteeing its own political survival, and designing a political agenda that will consolidate the neocolonial status quo under the guise of implementing a structural adjustment program. In fact, the MMD has attempted to carry out a new political agenda within the undemocratic and repressive environment constructed and operated for twenty-seven years by Kenneth Kaunda. It has tried to use the same decadent, inefficient, illegitimate, repressive, violent, and non-hegemonic state which Kaunda and the UNIP had used to suffocate civil society for decades, to mobilize the people and promote the democratic enterprise. To the extent that the conservative agenda of the MMD does not transcend the adoption of received models of economic and political restructuring and hardly reflects or incorporates the experiences and aspirations of the majority of Zambians, conflicts will continue to deepen with far-reaching implications for state and society. Finally, deepening conflicts can only be managed or contained through the following:

1. the deepening of the political process beyond mere procedural liberalization;
2. the visible guarantee of basic liberties, the mobilization of the people, and the construction of new, efficient, predictable, and transparent institutions;

3. the strengthening of civil society through the empowerment of the people, their communities, and their constituencies;
4. the introduction of a clear and viable alternative economic and social program which protects vulnerable groups and does not pursue reform at the expense of the survival of the people;
5. the dismantling and recomposition of the violent and undemocratic state in the democratization process;
6. the open involvement of popular groups in the transition process; and
7. the promotion of autonomy for ethnic and other primordial groups as well as the incorporation of their needs and aspirations in the national democratic project.[77]

NOTES

Research in Zambia for this study was supported by grants from the National Endowment for the Humanities and the American Philosophical Society.

1. Peter Burnell, "Zambia at the Crossroads," *World Affairs* 157 (Summer 1994): 27.

2. Interview with Honorable Frederick Hapunda, ex-UNIP minister for defense,) now MMD MP for Siavonga and chairman of the Southern Province, Lusaka, June 1993.

3. See Guy Martin, "Preface: Democratic Transition in Africa," *Issue: A Journal of Opinion* 21, nos. 1–2 (1993): 6–7.

4. See Larry Diamond, " 'The Second Liberation,' " *Africa Report* 37 (November–December 1992): 38–41.

5. Larry Diamond, "Promoting Democracy," *Foreign Policy* 87 (1992): 25.

6. Sadig Rasheed, "Africa at the Doorstep of the Twenty-First Century: Can Crisis Turn to Opportunity?" in *Africa within the World: Beyond Dispossession and Dependence*, ed. Adebayo Adedeji (London and Ijebu-Ode, Nigeria: Zed Books and ACDESS, 1993), 47.

7. For a discussion, see G.A. Almond, *The Civic Culture* (Princeton, NJ: Princeton University Press, 1963); Samuel Huntington, *The Third Wave: Democratization in the Late Twentieth Century* (London and Norman: Oklahoma University Press, 1993); S.M. Lipset, "Some Social Requisites for Democracy: Economic Development and Political Legitimacy," *American Political Science Review* 53, no. 1 (1976): 69–105; and Barrington Moore, Jr., *The Social Origins of Dictatorship and Democracy* (London: Allen Lane, 1967).

8. Arthur A. Goldsmith, "Political Freedom and the Business Climate: Outlook for Development in Newly Democratizing States," *Social Science Quarterly* 75 (March 1994): 115.

9. See Julius Ihonvbere, "Transitions and Non-Transitions in Africa: A Critical Evaluation of the New Political Parties and Prodemocracy Movements," text of lecture delivered under the auspices of the Students for a Free Africa (SFA) and the Coalition against Global Oppression (CAGO), University of Pittsburgh, PA, April 3, 1996.

10. Nicephore Soglo, President of Benin, quoted in *Jeune Afrique* 1632 (April 16–22, 1992).

11. Denis Venter, "Malawi: The Transition to Multi-Party Politics," in *Democracy and Political Change in Sub-Saharan Africa*, ed. John Wiseman (London: Routledge, 1995), 180.

12. See Julius Ihonvbere, "Where Is the Third Wave? A Critical Evaluation of the Transition Processes in Africa," seminar presentation, Faculty of Social Sciences, University of the West Indies, Mona, Jamaica, March 26, 1996.

13. See Claude Ake, *Revolutionary Pressures in Africa* (London: Zed Books, 1978).

14. See Julius Ihonvbere. "The 'Irrelevant' State, Ethnicity, and the Quest for Nationhood in Africa," *Ethnic and Racial Studies* 17 (January 1994): 42–60.

15. See Michael Chege, "Remembering Africa," *Foreign Affairs* 71, no. 1 (1991–92): 146–163; and Ellen Johnson Sirleaf, "Some Reflections on Africa and the Global Economy," in *U.S. Foreign Policy: An Africa Agenda*, ed. William Minter (Washington, DC: Africa Policy Information Center, 1994), 7–12.

16. See Julius Ihonvbere, "On the Threshold of Another False Start? A Critical Evaluation of Prodemocracy Movements in Africa," paper presented at the 11th Annual Meeting of the Council of Nigerian People and Organizations (CONPO), Washington, DC, September 14–17, 1995.

17. See Rene Lemarchand, "African Transitions to Democracy: An Interim (and Mostly Pessimistic) Assessment," *Africa Insight* 22, no. 3 (1992); J. Healey and M. Robinson, *Democracy, Governance and Economic Policy: Sub-Saharan Africa in Comparative Perspective* (London: Overseas Development Institute, 1992); and Robert Pinkney, *Democracy in the Third World* (Boulder, CO: Lynne Rienner, 1994).

18. According to Healey and Robinson, political liberalization involves a situation "in which the fear of repression is relaxed and there are constitutional guarantees of a range of political freedoms (especially the recognition of the right of opposition groupings to function and to express dissent) in which there is greater independence for legislative assemblies where they still exist, and freedom of the press." Healey and Robinson, *Democracy, Governance and Economic Policy*, 151.

19. Huntington, *The Third Wave*, 263.

20. See the contributions of T. Vincent Maphai (South Africa), Masipula Sithole (Zimbabwe), Githu Muigai (Kenya), and Hussein Adam (Somalia), in *Ethnic Conflict and Democratization in Africa*, ed. Harvey Glickman (Atlanta: The African Studies Association Press, 1995).

21. According to Huntington, democracy is even more difficult to consolidate when the system is characterized by "stalemate, the inability to reach decisions, susceptibility to demagoguery, domination by vested economic interests." *The Third Wave*, 210, also 262–263.

22. Ibid., 262.

23. Ibid., 258.

24. Ibid., 259.

25. As the saying goes, the devil you know is certainly better than the one you do not know, even better than the angel you do not know. When the new politicians display such shameless opportunism, confusion, disorganization, corruption, limited vision, reliance on primordial manipulation, and impatience with democracy, many citizens simply feel that a return to the status quo might just be better than relying on the new dispensation. In Nigeria, after the so-called "new breed" politicians displayed their total lack of faith in the democratic enterprise in 1992, General Ibrahim Babangida was forced to lift the ban on the politicians of the First and Second Republics.

26. Huntington, *The Third Wave*, 255.

27. See Julius Ihonvbere, *Economic Crisis, Civil Society, and Democratization: The Case of Zambia* (Lawrenceville, NJ: Africa World Press, 1996).

28. Richard Joseph, "Zambia: A Model for Democratic Change," *Current History* (May 1992): 200. See also his "Africa: Rebirth of Political Freedom," *Journal of Democracy* 2 (Fall 1991).

29. See Michael Bratton, "Economic Crisis and Political Realignment in Zambia," in *Economic Change and Political Liberalization in Sub-Saharan Africa*, ed. Jennifer Widner (Baltimore: Johns Hopkins University Press, 1994).

30. Ibid., 252–255.

31. Jowie Mwiinga, "Chill for Chiluba," *Africa Report* (March–April 1994): 60.

32. Movement for Multi-party Democracy, *Manifesto* (Lusaka: MMD National Secretariat, n.d.), 4.

33. According to a report in *Africa Confidential*, "Unlike Kaunda, Chiluba has no real political base to fall back on in times of crisis. The basis of the 1991 landslide was the 400,000 white-collar workers he led for 16 years as President of the Zambia Congress of Trade Unions (ZCTU). They are now disillusioned by the depth of job losses and the deterioration in living standards under the Structural Adjustment Programme backed by the World Bank and the International Monetary Fund." See "Zambia–The Return of 'Super Ken,' " *Africa Confidential* 26 (January 20, 1995): 7.

34. The privatization program of the government has also worsened the unemployment situation as privatized and commercialized corporations simply lay off thousands of workers who join the army of the unemployed and swell the ranks of criminals.

35. Republic of Zambia, *Economic Report 1992* (Lusaka: Ministry of Finance, 1992), 21.

36. E. G. Kasonde, *Budget Address by Minister of Finance to the National Assembly on 29th January 1993* (Lusaka: Government Printer, 1993), 9. For 1993, the primary objective of government recovery programs focused on introducing tighter fiscal policies; reducing domestic borrowing by government and parastatals; bringing inflation down to 10 percent; abolishing supplementary appropriations to government ministries; repaying much of government's outstanding debt to the banking system; freeing resources for private sector expansion; and running the government on a cash basis. The Bank of Zambia was instructed to "deny any government transaction unless there are adequate funds in the appropriate accounts."

37. Ibid.

38. The predicament of the Chiluba government is evidenced in the politics of privatization at the Zambia Consolidated Copper Mines (ZCCM) where privatization would lead to more job losses, thus jeopardizing the reform program and further eroding support for the government. Before the election in late 1996, the government preferred to sacrifice economic reform for political survival. See "Zambia—Down the Mines," *Africa Confidential* 36 (April 28, 1995): 4–5.

39. Jowie Mwiinga, "Zambia Economy: Stock Exchange Finds Its Feet," Inter-Press Service, Peace Net, May 10, 1995.

40. Ibid.

41. Interview with Mark Mwansa, Mamba Collieries Guest House, Lusaka, June 1993.

42. "Zambia—Down the Mines," 5.

43. "Zambia—The Market Democrats," *Africa Confidential* 36 (May 12, 1995): 6. This report also noted that "discontent was rising fast enough to deprive Chiluba's party of a majority in the 1996 parliamentary elections."

44. Ibid., 6.

45. See Jowie Mwiinga, "Zambia—Politics: Land Grabbers on Rampage," Inter-Press Service, Peace Net, May 10, 1995.

46. Jowie Mwiinga, "Zambia—Politics: Narcotics-Drug War Heats Up," Inter-Press Service, Peace Net, May 18, 1995.

47. Ibid.

48. See Donatella Lorch, "In Zambia, a Legacy of Graft and a Drug Scandal Taint Democratic Reforms," *New York Times* (January 30, 1994).

49. Jan Kees van Donge, "Zambia: Kaunda and Chiluba," in Wiseman, *Democracy and Political Change in Sub-Saharan Africa*, 199.

50. Chiluba himself is a Bemba from Luapula Province. Yet it needs to be pointed out that the Bembas are not united. For historical reasons, some Bembas are not regarded as "authentic"; even if such claims lack material foundations, they do have emotive and perceptual foundations.

51. "Zambia—Tribal Cracks in MMD," *Africa Research Bulletin* (March 1–31, 1995): 11787.

52. Elias Nyakutembe, "Zambia: Chiluba's Challenge," *New African* (November 1995).

53. See A.D. Roberts, "The Lumpa Church of Alice Leshina," in *Protest and Power in Black Africa*, ed. R. Rotberg and A.A. Mazrui (New York: Oxford University Press, 1970); and G.F. Lungu, "The Church, Labour and the Press in Zambia: The Role of Critical Observers in a One-Party State," *African Affairs* 85 (1986).

54. Movement for Multi-Party Democracy, *Manifesto*, 10.

55. For details see "Zambia—Splitology," *Africa Confidential* 36 (August 25, 1995). This strategy might not be reliable during major elections especially with a vigorous opposition campaign. The crisis of legitimacy made the use of food as a political instrument ineffective.

56. UNIP victories in the September 1995 by-elections in Mpulungu, Mbala, and Mkushi North, all in the Northern Province which had been an MMD stronghold, as well as victories in Feira (Lusaka), Chama North, Msanzala, and Lundazi (Eastern Province) and Kalabo (Western Province) convinced the MMD that it was not going to have an easy ride in the 1996 presidential and general elections. Some of the victories, especially those in the Northern Province, which had prompted MMD youths to march to the state house to protest the obvious weakness of the party, convinced Chiluba that the deportation of Kaunda (and leading UNIP officers—Patrick Mvunga, Ruphia Banda, Sketchley Sachika, and Lucy Sichone) would be a solution to his party's problem.

57. "Zambia—MMD Defections," *Africa Research Bulletin* (July 1–31, 1995): 11910.

58. "Zambia—Splitology," *Africa Confidential* 36, (August 25, 1995): 4.

59. Ibid. This report also noted that public servants in the parastatals, armed forces, and the intelligence services "are losing faith in the government." Of course, with such open expression of disrespect and a lack of confidence in the nation's security agencies, classified information and other official secrets and documents have found their way to opposition mailboxes from "nowhere." This has strengthened the opposition in its attacks against the MMD government. It is well known that the security forces are poorly trained and badly equipped and have low morale, and that the promotion of inexperienced officers from Chiluba's home province, Luapula, has contributed to poor leadership and inefficiency.

60. Kaunda has openly declared his intention to regain his old job. He has campaigned

across the nation exploiting the failures and weaknesses of the MMD and declaring his commitment to exactly the opposite of what the ruling party represents. He has promised to slow down the privatization program because it has been employed to enrich a few government officials, to stop the retrenchment of workers, to increase wages, and to reintroduce food subsidies. He has described the MMD government as a body of "crooks, thieves and drug dealers" and accused it of "mismanagement, corruption, abuse of office and tribalism in a country that has been spared ethnic chaos." See "Kaunda's Comeback Strategy," *Africa Research Bulletin* (July 1–31, 1995): 11910.

61. Kaunda overwhelmingly crushed his opponent, incumbent Kebby Musokotwane, at the UNIP Party Congress on June 27, 1995, when he won 1,916 votes to Musokotwane's 400. Musokotwane even had to rely on Kenneth Kaunda's assistance to obtain the required ten nominations in each province to enable him to file his nomination paper for the leadership elections.

62. "Zambia: Draft Constitution," *Africa Research Bulletin* (June 1–30, 1995): 11880.

63. "Zambia: Chiluba Defends Requirement for President," London: BBC World Service in English, September 27, 1995. The government White Paper also stipulated that "no person who has been elected president twice should be eligible to stand again." See "Kaunda, Minister Respond," London, BBC World Service in English, September 27, 1995. Legal Affairs Minister Remmy Mushota has, however, denied that this was mainly directed at Kaunda. Following statements by Home Affairs Minister Chitalu Sampa that Kaunda would be arrested and deported to Malawi, the government quickly stepped in to contain a situation which had generated tension and led to riots at the University of Zambia, announcing that the minister's statement had no official support.

64. Nyakutembe, "Chiluba's Challenge."

65. Ibid.

66. "Zambia—Disorderly Deportation," *Africa Confidential* 36 (December 1, 1995): 6. Kaunda had actually renounced his Malawian citizenship in the 1970s. The plan to deport Kaunda had the blessing of Malawi's new democratic president, Bakili Muluzi, but did not enjoy the support of the MMD cabinet. Chiluba was encouraged along by four powerful ministers, Michael Sata (health), Ben Mwila (defence), Chitalu Sampa (Home Affairs), and Ronald Penza (Finance).

67. "Zambian Said Intimidated for Challenging Chiluba," Reuters, May 19, 1995.

68. "Zambia—Dr. Kaunda's Comeback," *Africa Research Bulletin* (May 1–31, 1995): 11851. In the same statement, Kaunda pointed out that "The rural areas are devastated, our agriculture has gone, and in the urban areas 200,000 of 350,000 jobs have disappeared. As a nation, we are now making nothing, just reselling goods we have imported and paid for with donor funds."

69. Movement for Multi-party Democracy, *Manifesto*, 3.

70. "Zambia: Disorderly Deportation," 7. His defection, which was encouraged by Chiluba, and his death even before he was rewarded with the vice-presidential appointment weakened the NP. The public outrage over the incident, with the media openly raising several suspicious questions, forced Chiluba to appoint a commission of inquiry.

71. "Zambia—The Market Democrats," 6.

72. For details, see Julius Ihonvbere, "The 'Zero Option' Controversy in Zambia: Western Double Standards vis-à-vis Safeguarding Security?" *Afrika Spectrum* 30 (1995): 93–104.

73. See Ihonvbere, "The 'Zero Option' Controversy in Zambia," and "A Radical Pro-

gram of Action for UNIP (Alias the 'Zero Option')," *National Mirror*, Lusaka (March 15–21, 1993).

74. Nyakutembe, "Chiluba's Challenge."

75. "Zambia—Splitology," 5.

76. Ibid.

77. See Richard Sandbrook and Mohamed Halfani, eds., *Empowering People: Building Community, Civil Associations and Legality in Africa* (Toronto: Center for Urban and Community Studies, University of Toronto, 1993).

Selected Bibliography

Adedeji, Adebayo, ed. *Africa within the World: Beyond Dispossession and Dependence*. London and Ijebu-Ode, Nigeria: Zed Books and ACDESS, 1993.

Agbese, Dan. *Fellow Nigerians*. Lagos, Nigeria: Africa NewsWatch Publishing, 2000.

Agbese, Pita Ogaba, and George Klay Kieh, Jr. "Military Disengagement from African Politics: The Nigerian Experience." *Afrika Spectrum* 27 (1992): 5–23.

Ake, Claude. *Political Economy of Democratization in Africa*. London: Longman, 1995.

———. *Revolutionary Pressures in Africa*. London: Zed Books, 1978.

Almond, G.A. *The Civic Culture*. Princeton, NJ: Princeton University Press, 1963.

Anyidoho, Henry K. *Guns over Kigali*. Accra, Ghana: Woeli Publishing Services, 1997.

Auvinen, Juha. "Political Conflict in Less Developed Countries." *Journal of Peace Research* 34, no. 2 (1997).

Babangida, Ibrahim. *For Their Tomorrow We Gave Our Today: Selected Speeches of IBB*. Vol. 2. Ibadan: Safari Books, Ltd., 1991.

Berdal, Mats. *Whither UN Peacekeeping?* Adelphi Papers 281. London: Brassey, 1993.

Boley, G.E.S. *Liberia: The Rise and Fall of the First Republic*. London: Macmillan Press, 1983.

Boswell, Terry, and William Dixon. "Marx's Theory of Rebellion: A Cross-National Analysis of Class Exploitation, Economic Development and Violent Revolt." *American Sociological Review* 58 (1993).

Bread of the World Institute. *Causes of Hunger*. Silver Springs, MD: Communications and Graphics, 1994.

Cabral, Amilcar. *Revolution in Guinea*. London: Stage 1, 1969.

Chege, Michael. "Remembering Africa." *Foreign Affairs* 71, no. 1 (1991–92): 146–163.

Clapham, Christopher, and George Philip, eds. *The Political Dilemmas of Military Regimes*. Totowa, NJ: Barnes and Noble, 1985.

Crowder, Michael. *Senegal: A Study of French Assimilation Policy*. London: Methuen and Company, 1967.

Danopoulos, Constantine, ed. *The Decline of Military Regimes: The Civilian Influence*. Boulder, CO: Westview Press, 1988.

Deng, Francis, and I. William Zartman, eds. *Conflict Resolution in Africa*. Washington, DC: Brookings Institution, 1991.

Durch, William. *The Evolution of UN Peacekeeping*. New York: St. Martin's Press, 1993.

El-Ayouty, Yassin, and I. William Zartman, eds. *The OAU after Twenty Years*. New York: Praeger, 1984.

Essack, Karrim. *Civil War in Rwanda*. Dar es Salaam: Newman Publishers, 1991.

Fabian, Larry. *Soldiers without Enemies*. Washington, DC: Brookings Institution, 1971.

Falola, Toyin, and Julius Ihonvbere. *The Rise and Fall of Nigeria's Second Republic*. London: Zed Books, Ltd., 1985.

Fox, Mary. *Somalia*. New York: Children's Press, 1996.

Freedom House. *Freedom in the World: An Annual Survey of Political Rights and Civil Liberties, 1997–1998*. New York: Freedom House, 1998.

Garuba, Chris. *Capacity Building for Crisis Management in Africa*. Lagos, Nigeria: Gabumo Publishing Company, 1998.

Geertz, Clifford. "The Integrative Revolution: Primordial Sentiments and Civil Politics in New States." In *The Interpretation of Culture: Selected Essays*. New York: Basic Books, 1973.

Glickman, Harvey, ed. *Ethnic Conflict and Democratization in Africa*. Atlanta: The African Studies Association Press, 1995.

Goldsmith, Arthur A. "Political Freedom and the Business Climate: Outlook for Development in Newly Democratizing States." *Social Science Quarterly 75* (March 1994).

Graf, William. *The Nigerian State: Political Economy, State, Class and Political System in the Post-Colonial Era*. London: James Currey, 1988.

Groom, A.J.R. *Peacekeeping*. Bethlehem, PA: Lehigh University, 1973.

Guichaoua, André. *Les Crises politiques au Burundi et au Rwanda, 1993–1994: Analyses, faits et documents*. Villeneuve d'Ascq, France: Université des Sciences et Technologies de Lille, Faculté des Sciences Économiques et Sociales, 1995.

Gurr, Ted Robert. *Why Men Rebel*. Princeton, NJ: Princeton University Press, 1970.

Hadjar, Kofi. *On Transforming Africa*. Trenton, NJ: Africa World Press, 1987.

Healey, J., and M. Robinson. *Democracy, Governance and Economic Policy: Sub-Saharan Africa in Comparative Perspective*. London: Overseas Development Institute, 1992.

Huntington, Samuel. *The Third Wave: Democratization in the Late Twentieth Century*. London and Norman: Oklahoma University Press, 1993.

Ihonvbere, Julius. "Beyond Warlords and Clans: The African Crisis and the Somali Situation." *International Third World Studies Journal and Review* 6 (1995): 7–19.

———. *Economic Crisis, Civil Society, and Democratization: The Case of Zambia*. Lawrenceville, NJ: Africa World Press, 1996.

———. "The 'Irrelevant' State, Ethnicity, and the Quest for Nationhood in Africa." *Ethnic and Racial Studies* 17 (January 1994): 42–60.

Katsuyoshi, Fukui, and John Markakis, eds. *Ethnicity and Conflict in the Horn of Africa*. London: James Currey, 1994.

Khapoya, Vincent. *The African Experience*. 2d ed. Upper Saddle River, NJ: Prentice Hall, 1998.

Kieh, George Klay, Jr. "Combatants, Patrons, Peacemakers, and the Liberian Civil Conflict." *Studies in Conflict and Terrorism* 15 (1992): 127–128.

———. "International Organizations and Peacekeeping in Africa." In *Peacekeeping in Africa: ECOMOG in Liberia*, ed. Karl Magyar and Earl Conteh-Morgan. London: Macmillan Press, 1998.

Konneh, Augustine. "Indigenous Entrepreneurs and Capitalists: The Role of the Mandingo in the Economic Development of Modern-Day Liberia." Ph.D. disseration, Indiana University, 1992.

———. "Mandingo Integration in the Liberian Political Economy." *Liberian Studies Journal* 18, no. 1 (1993).

Kourvetaris, George. "Ethnonationalism and Subnationalism: The Cases of Former Yugoslavia." *Journal of Political and Military Sociology* 24 (Winter 1996).

Kriesberg, Louis. *International Conflict Resolution*. New Haven, CT: Yale University Press, 1992.

Krymkoski, David, and Raymond Hall. "The African Development Dilemma Revisited: Theoretical and Empirical Explorations." *Ethnic and Racial Studies* 13, no. 3 (1990).

Lemarchand, René. "African Transitions to Democracy: An Interim (and Mostly Pessimistic) Assessment." *Africa Insight* 22, no. 3 (1992).

Logiest, Guy. *Mission au Rwanda*. Brussels: Didier Hatier, 1988.

Lowenkopf, Martin. *Politics in Liberia*. Stanford, CA: Hoover Institution Press, 1976.

Lungu, G.F. "The Church, Labour and the Press in Zambia: The Role of Critical Observers in a One-Party State." *African Affairs* 85 (1986).

Lyons, Terrence, and Ahmed Samatar. *Somalia: State Collapse, Multinational Intervention and Strategies for Political Reconstruction*. Washington, DC: Brookings Institution, 1995.

Makinda, Samuel. *Seeking Peace from Chaos*. Boulder, CO: Lynne Rienner, 1993.

Mamdani, Mahmud. *Citizen and Subject: Contemporary Africa and the Legacy of Late Colonialism*. London: Heinemann, 1976.

———. *Politics and Class Formation in Uganda*. London: Heinemann, 1976.

Maniruzzaman, Talukder. *Military Withdrawal from Politics: A Comparative Analysis*. Cambridge, MA: Ballinger Press, 1987.

Marx, Karl. *Capital*. Vol. 1. New York: International Publishers, 1967.

Mbaku, John. *Preparing Africa for the Twenty-First Century: Strategies for Peaceful Co-existence and Sustainable Development*. Brookfield, VT: Ashgate Publishing, 1999.

Mbaku, John, and Julius Ihonvbere, eds. *Multiparty Democracy and Political Change: Constraints to Democratization in Africa*. Brookfield, VT: Ashgate Publishing, 1998.

McClintock, Liz "Angola." In *International Negotiation Network, The State of the World Conflicts Report*. Atlanta: The Carter Presidential Center, 1996.

Midall, Hugh. *The Peacemakers*. New York: St. Martin's Press, 1992.

Minear, Larry, et al. *Humanitarianism under Siege: A Critical Review of Operation Lifeline Sudan*. Trenton, NJ: Red Sea Press, 1990.

Moore, Barrington, Jr. *The Social Origins of Dictatorship and Democracy*. London: Allen Lane, 1967.

Mutisya, Godfrey. *Conflict Watch*. Durban, South Africa: ACCORD, 1999.

Nabudere, Dan. *Imperialism and Revolution in Uganda*. Dar es Salaam: Tanzania Publishing House, 1980.

Nwolise, O.B.C. "ECOMOG Peacekeeping Operations in Liberia: Effects on Political Stability in the West African Sub-Region." *African Peace Review* 1, no. 1 (1997).

Nyerere, Julius. *Freedom and Socialism*. Dar es Salaam: Oxford University Press, 1968.

Olukoshi, Adebayo and Liisa Laakso, eds. *Challenges to the Nation-State in Africa*. Uppsala, Sweden: Nordiska Afrikainstitutet, 1996.

Onimode, Bade. *The Political Economy of the African Crisis*. London: Zed Press, 1988.

Osaghae, Eghosa E. "Conflict Research in Africa." *International Journal of World Peace* 16 (December 1999): 53–72.

Pinkney, Robert. *Democracy in the Third World*. Boulder, Co: Lynne Rienner, 1994.

Polychroniou, Chronis, and Harry Targ, eds. *Marxism Today*. Westport, CT: Praeger, 1996.

Rabow, Gerald. *Peace through Agreement*. New York: Praeger, 1990.

Ramseys, F. Jeffress. *Global Studies: Africa*. Guilford, CT: Dushkin/McGraw Hill, 1999.

Ricciuti, Edward R. *Somalia: A Crisis of Famine and War*. Brookfield, CT: The Millbrook Press, 1993.

Roberts, A. D. "The Lumpa Church of Alice Leshina." In *Protest and Power in Black Africa*, ed. R. Rotberg and A. A. Mazrui. New York: Oxford University Press, 1970.

Rodney, Walter. *How Europe Underdeveloped Africa*. Washington, DC: Howard University Press, 1982.

Samatar, Ahmed I. *Socialist Somalia: Rhetoric or Reality?* London: Zed Press, 1988.

Sandbrook, Richard, and Mohamed Halfani, eds. *Empowering People: Building Community, Civil Associations and Legality in Africa*. Toronto: Center for Urban and Community Studies, University of Toronto, 1993.

Sebudandi, Gaetan, and Pierre-Olivier Richard. *Le Drame burundais: Hantise du pouvoir ou tentation suicidaire*. Paris: Karthala, 1996.

Seyon, Patrick. "Liberia's Second Republic: Superpower Geopolitics in Africa." *Liberian Studies Journal* 12, no. 1 (1987): 64.

Shaw, Carolyn M. "Hegemonic Participation in Peacekeeping Operations: The Case of Nigeria and ECOMOG." Paper presented at the 27th Annual Liberian Studies Conference, Dayton, Ohio, April 19–22, 1995.

Shivji, Issa, ed. *State and Constitutionalism: An African Debate on Democracy*. Harare, Zimbabwe: SAPES Trust, 1991.

Sirleaf, Ellen Johnson. "Some Reflections on Africa and the Global Economy." In *U.S. Foreign Policy: An Africa Agenda*, ed. William Minter. Washington, DC: Africa Policy Information Center, 1994.

Soyinka, Wole. *The Open Sore of a Continent: A Personal Narrative of the Nigerian Crisis*. New York: Oxford University Press, 1996.

Suberu, Rotimi T. "The Democratic Recession in Nigeria." *Current History* (May 1994).

Tansey, Stephen. *Politics: The Basics*. New York: Routledge, 1995.

Touval, Saadia. *The Peace Brokers*. Princeton, NJ: Princeton University Press, 1982.

Udogu, E. Ike, ed. *Democracy and Democratization in Africa: Towards the Twenty-First Century*. Leiden: E.J. Brill, 1997.

United Nations Economic Commission for Africa (UNECA). *African Alternative Framework to Structural Adjustment Programs for Socio-Economic Recovery and*

Transformation: A Popular Version. Addis Ababa, Ethiopia: UNECA Secretariat, 1991.

———. *Economic Report on Africa 1999*, E/ECA/CM.24/3. Addis Ababa, Ethiopia: UNECA, May 1999.

United Nations High Commission for Refugees. *The State of the World's Refugees, 1995*. New York: Oxford University Press, 1995.

Van de Goor, L., K. Rupesinghe, and P. Sciarone, eds. *Between Development and Destruction: An Inquiry into the Causes of Conflict in Postcolonial States*. New York: St Martin's Press, 1996.

Venter, Denis. "Malawi: The Transition to Multi-Party Politics." In *Democracy and Political Change in Sub-Saharan Africa*, ed. John Wiseman. London: Routledge, 1995.

Wainhouse, David. *International Peacekeeping at the Crossroads*. Baltimore: The Johns Hopkins University Press, 1973.

Wallensteen, Peter, and Karen Axell. "Conflict Resolution and the End of the Cold War, 1989–1993." *Journal of Peace Research* 31, no. 3 (1994).

Widner, Jennifer, ed. *Economic Change and Political Liberalization in Sub-Saharan Africa*. Baltimore: Johns Hopkins University Press, 1994.

World Bank. *Trends in Developing Economies 1995*. Washington, DC: World Bank, 1995.

Zartman, I. William, ed. *Collapsed States*. Boulder, CO: Lynne Rienner, 1995.

Index

About the Contributors

Pita Ogaba Agbese is Professor of Political Science at the University of Northern Iowa. His research has appeared in journals such as *Africa Today*, *Afrika Spectrum*, *Austrian Journal of African Studies*, *Journal of Asian and African Studies*, *Journal of Commonwealth and Comparative Politics*, *Journal of Peace Research*, and *Bulletin of Peace Proposals (Security Dialogue)*. He is editor of *Constitution, Government, and Ethnic Relations in Africa* (forthcoming), and coauthor of *The State and the Politics of Structural Adjustment in Nigeria* (forthcoming).

Julius Ihonvbere is Program Officer in the Social Justice and Civil Society Unit at the Ford Foundation. He is author and coeditor of numerous books. The most recent include *Africa and the New World Order*, *Nigeria: The Politics of Adjustment and Democracy*, *Economic Crisis, Civil Society, and Democratization: The Case of Zambia*, and *Multiparty Democracy and Political Change: Constraints to Democratization in Africa*. His articles have appeared in numerous journals including *Africa Today*, *Asian and African Studies*, *Futures*, *Journal of Modern African Studies*, *Journal of Asian and African Studies*, *Journal of Political and Military Sociology*, and *World Development*.

George Klay Kieh, Jr., is Professor of Political Science at Morehouse College. He is the author of *Dependency and the Foreign Policy of a Small Power*, and a coauthor of *American Democracy in Africa in the Twenty-First Century?* His articles have appeared in several journals, including *Afrika Spectrum*, *African Journal on Conflict Management*, *Prevention and Resolution*, *Austrian Journal* *of African Studies, Journal of Asian and African Studies, Journal of Peace Studies, Peace Review, Small Wars and Insurgency, Low Intensity Conflict and Law Enforcement, Studies in Conflict and Terrorism, Journal of Third World Spectrum*, and *Western Journal of Black Studies.*

Augustine Konneh is Associate Professor and Chair of the Department of History at Morehouse College. He is the author of *Religion, Commerce, and the Integration of the Mandingo in Liberia*. His articles have appeared in journals such as *African Studies Review, Journal of African History, Journal of the Georgia Association of Historians, Journal of Social and Behavioral Sciences*, and *Liberian Studies Journal.*

Ida Rousseau Mukenge is Professor of Sociology and Director of the NIMH-MRISP Faculty Development Project in Mental Health Research at Morehouse College. She has also taught, consulted, and conducted research on women, education, and development in several African countries, including Sierra Leone, Zaire (the Democratic Republic of the Congo), Senegal, Mali, and Côte d'Ivoire. Her writings on women in development include "African Women: Identity Crisis," a chapter in the seminal volume in this field, *Women Cross-Culturally: Change and Challenge.*

Musifiky Mwanasali is an analyst in the Conflict Management Division of the Secretariat of the Organization of African Unity (OAU), Addis Ababa. His primary research interest is in the area of conflict studies. He has contributed to various volumes, including his chapter on "Criminal Agendas in Civil Wars," in the book, *Economic Agendas in Civil War.*